D1496136

BETRAYED WITHOUT A KISS

BETRAYED WITHOUT A KISS

Defending Marriage after Years of Failed Leadership in the Church

JOHN CLARK

Foreword by

CATHERINE GODFREY-HOWELL, JCD

TAN Books
Gastonia, North Carolina

Cover design by Caroline Green

Cover image: *Catharine of Aragon pleading her cause before King Henry VIII.* Coloured mezzotint by W. Ward, 1802, after R. Westall. Wellcome Collection. Public Domain via Wikimedia Commons.

Library of Congress Control Number: 2023934826

ISBN: 978-1-5051-2763-8
Kindle ISBN: 978-1-5051-2764-5
ePUB ISBN: 978-1-5051-2765-2

Published in the United States by
TAN Books
PO Box 269
Gastonia, NC 28053
www.TANBooks.com

Printed in the United States of America

To Athanasius, Veronica, Demetrius, Tarcisius, Philomena,
Dominica, Bonaventure, Immaculata, and Mary Katherine—
the primary purposes of our marriage.

To Joseph Seraphim, Christiana Cherubim, and
Raphael Francis—three children in heaven patiently
waiting for Mom and Dad to come home.

For Lisa.

Contents

Foreword

THE NOTION THAT marriage today is in crisis is absolutely untrue. The spousal identity, with or without an institution, is a reality that we have perceived long before Christ elevated it to sacramental dignity because of the destiny it entails. We now know how to articulate the meaningfulness of this attraction to claim the right to marry (*ius connubii*) and how it indicates a reality beyond ourselves that makes this possible, and simultaneously our capacity to be remade through it. We also know now, more than ever, that fighting to maintain the spousal relationship leads to happiness and salvation. Whatever else there may be left in this world to possess, it cannot be greater than either of these. No, marriage is not in crisis. Chaos and suffering grow to unbearable weight because we refuse to let marriage speak for itself. This is what John Clark sets out to do—namely, to give marriage a chance to give an account of itself.

There are a few premises that need to be set in place (again). First, marriage entails a bond. Not an emotional reason to stay close to someone, but a reality that comes to be at the call of a man and woman who, with the fullness of their human faculties, profess a covenant between themselves. They have new identity in this moment that they can never forsake. This sounds like a tether, but it is the reverse—the marriage covenant is a promise that living well will yield ten-fold fruit, as each spouse helps the other reach heaven. The bond of Christian marriage, the spoken oath and covenant, is *created* and is also the nursery for further human collaboration in creation. The identity given in marriage is something altogether new in this life, as is the conception of those souls that will come after because we, too, have spoken the right words of creation. Marriage is a sacrament, but as Clark vehemently exhorts the reader to see, its closeness to the Eucharist is the same proximity as the heart is to the soul.

And the hearts of spouses unified (even in imperfect participation) is the image of the same covenant that God has with His people. It is not lightly that the Code of Canon Law reproduces the importance of the marital covenant as the nursery of all vocations; in the light of spouses' vocation (some might say justice toward God in the way cult or liturgy embodies), these two are entrusted with fostering in that same spousal bond the vocations in their children, and especially to the priesthood.[1] What the covenant of spouses and the covenant the Eucharistic celebration acknowledges is explicitly bound together in their use of the same language, a

[1] This is not to say that priesthood is of greatest value, but that priesthood comes most robustly from good marriages. Cf. C. 226: §1 "Those who are married are bound by the special obligation, in accordance with their own vocation, to strive for the building up of the people of God through their marriage and family." §2 "Because they gave life to their children, parents have the most serious obligation and the right to educate them." The first encounter with sacramental covenant is with one's parents. If this is not the case, priests will be required to represent this before an explanation of faith seems possible. In any event, immutability needs to be expressed in human will, and if not by parents, then it will be difficult and quite reliant on grace.

language children hear first in their mother and father long before they grasp their own faith or receive the Eucharist.

Clark has written a book here about marriage and the Eucharist. Only a man who passionately loves his own wife could write this book. And I think it is actually a love letter to the Eucharist. After these years of pandemic and exclusion, Clark has had indeed more time with the former and so probably more to say to the latter. But the questions he asks are critical and reflective. Neither marriage nor the Eucharist rely on disposition or personality. Both call upon the highest human attributes even in the smallest or unannounced moments. Both are imbued with consistency, constancy, *words* pronounced, and actions that follow necessarily. The Eucharist is clearly a primary inspiration to Clark's marriage.

Another premise that needs to be re-presented is that in Christian (Trinitarian) anthropology, the most basic and irreducible relation among human beings is that of spouses, that of a man and a woman. Closer than even mother and child, spouses mark "the beginning," or primary reference, for all human relations in the way that creation in Genesis indicates the literal beginning for all things. To say this now may be highly contested given that a proper anthropology has been lost in all arenas save Christianity, but it remains true. The divine will for our lives is that our greatest expression of love (not to be confused with affection) is in a context of full reciprocity, equality, freedom, and individuality. To say the word "family" is, at its core, a reference to the spouses themselves. The blessing of children notwithstanding, the husband and wife together claim this enduring epithet, and it should not be taken from them.

Clark's treatment of marriage brings a lot to the surface, even if this was not initially intended. The history of the institution mirrors much of the turmoil spouses live daily, although in private. Marriage is not easy or hard, clear or complicated. Marriage is marriage. It *requires* shaming the ego, which can be sweet in the way it brings us closer and more worthily to the Eucharist. It mandates another to witness the decline and underestimation of everything around him, and remark on the wealth of human existence even in the settling of the dust. Marriage is also a battleground. A marriage is never lost or won in a given day and then set to cruise—rather, the stakes have been raised to include more than spouses themselves in their own marriages. Marriage is now a place wherein the profane struggles of the world seek to extract a kind of booster to endure when folly doomed their schemes from the outset. Servant of God Sister Lúcia, one of the Fatima visionaries, once wrote that the last battle for the world would be over marriage and the family, and Carlo Cardinal Caffarra has confirmed as much: "[The family] finds itself to be the battlefield where the power of this world meets the voice of God."[2] If family means spouses, then we can be sure that marriage is ground zero. Every era of history has been divided by two principle shaping forces—namely, those who seek ways to destroy reality and those who give life and make way for the new. Marriage is a battleground because it is a place for creation. Clark and his wife live in this arena of struggle. The issues surrounding marriage as a sacrament, object of law, and its pastoralism are not to be taken lightly.

2 "Dio ci guardi dall'aver paura . . ."

A further merit of this book is a reorientation toward recognizing the stupidity of how we often talk about the future of civilization. There will always be judgment involved in living well. We cannot avoid calling things as they are when we try to be smart, and drowning out marriage is nothing more than an attempt to get rid of the sting of being stupid. A positive image of this harsh remark comes to us in John Paul II's *The Jeweler's Shop.* A man and woman meet the jeweler who enacts the image of weighing and watching, who wills them to walk into the future that they believe to be there before them. It is only together in covenant that the unknown causes no more anxiety, as Andrew says: "The future for us remains an unknown quantity, which we now accept without anxiety. Love has overcome anxiety. The future depends on love." But his love has a concrete object. Christian marriage presupposes many judgments, but there is also the affirmation of the causal relation between the seen and unseen. Certain realities *cannot be* without such words. The future of mankind requires such words, and they will be uttered by spouses. The future does not just happen; it is made and it is prayed in the lives of sacramental marriage. The priesthood will not go to ruin if bishops all lose their legs. It dies with marriage.

The present work is less about doom and is quite hopeful. In this world, to be true to oneself and at the same time true to nature usually means a call to arms, but confusedly also an attempt to express some modicum of affection for others. I believe the purpose of this book is very well intentioned especially in the questions it asks, which will require an account from various groups within the Church, and always in a spirit of fraternity. Nevertheless, it begins to draw a line that signifies where one speaks well of marriage or where one speaks badly (or not at all), and therefore cannot be of service to it. If the future is love, true love does require judgment even if in mercy we bear the weight of folly on our own shoulders. If you are a spouse, you know that regardless of the process, you married a person you must in some way carry. This is love. But *before* it is love, it is called marriage. No other word describes love more fully save one—namely, Eucharist.

In sum, John Clark poses a serious series of questions regarding how we are encouraged to think about marriage today: Why is marriage presented as much less than it actually is? Why is the process of declaration of nullity not rightly understood and so often misrepresented? Why is there no concerted effort to clarify the challenges identified by the laity regarding the vocation? (If marriage is the last stronghold, why are family issues not given due attention and reinforcement?) Why does the process for the declaration of annulment still elicit so many misunderstandings and allow itself to be instrumentalized in doctrinal disputes that only partially touch marriage, and yet seem to end up aiming at the Eucharist? As Clark rightly observes, if marriage "loses its sacramental limbs" and is reduced to sociological constructs, how will the world be able to meet Christ here on earth if it is determined to believe that there is no link between the seen and unseen, if words cannot in faith still *create*? And if we believed this, truly, how much more would we be emboldened to live steadfastly and in resolution toward our spouses, as others that require of us understanding as much as self-expression, with Christ as our example in all things? One's spouse is what one will be judged against, Nobel Prize notwithstanding.

There is a reason there is a juridical process that declares nullity of marriage. When words do not mean anything, this must be exposed. It is a lie and fraud, or it is a reality that in some cannot be achieved because words do not enjoy a full expression of intellectual integrity. These cases occur, and it is a very good thing that the Church declares an attempted sacrament to be failed. Otherwise it would amount to people living without any real reference to truth. This is required for clarity in one's road to sanctity and opposes abuse and abject degradation. But, on the flipside, if words have weight and create, to deny this in the face of marriage, how can we save face when we say we believe in what is present in the Eucharist? Clark is relentless: "Take every question seriously!" he seems to shout. All in all, there are a host of serious things to talk about.

A professor and renowned teacher on the thought of John Paull II and the catechism of human love, Adrian Reimers, recently celebrated his fiftieth wedding anniversary. I asked him (myself barely five years wed) what he would say is the true stuff of a good marriage. His answer was something learned from his wife, Marie: One must have reverence, above all reverence toward one's spouse. My interpretation is that one must act as if this person is the altar on which you hang your prayer and sacrifice to God Himself, as if you yourself are priest. In this brilliance, the Reimers are a real jolt. So is John Clark. If it is not spousal love that is given the chance to guide us into the future, it begs the question:

Will there be a future at all? What will Christ find when He returns to this place? And will spouses be judged more harshly than the ministers of the Church? How do we live now so that our spouses will be the happiest faces we see in heaven, both because of us and for us?

Catherine Godfrey-Howell, JCD

Preface

THE YEAR 1969 witnessed more than 426,000 Catholic weddings in America. By 1989, the number had fallen to 326,000. By 2014, the number had dwindled to under 148,000. In 2020, the number fell to under 100,000.[3] Some might think that figure was significantly reduced due to Covid restrictions; however, it was consistent with a well-established downward trajectory. And while fewer Catholics chose to begin a marriage, more Catholics chose to end one. In the year 1968, there were fewer than 350 annulments in America. By 1989, that number had skyrocketed to over 70,000. That is an increase of 20,000 percent in one generation. Some people have expressed relief that the annulment numbers have decreased in recent years. In 2014, for instance, there were only 23,000 annulments. But this simply reflects mathematical reason: fewer people are attempting annulment because fewer people are attempting marriage.

It's impossible to do a comprehensive damage assessment regarding the rejection of Matrimony, but we might look at it this way. It is proper to say that the sacrament of Matrimony serves as the heart of the Mystical Body of Christ. The graces and fruits of Matrimony nourish the Church Militant, relieve the Church Suffering, and increase the Church Triumphant. But Matrimony's treatment over the past fifty

[3] "Frequently Requested Church Statistics."

years has resulted in endocarditis—heart damage—to the Mystical Body of Christ.

Many Catholics are likely unfamiliar with the above statistics. They may vaguely notice fewer weddings today; they're likely friends with fellow Catholics who have undergone annulments. But they are largely unaware that the catastrophe surrounding Matrimony is epidemic. Largely, the problem is not spoken of inside churches or outside churches: for all its central importance, the word "Matrimony" is seldom uttered in Catholic churches. (As we'll see, that is part of the problem.) What we Catholics hear instead is that there is a crisis of priestly vocations. Certainly, we need more priests. But the years 1994 to 2014 actually saw an *increase* of ordinations.[4] Lest we forget, there are only two vocational sacraments: Holy Orders and Matrimony—and it is the latter that is in decline.

This book seeks to address a very basic question: Considering its irreplaceable vitality, how has marriage reached a stage of indifference, neglect, and rejection? To be sure, there is not one single answer. It is easy to blame the American culture broadly. The sexual revolution of the 1960s—which loudly rejected marriage—is an overwhelming culprit. American society has grown more pornographic by the day, presenting the marital act as a nonmarital act, as well as a violent and hateful one. Children, the primary purpose of marriage, are seen as an unwanted and unnecessary obstacle to the good life. But it is unfair and unhelpful to blame marriage's demise on American society alone. If we are going to have a serious discussion about marriage—if we desire to protect

[4] "Frequently Requested Church Statistics."

and nourish Matrimony—then we must focus on what has been happening *inside* the Catholic Church. The promotion of same-sex marriage by celebrity prelates seems to be an obvious starting point. Taken together, there is considerably more ecclesiastical outreach to same-sex couples than those couples who are sacramentally married. Masses for LGBT Catholic couples have become standard practice in numerous dioceses, but when was the last time you saw a Mass for sacramentally married couples promoted? The promotion of same-sex marriage among Catholics, however, is not the root cause of Matrimony's crisis; rather, it is the effect.

What is the root cause of Matrimony's problems? Broadly, it is the failure to appreciate Matrimony as a sacrament. Simply, Matrimony is not treated with the reverence and respect of the other sacraments. Consider: what other sacrament finds itself under the siege of unrelenting scrutiny? Do panels convene to determine the legitimacy of a first confession? Are there brochures in the vestibules questioning the validity of a Eucharistic consecration? After an unpleasant sermon, is there a demand to investigate the validity of the priest's ordination? Thirty years after the fact, do we hire high-priced canon lawyers to argue against the legitimacy of a man's reception of Anointing of the Sick? Most Catholics, priests and laity alike, would never consider doing any of these; yet, when it comes to Matrimony, questions and doubts are often encouraged. That's where we are, and denial will only lead to more damage to the ventricles of the Mystical Body's heart.

As always, however, there is hope—specifically, there is hope that the prelates of the Church will work to restore the prominence of this great sacrament. There is also hope that the laity will come to a greater love of their own marriages and a more comprehensive understanding of Matrimony itself. We need to understand how God intended marriage from the beginning. We need to be inspired by those who laid down their lives for marriage. We need to know that though the world will tempt us to reject marriage, God's grace will see us through. We need to recognize that the sacraments rise together, and a reverence for the Eucharist requires a reverence for Matrimony by design. We need to contemplate a central fact too often forgotten: God loves marriage. He loves your marriage, and He loves mine. Mary, the Mother of God, loves marriage too. Just when your marriage might seem troubled—just when it seems to have run out of wine—Jesus wills to replenish sacramental graces to the brim. It could just be that Jesus has saved the best graces for last.

The beauty, the majesty, the truth, the purpose, the permanence, the indissolubility, the sacramentality of marriage—these things must be embraced and championed throughout the cathedrals and domestic churches of the world. My hope is that this book can be part of that process of pondering and analyzing the theology of Matrimony, and that the sacrament can be restored to widespread glory.

John Clark
November 1, 2022
The Feast of All Saints

Acknowledgments

No one writes a book alone.

My parents, Bruce and Mary Kay Clark, taught me a five-decade class about marriage. Without my parents' example to guide me—especially in the inspirational final years of their marriage on earth—this book would have never been written.

My wife and I have been married for thirty years. Lisa made it incredibly easy for me to write about the happiness and fulfillment of marriage.

Monsignor Ignacio Barreiro, Father Frank Papa, and Archimandrite Constantine Belisarius were my dear priestly friends in life. When I doubted, they assured me. When I hesitated, they encouraged me. When I wandered, they led me back. Though they passed on to their eternal rewards before this book was written, I have no doubt that these men assisted me from heaven.

The writing and classes of Dr. Warren Carroll, my history professor at Christendom College, proved essential for the book's historical references. Dr. William Marshner's Sacraments class proved to be the genesis of this book. Erin Duffy, my freshman Composition professor at Christendom, helped me believe I could be a good writer. That belief has made all the difference.

I especially need to thank Catherine Godfrey-Howell for the wonderful foreword, as well as her assistance and patience in helping me understand canon law in greater detail. Thanks also to Dr. Matthew Tsakanikas for his help in explaining sacramental theology. Many others who encouraged and assisted me included Anthony D'Andrea, Leila Miller, Krista Thomas, Bai MacFarlane, Bennett Ellis, Mary Beth Ellis, and the devoted staff at TAN Books. Dr. Matthew Levering also deserves my thanks for his assistance not only with sacramental theology but for the reminder to write with charity. I hope and pray I accomplished that in this book.

1

In the Very Beginning: From Eden to Cana

"He said to them, 'For your hardness of heart Moses allowed you to divorce your wives, but from the beginning it was not so.'"

—Matthew 19:8

THE FIRST MARRIAGE had no guests. The bride and groom had a quiet wedding followed by a short but perfect honeymoon—all in a place designed for them and their happiness. Their honeymoon would have continued indefinitely had it not been spoiled by an uninvited guest and their decision to let him remain. Because they failed to command this inhuman visitor to leave, their honeymoon ended in shame and disgrace. The couple's argument that followed was brutally accusatory. Worse, they refused to apologize to the owner of the paradisal abode. Thus, they were told to leave and never return. Their marriage witnessed more devastation than any marriage since. Through it all, they never seem to have considered divorce. Perhaps they never forgot how happy marriage could be.

Their names were Adam and Eve.

Even in texts that examine the nature of Christian marriage, little attention is paid to this first marriage. That is unfortunate because the marriage of Adam and Eve can help us understand how God intended marriage from the very beginning—before the Fall. When we consider that Christ's elevation of marriage to a sacrament was restorative in nature, it invites us to investigate what marriage looked like before the Fall—before marriage found itself in need of restoration. So, to initiate our glimpse of marriage, that is where we will begin: in the Garden of Eden.

The Marriage of Eden

Genesis tells us, "And God saw everything that he had made, and behold, it was very good" (Gn 1:31). From the moment of Adam's creation, he was surrounded by good, beautiful, and wondrous things. Genesis only gives us a tiny glimpse of Eden. But even that little window reveals that Adam touched, tasted, smelled, saw, and heard earthly pleasures that we—living in our fallen world today—cannot imagine.

Yet, even with all that, Adam was unfulfilled. No matter where he looked, nothing in the Garden was like him. Perhaps he felt another reality: humanity itself was incomplete. But Adam would soon feel complete. "God said, 'It is not good that the man should be alone; I will make him a helper fit for him'"(Gn 2:18). The creation of Eve was not an afterthought of the omniscient God; it was always God's plan to create humanity. Father Peter Elliott, author of What God Has Joined: The Sacramentality of Marriage, explains that the creation of Adam and Eve "is part of the one act of God creating the human person."[5] In the creation of Eve, male and female profoundly complement each other, and humanity is realized. Her method of arrival was unique. During Adam's sleep, God formed Eve from flesh and bone from Adam's side. In subsequent marriages, two become one flesh. In Adam and Eve's marriage—this first marriage—one flesh becomes two, and then it becomes one again. The complementarity of the sexes could not be more pronounced.[6]

When Adam arises from a "deep sleep" (Gn 2:21) to set his eyes on Eve for the first time, he experiences fulfillment. Upon seeing her, Adam exhibits love and wonder, "This at last is bone of my bones and flesh of my flesh" (Gn 2:23). Saint John Chrysostom explains that "like himself" means "of his kind, with the same properties as himself, of equal esteem, in no way inferior to him."[7] We do not know how long Adam was in the garden without Eve; perhaps it was days, hours, or mere minutes. However long it may have been, we know this: Adam waited his whole life for Eve.

Though their bodies were designed for reproduction, Saint Thomas Aquinas speculates that sexual consummation did not occur before the Fall.[8] Still, the more critical point for Saint Thomas was this: sexual intimacy was consistent with Adam and Eve's innocence. He writes, "Therefore, even if man had not sinned, there would have been such intercourse, to which the distinction of sex is ordained."[9] Aquinas fur-

---

[5] Elliott, *What God Has Joined*, 8.

[6] Elliott, 7.

[7] Chrysostom, *Homilies on Genesis*, "Homily 15."

[8] Aquinas, *The Summa Theologiæ of St. Thomas Aquinas,* "Supplement," Q. 42, Art 4.

[9] Aquinas, *Summa Theologiae*, I, Q. 98, Art. 2.

ther explains that intercourse would have been significantly more pleasurable to Adam and Eve before their fall because "sensible delight" would "have been the greater in proportion to the greater purity of nature and the greater sensibility of the body."[10] Likewise, Saint Augustine strenuously objects to those who claim that intimacy would have been impossible before the Fall. Augustine points out that if it were true that man could not copulate without sin, the procreation of children would be sinful. Man would be left in a position where sin would be necessary to continue the human race. If that were true, Augustine says, it would be impossible for Christian parents to bring souls to heaven without committing a sinful act.[11] Every child, with the glorious exception of the Immaculate Conception, bears the mark of original sin on his or her soul, but that is profoundly different from claiming that the commission of actual sin is necessary to produce a child.

In this discussion of sexual intimacy in the garden, however, we should recognize a more profound reality that Saint Ambrose recognized: Adam and Eve were formed to be united in body but also—and more profoundly—in spirit.[12] Unity of body is a sign, a reflection, of unity of spirit—not the other way around. Taken and lived properly, marriage is a unity of spirit. Further, Adam and Eve were united with God as a married couple, for God had brought them together. Their friendship was rooted in their friendship with God.

---

[10] Aquinas, *Summa Theologiae*, I, Q. 98, Art. 2. See also Messenger, *Two In One Flesh*, 18.

[11] Dods, *The Works of Aurelius Augustine, Bishop of Hippo*, vol. 2, *The City of God*, 39.

[12] Savage, *The Fathers of the Church*, vol. 42, *Saint Ambrose: Hexameron, Paradise and Cain and Abel*, 174.

To be sure, Eden was not heaven; Adam and Eve did not have the "vision of the Divine Essence" reserved solely for the saints and good angels.[13] Here on earth, however, God does offer us foretastes of heaven. Insofar as divine mercy allows us tiny morsels of heaven in this fallen world, Adam and Eve enjoyed entrees. And much of that foretaste was found in marriage. As Saint Augustine observes, "And what could those persons fear or suffer in such affluence of blessings, where neither death nor ill-health was feared, and where nothing was wanting which a good will could desire, and nothing present which could interrupt man's mental or bodily enjoyment? Their love to God was unclouded, and their mutual affection was that of faithful and sincere marriage; and from this love flowed a wonderful delight."[14] Tragically, Adam and Eve's honeymoon did not last long; Augustine and Aquinas concur with what Scripture seems to attest: the Fall happened very soon after Eve arrived in the garden.[15]

Attacker of the Bond

Lucifer—brightest of the angels in being but darkest in deed—is envious. A "murderer from the beginning" (Jn 8:44), he seeks to end the first marriage. He seeks to attack the bond of marriage. And he intuits something right from the beginning: Adam and Eve's marriage is not merely a

---

[13] Aquinas, *Summa Theologiae*, Supplement, Q. 92

[14] Dods, *The Works of Aurelius Augustine, Bishop of Hippo*, vol. 2, *The City of God*, 21.

[15] Aquinas, *Summa Theologiae*, First Part, Q. 98, Art. 2. See also Messenger, *Two In One Flesh*, 18.

partnership between a man and a woman. Instead, marriage is a triangular relationship among a man, a woman, and God. If only he could make the husband and wife enemies of God, they will become enemies with each other.

And that is exactly what he did.

As Elliott explains, "Marriage is the target of the serpent, first as his tactic of seduction, playing upon the nuptial bond between man and woman to get them to fall, and then in disrupting that bond."[16] To the detriment of the whole world, they fell.

Because Eve is mentioned first in the Genesis text, the reader might assume that Eve was alone with the serpent. But she was not alone; Adam was with her—a fact confirmed using the Hebrew word immāh, which means, "who was with her."[17] Adam failed to protect his wife from danger. Adam allows his wife to be tempted; then she eats the forbidden fruit, then offers it to him. This married couple sinned together—a fact emphasized by the Church fathers.[18] This couple acted together, not to divorce each other, but to divorce God.

At the first moment of their fall, Adam and Eve run for cover, using fig leaves as makeshift clothing. Innocence has been lost, Adam and Eve's intellect is darkened, and they have their first inclinations of concupiscence, defined as "a desire of the lower appetite contrary to reason."[19] This requires

---

[16] Elliott, *What God Has Joined*, 9.

[17] Bergsma, *A Catholic Introduction to the Bible*, vol. 1, *The Old Testament*, loc. 2159 of 30084, Kindle. The authors translate the word to mean "who was with her."

[18] Levering, *Engaging the Doctrine of Marriage*, 98, Kindle.

[19] *The Catholic Encyclopedia,* vol. 4, s.v. "Concupiscence."

some explanation. Concupiscence is not synonymous with lust (because concupiscence is far broader than inordinate sexual desire and can include things like gluttony and sloth). Still, lust is a powerful component of concupiscence. Sexual desire, per se, is not wrong; in fact, God placed sexual desire in Adam and Eve. Ordinate sexual desire—like ordinate eating and drinking—is good. But concupiscence disrupts reason and produces unreasonable and improper desires. After their sin, Adam and Eve experienced concupiscence for the first time, and they were frightened. Suddenly, their world has been turned upside down.

As the devil watched with delight, he likely presumed that Adam and Eve would suffer his same fate: damnation. From the devil's perspective, Adam and Eve had committed the same sin of attempting to appropriate divinity to themselves. He also likely presumed that marriage itself was doomed; after all, this marriage had only endured for a brief amount of time. What chance did marriage have?

The devil must have been shocked that neither of these was the case.

First, Adam and Eve were not damned. They were cast out of the garden, never to return. All creation would suffer. Man's passions, for all generations, would become disordered by concupiscence through this ancestral sin. But they were not damned; quite the contrary: they were promised a Savior.

Second—and this must have infuriated the devil—marriage was not destroyed. Because of the Fall, marriage was damaged but not destroyed. The earth is cursed because of Adam and Eve's sin, but they are not cursed, nor is the marriage. God's vengeance was exacted on the serpent—the attacker of the bond—whom God primarily blames for disrupting that marriage. Speaking to the serpent, God says, "Because you have done this, cursed are you above all cattle, and above all wild animals"(Gn 3:14). Even though Adam and Eve had infinitely offended God, and their marriage would now suffer the effects of concupiscence, their marital bond remained strong. Adam and Eve left the garden in disgrace, but they left it together. Like man and the rest of creation, marriage stands in desperate need of healing.[20] Eve's villainy in the garden had left marriage in a precarious state; the heroism of another woman, however, would work to restore marriage to its former glory. And her divine Son would establish Matrimony not as a sacrament of the Old Law but as a sacrament of the New Law.

Children as Primary from the Beginning

The Catholic faith has continually upheld three ends of Matrimony: first, the procreation and education of children; second, mutual assistance of the husband and wife; third, to remedy concupiscence. Remedying concupiscence and mutual assistance have been recognized as secondary to the primary end. In fact, these secondary ends serve the primary end. As the sacrament of Matrimony is restorative, and insofar as that restoration refers to Adam and Eve's marriage, we might naturally ask: do these three ends describe Adam and Eve's marriage?

---

[20] Elliott, *What God Has Joined*, 10.

There was no concupiscence before the Fall; therefore, it cannot be said that an end of their marriage—in its original condition—was to remedy concupiscence.

What about "mutual assistance?" To address that question, we can look back to Genesis, which describes Eve as "a helper fit for him" (Gn 2:18). That phrasing implies mutual assistance. Eve was not to be a slave or employee of Adam; she was a helper for him. She was a helper with him in tending the Garden of Eden. So, we can conclude that mutual assistance was an end of the first marriage. But are we to conclude that mutual assistance was confined to caring for the garden? Or could it be that mutual assistance went far beyond caring for the flora and fauna of paradise? We will revisit that question in a moment. And that brings us to the next end: children.

The procreation and education of children is not merely an end but the primary end of marriage. This primary end teaching is the common opinion of the Church fathers, both testaments of Scripture, and the Magisterium; the teaching enjoys infallibility.[21] In his 1930 encyclical, Casti Connubii, Pope Pius XI references the 1917 Code of Canon Law: "The primary end of marriage is the procreation and education of children; the secondary [end] is mutual support and a remedy for concupiscence."[22] Further, Pope Pius XI points to the Garden of Eden to affirm this primary end: "Thus amongst the blessings of marriage, the child holds the first place. And indeed the Creator of the human race Himself,

---

[21] Marshner, *Annulment or Divorce?*, 7.

[22] Peters, *The 1917 or Pio-Benedictine Code of Canon Law*, Canon 1013.1; Pope Pius XI, *Casti Connubii*, no. 17.

Who in His goodness wishes to use men as His helpers in the propagation of life, taught this when, instituting marriage in Paradise, He said to our first parents, and through them to all future spouses: 'Increase and multiply, and fill the earth.'"[23]

Adam and Eve's bodies—in their maleness and femaleness—were created to transmit human life. And not only could they, but they were commanded to do just that. It is to their shame that Adam and Eve fell before they had the chance to conceive children in paradise, but they were certainly designed to do so. And not only were Adam and Eve intended to conceive children but so were *all* the future men and women in Eden. Aquinas states that, had Adam and Eve not fallen, *everyone* would have been called to fruitful marriage: "Hence it was fitting that all should generate, and not only the first parents. From this it seems to follow that males and females would have been in equal number."[24]

Augustine writes, "To increase and multiply and replenish the earth in virtue of the blessing of God, is a gift of marriage *as God instituted it from the beginning* before man sinned."[25] But it was not only earth that was to be replenished but heaven. It is the opinion of Saint Augustine, Saint Bonaventure, and Saint Anselm that the saved human souls will replenish the number of souls lost at Lucifer's rebellion.[26] God designed marriage to restore what Lucifer had stolen,

---

[23] Pope Pius XI, *Casti Connubii*, no. 11.

[24] Aquinas, *Summa Theologiae*, I, Q. 99, Art. 2.

[25] Dods, *The Works of Aurelius Augustine, Bishop of Hippo*, vol. 2, *The City of God*, 38, emphasis added.

[26] Augustine, "The Enchiridion on Faith, Hope and Love"; Anselm, *Cur Deus Homo*, 32. Messenger, *Two In One Flesh*, 29.

which might partially explain the devil's antipathy not only for Adam and Eve's marriage but for all Christian marriages.

Indissoluble from the Start

The recognition of the primacy of the *procreation and education of children* points to the indissolubility and fidelity of marriage.

When we use the word "procreation" from the perspective of sacramental theology, it can be defined as "the normal use of the sexual act with resultant conception and birth of a child."[27] Procreation is a momentary act, but it is sacramentally inseparable with *education*, which is lifelong. In common parlance, *education* tends to refer almost exclusively to academics—as in reading, writing, and arithmetic—but within the context of marriage, education is much more comprehensive. The word derives from the Latin *educatus*, which means "to bring up, train, and teach." This principle is established in Scripture. Proverbs reads, "Train up a child in the way he should go, and when he is old he will not depart from it" (Prv 22:6). Ephesians instructs, "Fathers, do not provoke your children to anger, but bring them up in the discipline and instruction of the Lord" (Eph 6:4). Deuteronomy commands, "And these words which I command you this day shall be upon your heart; and you shall teach them diligently to your children, and shall talk of them when you

[27] Ford, "Marriage: Its Meaning and Purposes," 345. This distinction of "normal use" is important here. "Procreation" might be used to broadly apply to medical procedures such as *in vitro* fertilization that the Church declares unlawful. That is, if a married couple partakes in an *in vitro* fertilization, they are not engaging in "procreation" but in an objectively sinful act.

sit in your house, and when you walk by the way, and when you lie down, and when you rise" (Dt 6:6–7).

These passages indicate a reality that Adam and Eve discovered; namely, bringing up and training a child is not an event but rather a process—a lifelong process of the husband and wife. It is a process in which mutual assistance, a secondary end, serves the education of children, the primary purpose. We might assume that "mutual assistance" implied a relationship between Adam and Eve that exclusively focused on each other. But in its highest manifestation, "mutual assistance" referred to the procreation and education of children. The procreation *of children* and *education of those children* are inextricably linked. A husband and wife form a bodily and spiritual unity to procreate; the husband and wife then educate until it is time for the child to "leave his father and mother and be joined to his wife" (Mt 19:5) to begin the process anew. God sent Adam a helper, not merely to tend the garden but to bring children into the world and then into heaven. As Saint Ambrose writes, "We understand that to mean a helper in the generation of the human family."[28] And that is how it was meant to be from the beginning.

This primary purpose is evident not only in Adam and Eve's marriage but throughout Scripture. Matthew Levering makes a fascinating observation in this regard:

> The association of marriage with the procreation and raising of children is treated by the Bible as a self-evident element of human life. When a married couple cannot conceive a child, this leads to sadness.

---

[28] Ambrose, "St. Ambrose on Gen. 2-3," 327.

> In numerous biblical instances, God brings about the miraculous conception of a child. This is part of the stories of Abraham and Sarah, Jacob and Rachel, and other significant biblical couples. In a poignant moment, the hapless husband Elkanah tells his childless wife, "Hannah, why do you weep? And why do you not eat? And why is your heart sad? Am I not more to you than ten sons?" (1 Sam 1:8). Of course he is not![29]

Adam and Eve's marriage was indissoluble; the very authority of Christ confirms this truth. In the nineteenth chapter of Matthew, Jesus is asked, "Is it lawful to divorce one's wife for any cause?" (Mt 19:3). Though He does not mention the names Adam and Eve, Jesus answers their question by clearly referencing their marriage. He says, "For your hardness of heart Moses allowed you to divorce your wives, but from the beginning it was not so" (Mt 19:8). The message is clear: Adam and Eve's marriage was indissoluble by divine design, and Jesus rebukes the Pharisees for failing to recognize that fact: "Have you not read that he who made them from the beginning made them male and female, and said, 'For this reason a man shall leave his father and mother and be joined to his wife, and the two shall become one'?" (Mt 19:4–5).

The Pharisees were correct in one respect: Moses had allowed divorce. In Old Testament times, God permitted men to divorce their wives—that is true. But the Pharisees should have been asking why. Aquinas references that

---

[29] Levering, *Engaging the Doctrine of Marriage*, 141.

marriage was considered indissoluble under Mosaic Law, but "the indissolubility of marriage was suspended in the law of Moses in order to avoid a greater evil, namely wife-murder."[30] Divorce, an evil, was allowed to prevent the greater evil of murder. This is hardly a ringing endorsement of divorce. The divine view of divorce is succinctly expressed in the book of Malachi: "For I hate divorce, says the LORD the God of Israel" (Mal 2:16).

This indissolubility is also inseparably linked to fidelity. Though bigamy was also allowed in Mosaic Law, marriage in the state of innocence was designed for two—only two—to become one flesh. Tertullian reminds us that bigamy was introduced to the world through the actions of Lamech, who was in the line of Cain. Lamech was a murderer like Cain and a bigamist who took two women as his wives. Tertullian writes, "Plurality of marriage began with an accursed man. Lamech was the first who, by marrying himself to two women, caused *three* to be (joined) 'into one flesh.'"[31]

We should note something here to eliminate any confusion regarding indissolubility and divorce. Within His teaching on marriage, Jesus said, "Whoever divorces his wife, *except for unchastity*, and marries another, commits adultery; and he who marries a divorced woman, commits adultery" (Mt 19:9, emphasis added). Is Jesus allowing divorce in the case of unchastity? If so, how does that stand alongside the permanence of marriage? Does this teaching constitute an exception for divorce? It does not.

---

[30] Aquinas, *Summa Theologiae*, Supplement, Q. 67, Art 3, Reply to obj. 5.

[31] Tertullian, "On Exhortation to Chastity."

Author John Meier explains that Matthew's word, often translated into English as "unchastity," is *porneia*, a word that "carries the sense of incestuous union."[32] Jesus was saying that in the case of incestuous "marriage," the consanguinity prohibition applied: there was never a true marriage in the first place. For confirmation of his argument, Meier indicates that the same word "porneia" was used in 1 Corinthians 5:1: "It is actually reported that there exists among you *porneia*, and such *porneia* as does not even exist among the pagans; that a man should have his father's wife."[33] It might reasonably be asked: Why would Jesus bring the matter of incestuous marriage up at all? The reason, as Meier explains, is that the Jewish people at that time were "almost unique in their strict prohibitions of incestuous marriages."[34]

In addition to Meier, other theologians note the use of *porneia* and draw similar conclusions. Father E. C. Messenger, for instance, notes that porneia "is certainly not the word usually employed to signify adultery,"[35] that is, sexual sin committed *within* marriage. In Matthew 19:9, Jesus was not referring to a problem that occurred *during* the marriage but rather an impediment that preexisted in what appeared to be a marriage. Jesus is essentially saying, *And I say to you: whoever divorces his wife, except in the case where there was never a valid marriage, and marries another, commits adultery.* Jesus's essential teaching is that a lawfully married person cannot marry another; to do so is to perform the act of adultery.

---

[32] Meier, *The Vision of Matthew*, 256.

[33] Meier, 256.

[34] Meier, 254.

[35] Messenger, *Two In One Flesh*, 110.

Jesus's teaching is clear: Matrimony was designed to be an indissoluble union for the primary purpose of procreation and upbringing of children.

The Lessons of Tobias

In the garden, the serpent showed his hand: he is the cunning adversary of humanity who hated (and still hates) marriage. Of course, the devil cannot destroy marriage; he can only tempt humans to destroy their own. He tried it with Adam, who refused to cast the serpent out of the garden, thus failing to protect his wife and his marriage. But what if Adam *had* cast out the serpent? What might his marriage have been like if Adam had exorcised that envious creature? Scripture does not tell us precisely, but it gives us a fascinating peek in the Old Testament book of Tobit.

The book recounts the history of Tobit and his family during the Assyrian captivity, some seven centuries before Christ. As the head of the family, Tobit has been blind for years. His blindness rendered him unable to work and has devastated his marriage to the point where Tobit prays for death. At the same time, Tobit is offering this prayer, we learn the story of a beautiful young woman named Sarah, who lives in the town of Med'ia. Sarah has been married seven times, and each of her husbands died on his wedding night. Sarah did nothing wrong, but her father's servants accused her of causing these men's death. Sarah desperately wants to be married and have children, but a lasting marriage has escaped her for some unknown reason. Like Tobit, Sarah prays to die. Tobit's marriage is falling apart; none of

Sarah's seven marriages even make it to the point of consummation. And both are desperately miserable.[36] When we readers are introduced to Tobit and Sarah, their paths are about to cross.

Tobit has entrusted "ten talents of silver" (Tb 4:20) to a relative in Med'ia, so he instructs his son, Tobias, to retrieve that wealth. Tobias prays for help and locates a guide to help him on his journey. (Tobias later discovers that this is no ordinary guide; rather, it is the archangel Raphael.) Along the way, Tobias stepped into the Tigris River, where a massive fish jumped from the water, seemingly attempting to swallow Tobias. But Raphael instructed Tobias: "Catch the fish" (Tb 6:3). Tobias caught the fish, fileted it, ate it, and—following the instruction of Raphael—carefully preserved the heart, liver, and gall and dutifully stored them in his pack.

At the end of their journey, Tobias asked Raphael why he had instructed him to keep the organs of the fish. Raphael told him, "As for the heart and liver, if a demon or evil spirit gives trouble to any one, you make a smoke from these before the man or woman, and that person will never be troubled again. And as for the gall, anoint with it a man who has white films in his eyes, and he will be cured" (Tb 6:7–8). Raphael also informed him that he should marry Sarah, who he described as "sensible, brave, and very beautiful" (Tb 6:12). Tobias made an obvious objection: marriage to Sarah seemed to carry an immediate death sentence. Raphael explained that the lust demon named Asmodeus

---

[36] Bergsma, *A Catholic Introduction to the Bible*, loc. 9884–9949 of 30084, Kindle.

had killed each of these seven men on his wedding night. But Raphael assured Tobias with this beautiful soliloquy:

> Now listen to me, brother, for she will become your wife; and do not worry about the demon, for this very night she will be given to you in marriage. When you enter the bridal chamber, you shall take live ashes of incense and lay upon them some of the heart and liver of the fish so as to make a smoke. Then the demon will smell it and flee away, and will never again return. And when you approach her, rise up, both of you, and cry out to the merciful God, and he will save you and have mercy on you. Do not be afraid, for she was destined for you from eternity. You will save her, and she will go with you, and I suppose that you will have children by her. (Tb 6:15–17)

Upon hearing of his destiny, Tobias fell in love with Sarah. On the night of their wedding, Tobias did what Raphael instructed, reciting this prayer:

> Blessed are you, O God of our fathers, and blessed be your holy and glorious name for ever. Let the heavens and all your creatures bless you. You made Adam and gave him Eve his wife as a helper and support. From them the race of mankind has sprung. You said, "It is not good that the man should be alone; let us make a helper for him like himself." And now, O Lord, I am not taking this sister of mine because of lust, but with sincerity. Grant that I may find mercy and may grow old together with her. (Tb 8:5–7)

Tobias and Sarah prayed together and then went to sleep, putting off the consummation of their marriage until the third night. Tobias returned to his father with the miraculous medicine from this fish, which restored his sight. Tobias lived for many years, faithful to Sarah, faithful to God, in a marriage richly blessed with children. His prayer's reference to Adam and Eve was appropriate, for Tobias and Sarah had done what Adam and Eve had failed to do: expel the serpent from their marital home and put their faith and hope in the mercy of God.

Tobias and Sarah's marriage serves as a powerful witness: strong marriages drive out demons.

Of course, it also illustrates something else: the devil hates marriage. That fact was immediately known to Sarah's seven suitors, as well as her and Tobias. But just as hell did not have the final say for Tobias and Sarah, nor will hell have the final say about marriage. If the devil thought he had destroyed marriage, he thought wrong. Marriage would triumph. And the triumph of marriage, the mystical and indissoluble union of man and wife before God, would have a mediatrix. That mediatrix, a married woman of perpetual virginity, would be the same woman who was promised to crush the head of the devil. While Eden's wedding had no human guests, another wedding did.

The Wedding Feast at Cana

In the opening chapters of Genesis, marriage faced a near apocalypse. Adam and Eve invited a serpent into their wedding abode, and marriage fell. But that was not the end of marriage. In the opening chapters of the Gospel of John, we learn the story of another married couple. Though they had no way of knowing it at the time, they had invited the Savior of the world to their wedding. From their first moments together as husband and wife, Christ physically stood at the center of the marriage.

The couple had also invited Mary, the Mother of God. Mary turned to her divine Son in a time of embarrassment for this couple. The couple had run out of wine, a significant social blunder. Mary told Jesus something He already knew: "They have no wine" (Jn 2:3). Mary knew the consequence of her words. Up until now, Jesus had not worked a public miracle; the Gospel of John informs explicitly of that fact. Why had Jesus not worked a miracle? Saint John Chrysostom explains that if Jesus had worked public miracles as a young boy, others would have "deemed the thing a delusion" and rejected Him.[37] But it would have had a more profound effect. As Chrysostom writes, "If while quite young He had wrought miracles," His persecutors would "have hurried Him sooner and before the proper time to the Cross, in the venom of their malice."[38] Mary knew that this miracle would begin the path of the public life of Jesus, and that His path would end on a cross. The response of Jesus underscores that fact as He tells His mother, "O woman, what have you to do with me? My hour has not yet come" (Jn 2:4). Mary's observation about the lack of wine led to Jesus beginning His public life. Jesus could have begun His public life at any time, yet He began it at a wedding at

[37] Chrysostom, "Homily 21 on the Gospel of John."
[38] Chrysostom, "Homily 21 on the Gospel of John."

Mary's urging. It is clear that Jesus loves marriage, as does His mother.

To the brim, the servants poured water into six huge waterpots, and Jesus turned ordinary water into the best wine. More than a hundred gallons of water was turned into wine. It is declared the best of wine; through this miracle, Jesus "manifested his glory; and his disciples believed in him" (Jn 2:11).

The Catholic Church definitively teaches that Jesus instituted each of the seven sacraments, but that definitive teaching does not inform us as to the exact moment that marriage was raised to a sacrament. But whether it was at the precise moment that Jesus turned water into wine, this wedding at Cana played a beautiful role in reversing what Adam and Eve had damaged. The first sacrament in the Old Testament appears to be the first sacrament of the New Testament.

The centrality of Matrimony was clear to early Christians and to the Christians who followed. It was the hill they would die on. As we are about to see, many illustrious martyrs of the Catholic Church would defend Matrimony to the death.

2

Letting No Man Put Asunder: When Catholics Defended Marriage to the Death

"Blessed Thomas More is more important at this moment than at any moment since his death, even perhaps the great moment of his dying; but he is not quite so important as he will be in about a hundred years' time. . . .If there had not happened to be that particular man at that particular moment, the whole of history would have been different."[39]

—G. K. Chesterton

IN THE ILLUSTRIOUS twenty centuries of Church history, many men and women have died in defense of Matrimony. This fact has often been obscured by vaguely referring to certain saints like Thomas More and Bishop John Fisher as martyrs for "the Faith." But if we are to study and learn from the lives of the saints, a practice that the Magisterium has so often recommended, we need to know their stories. Catholic martyrs provide an everlasting witness as to what

[39] Chesterton, "A Turning Point in History," in *The Fame of Blessed Thomas More: Being Addresses Delivered in His Honour in Chelsea, July 1929*, 63.

the Church believes. Across time and place, they tell their fellow Catholics what is worth *living* for, and what is worth dying for. Some men and women live their lives and give their lives to protect and cultivate the sacraments. Why? Because as Pope John XXIII reminded the faithful in his encyclical *Mater et Magistra*, the Church is our mother, and the sacraments are the mother's milk of Catholic life. In our present age of sacramental crisis—we see the sacraments under venomous attack—we need to open the pages of these biographies. We need to recognize that many saints died in defense of the sacraments, and we need to be inspired by that example.

In the year 258, Saint Tarcisius died for "the Faith." But to be more specific, Tarcisius, a young deacon in Rome, was discovered carrying the Eucharist when Christianity was a crime against the state. Tarcisius was beaten to death by ruthless attackers who possessed a Luciferian fury. Tarcisius never raised a hand to defend himself; instead, he died while desperately clutching the precious Body of Christ to his own. After he eventually succumbed to death, his murderers searched his body for the Eucharist, only to find that the Eucharist had disappeared.[40] Saint Tarcisius gave his life for the sacrament of the Eucharist. On June 6, 1944, US Army Captain Ignatius Maternowski parachuted into Normandy. While two million men carried out their singular mission on that fateful D-Day, Father Maternowski had his own mission. Once his boots touched ground, he administered Anointing of the Sick to the dying soldiers. For his efforts, Father Maternowski was shot in the back and killed by a

---

[40] Butler, *Butler's Lives of the Saints*, 335.

Nazi.[41] Father Maternowski gave his life for the Anointing of the Sick.

We should also include those who devoted their lives to the exercise of a sacrament; sometimes, these saints might be referred to as white martyrs. And in that regard, Saint John Vianney provides an excellent example. Father Vianney, a parish priest in the tiny town of Ars, France, offered absolution for eighteen hours a day for decades. Penitents came from all over France and Europe. Some even came from America by ship, so it can be said that Vianney's confessional line stretched back to New York harbor. As Father Vianney lay on his deathbed, penitents came to him, and he offered them deathbed absolutions. Vianney gave his life for the sacrament of Reconciliation.[42]

And that brings us to the biographies of those who died for the sacrament of Matrimony.

The Early Christian Martyrs

The rights, duties, and graces of the sacrament of Matrimony are not one-time events but rather realities that operate over a husband and wife's lifetime. As the Church has taught since her infancy, the primary purpose of marriage is the procreation and education of children.[43] Thus, the duty to protect the Catholic upbringing of children flows from the sacrament itself. Therefore, any comprehensive discussion

---

[41] Weidenkopf, "Father Ignatius Maternowski: D-Day Chaplain."

[42] Rutler, *The Cure d'Ars Today*, 186–92, Kindle.

[43] Marshner, *Annulment or Divorce?*, 33. Marshner notes that "the doctrine that marriage is primarily for the sake of procreation is already taught at a time when the ink is scarcely dry on the New Testament."

regarding the martyrs of marriage must reference parents who died to communicate the Faith to their children.

Accordingly, this list would include all those Christian parents who were martyred during the Roman persecution. For instance, during the reign of Emperor Claudius (circa AD 41–54), a married Catholic couple named Marius and Martha took a pilgrimage to Rome, bringing their two sons. They were captured and savagely "tortured on the rack with fire, lacerated with iron hooks," and had their hands cut off.[44] The entire family was murdered; Marius and his sons "were beheaded and cast into the flames."[45] In Rome, a man named Craton and his wife and children—who had all been baptized by "the holy bishop Valentine"—were martyred together.[46] In the town of Spoleto, husband and father Venustian was martyred along "with his wife and sons."[47] Claudius, husband and father, was executed by being fastened to a large rock and thrown into the river to drown. His sons were also executed. When Claudius's wife, Hilaria, was praying at the graves of her sons, she was arrested and executed.[48]

In the early second century, in the little town northeast of Rome called Tivoli, a scene occurred that was strikingly reminiscent of an account in the second book of Maccabees. In that Old Testament account, a mother and her seven sons were brought before the king, who insisted they eat the flesh of swine, or die. Recounted in one of Scripture's most harrowing and heroic chapters, the brothers refused. One by

---

44 *The Roman Martyrology*, 19.
45 *The Roman Martyrology*, 19.
46 *The Roman Martyrology*, 48.
47 *The Roman Martyrology*, 401.
48 *The Roman Martyrology*, 372.

one, they were tortured and killed. The king and his toadies seem to have thought the sight would sway the mother. But the mother encouraged each of them to be valorous to the end. When it was time for the seventh son to renounce his faith or die, he began to waver. His mother's response inspired him to the end. Scripture recounts her speech:

> My son, have pity on me. I carried you nine months in my womb, and nursed you for three years, and have reared you and brought you up to this point in your life, and have taken care of you. I beg you, my child, to look at the heaven and the earth and see everything that is in them, and recognize that God did not make them out of things that existed. Thus also mankind comes into being. Do not fear this butcher, but prove worthy of your brothers. Accept death, so that in God's mercy I may get you back again with your brothers. (2 Mc 7:27–29)

Inspired by his mother's words and divine grace, the seventh son defiantly shouted at the king and his attackers, "What are you waiting for? I will not obey the king's command, but I obey the command of the law that was given to our fathers through Moses" (2 Mc 7:30). Scripture recounts that he was treated worse than the previous six brothers. After seeing her seven sons die at the hands of a vicious tyrant, she was also killed.

The Roman Martyrology offers few details concerning the Christian mother of seven sons, but it does tell us this: "At Tivoli, in the time of the emperor Adrian, St. Symphorosa, wife of the martyr St. Getulius, with her seven sons,

Crescens, Julian, Nemesius, Primitivus, Justinus, Stacteus, and Eugenius. Their mother, because of her invincible constancy, was first buffeted a long time, then suspended by her hair, and lastly thrown into the river with a stone tied to her body. Her sons had their limbs distended by pulleys and bound to stakes, and terminated their martyrdom by different kinds of death."[49] Saint Symphorosa, a woman of "invincible constancy," was faithful to her baptism and the fruits of her Matrimony.

The *Martyrology* also recounts those married couples who seem to be childless since it does not mention sons or daughters. Under the Great Persecution of Decius, husband Galation and his wife, Epistemis, "were scourged, had their hands, feet and tongue severed from their bodies" and then were beheaded.[50] Husband and wife Chrysanthus and Daria were "thrown into a sandpit" and "buried alive."[51] Andronicus and his wife, Athanasia, were martyred in Jerusalem.[52]

Another such couple is Saints Timothy and Maura, who were married in the year 286 under the violent reign of Diocletian. The lector Timothy married seventeen-year-old Maura. But just a few days after their wedding, Timothy was arrested by the officials and threatened with torture and death if he did not surrender his Christian books. His persecutor thought Timothy would fold under pressure. He thought wrong. The persecutor asked, "You see, don't you, the instruments prepared for torture?" Timothy responded,

---

[49] *The Roman Martyrology*, 211.
[50] *The Roman Martyrology*, 342.
[51] *The Roman Martyrology*, 329.
[52] *The Roman Martyrology*, 312.

"But don't you see the angels of God, which are strengthening me?" Surely, the angels strengthened Timothy, for he was burnt with hot irons and blinded, yet remained steadfast.[53]

The officials brought Maura to Timothy in the hopes that she would convince Timothy to surrender his holy books. For her refusal to do so, she also suffered immense tortures. Maura's hair was ripped out and she was immersed in boiling water. Yet she lived. Aggravated by their faithfulness to Christianity, and perhaps even more infuriated that they seemed to draw strength from each other, the emperor nailed the couple to two crosses, facing each other. As they hung from their crosses, they sang Christian songs and prayed together. One might imagine that they comforted each other with the promise of Jesus to the good thief: "Truly, I say to you, today you will be with me in Paradise" (Lk 23:43). After nine days, crucifixion had taken both their lives.[54]

The Roman martyrology catalogs many husbands and wives suffering martyrdom together. They were faithful to their vows of baptism and marriage to the end. And though some were only married for a few days before their martyrdoms, they celebrated their honeymoons in heaven.

Henry VIII Sets the Stage for Martyrs

To understand the Church's position on Matrimony and annulment, it is vital to familiarize oneself with the case of Henry VIII and his marriage to Catherine of Aragon.

---

[53] Hunter-Kilmer, "Saints Timothy and Maura."

[54] *The Roman Martyrology,* 126; Hunter-Kilmer, "Saints Timothy and Maura."

Biographies of Henry VIII abound, yet historians commonly miss the most critical factors here from a Catholic perspective. They often overlook the quintessential fact about the case: Henry did not seek a divorce from Catherine—at least, not at first. Henry sought an annulment before seeking a divorce. Henry's actions gave rise to martyrs for Matrimony. But to understand that heroism and why it was heroic in the first place, we need to look back at the events that led up to it.

Henry Tudor, the future King Henry VIII, was born on June 28, 1491—one day before the feast of saints Peter and Paul and one year before "Columbus sailed the ocean blue" for the new world. Upon his birth, however, it was not Henry but his older brother Arthur who was in line for the throne of England, being Henry VII's oldest son and five years Henry's senior.

As was often a custom in those times, royalty often married royalty. In 1501, Princess Catherine of Aragon—daughter of Queen Isabel of Spain, who financed the voyage of Christopher Columbus—sailed from her native Spain to marry Arthur, the Prince of Wales. Though the union of marriage between Catherine and Arthur was strongly encouraged by Henry VII as a political alliance, the couple nevertheless welcomed the nuptials. Catherine and Arthur had exchanged letters over the years, and now it was time to meet and to marry.[55]

When fifteen-year-old Catherine arrived on the shores of England, she met ten-year-old Henry, who immediately

---

[55] Mattingly, *Catherine of Aragon*, 20–22; Bruce, *The Making of Henry VIII*, 127, Kindle.

developed what we would call a schoolboy crush.[56] Nevertheless, Catherine was to be Arthur's bride, and they married soon after her arrival. But it was an ill-fated marriage because Arthur had been extremely sick, unbeknownst to his family. By the spring of 1502, Arthur was dead. Catherine became a widow at sixteen, and Henry was now in line for king. In April of 1509, King Henry VII died of tuberculosis, and nineteen-year-old Henry took the throne as Henry VIII. Two months later, he married Catherine, making his former sister-in-law his wife and queen.

Then, as now, the idea of marrying a brother's widow may seem an unsightly breach of etiquette; more importantly, it raised an issue with canon law. At that time, the letter of canon law considered that an impediment existed to this proposed marriage, called an "impediment of affinity."[57] Though current canon law prohibits marriage between "direct line . . . blood relatives,"[58] the canon law of that time prohibited a man from marrying his brother's widow. In fact, it prevented a man from marrying a woman who had sexual relations with his brother, either inside or outside marriage.[59]

To underscore a critical point here, a marriage is not generally complete *unless and until* it is consummated.[60] On this point, Catherine repeatedly claimed that her marriage to

---

[56] Bruce, *The Making of Henry VIII,* 129–30.

[57] Blackburn, "Why did Henry VIII need a dispensation to marry his brother's widow, Catherine of Aragon?"

[58] *The Code of Canon Law*, Canon 1093.

[59] Blackburn, "Why did Henry VIII need a dispensation to marry his brother's widow, Catherine of Aragon?"

[60] There are a few exceptions to this rule, but none of them apply in this case.

Arthur had never been consummated. (This would become a relevant point years later.) But whether her marriage to Arthur was consummated or not, the pope had the power to provide a papal dispensation for Henry and Catherine to marry. And Pope Julius II granted this dispensation. It is noteworthy that this dispensation was not unique by any means; Pope Julius had granted other dispensations, as had previous popes; such dispensation was an established papal right.[61] In any case, in 1509, King Henry VIII married Catherine of Aragon, making her the queen of England.

Some might speculate that the marriage of Henry and Catherine was doomed from the beginning. After all, political alliances and romance tend to make strange bedfellows (and sometimes fail to make bedfellows at all). Yet, it was not primarily pressure from Henry VII toward his son to form political alliance that motivated Henry and Catherine. Quite the contrary: Henry's father had tried to halt the proposed marriage between his son and Catherine. All this might explain why Henry waited until after his father's death to marry Catherine. They were in love. By all accounts—most notably their own—Henry and Catherine had a happy marriage, at least for the first years of their marriage. Henry frequently expressed his love for Catherine in letters, and there is no doubt that Catherine loved her teenage husband. They were popular with both commoners and noble classes. Years later, Kipling wrote about those who could "talk with crowds and keep your virtue," and "walk with Kings" and

---

[61] A papal dispensation was issued by Julius II on behalf of husband William Skevyngton and wife Anne Digby, who were cousins.

not "lose the common touch."[62] As a young newlywed, that was Henry. But as popular as Henry was, Catherine was even more admired by the British. Catherine was a statuesque princess of gray eyes and reddish-blonde hair—a twenty-four-year-old queen whom the people of her new country loved.[63] It furthered the affection of their subjects that Henry and Catherine were devout Catholics in a Catholic nation. Henry frequently attended Mass several times a day and enjoyed arguing against Lutheran theology almost as much as he enjoyed hunting. Henry also penned—or at least lent his name—to writings defending the sacrament of Matrimony.[64]

But while their marriage had a storybook beginning, sadly, the tumult began in the early chapters. For while many wedding vows contain the promise to "love, honor, and cherish," queens are expected another duty: to produce a healthy male heir to the throne. But that proved impossible. Catherine had a baby boy on the first day of 1511, but the baby died before the end of February. Several stillbirths and miscarriages followed that tragedy. Though Catherine had multiple pregnancies, only one child saw her first birthday: Mary Tudor, born in 1516. It became increasingly clear to Henry that Catherine would not be able to produce a healthy son. That inability carried political implications, and Henry entertained thoughts of looking outside his lawful marriage to produce a male heir.

---

[62] Rudyard Kipling in his poem *If*.

[63] Mattingly, *Catherine of Aragon*, 29.

[64] Carroll, *The Cleaving Of Christendom*, 11; Bowle, *Henry VIII*, 91–93.

But another reason Henry was looking to end his marriage was his insatiable lust for other women. It is unknown when Henry first broke his vow of fidelity, but it was no later than 1514.[65] For a few years, Henry may have tried to hide his numerous infidelities, but in 1519, Henry fathered a child with lady-in-waiting Bessie Blount and his days of discreet liaisons were over. Two years later, he had an ongoing affair with a woman named Mary, who was married to a British diplomat.[66] Henry's gluttonies were not confined to the dinner table. By 1526, Henry became sexually involved with Mary's nineteen-year-old sister. Her name was Anne Boleyn. And it was Henry's pursuit of young Anne that would change history forever.

Anne quickly proved much shrewder than Henry's previous mistresses, insofar as she was not content to be—in the words of historian Warren Carroll—just "another trophy of the royal bedroom."[67] Come hell or high water, Anne was determined to be queen.

Of course, the idea of Anne becoming the new queen was absurd. Henry had taken lifelong vows to Catherine, and terminating a true marriage—then, now, and for all time—is theologically impossible. But Henry concocted a plot: What if his marriage to Catherine had been invalid in the first place? If there had never been a marriage, Henry was free to marry someone else.

So Henry enlisted the help of a powerful prelate to concoct the case for annulment: Cardinal Thomas Wolsey.

---

[65] Scarisbrick, *Henry VIII*, 147.
[66] Scarisbrick, 148.
[67] Carroll, *The Cleaving of Christendom*, 113.

Wolsey was both the cardinal primate of England (meaning that his ecclesiastical rank was above all the other clergy of the country) and high chancellor (meaning that he served as Henry's chief political advisor). He was also corrupt, insofar he chose State over Church, irrespective of morality—a fact he finally admitted a few days before his death.[68]

But even with Wolsey's political and canonical acumen, what was the case for annulment? After all, by this point, Henry and Catherine had been married for eighteen years. Corrupt as he was, Wolsey knew that an annulment has nothing to do with future events; a finding of *nullity* must be based on impediments *prior* to wedding vows and consummation. Nullity is not the stuff of *ex post facto*. Henry could cheat on Catherine with every woman in England, but that would not nullify the marriage. To argue nullity was to claim that an impediment existed *before* vows and consummation. Wolsey had the answer, or at least pretended to think he had the answer: that the papal dispensation to marry Catherine (as his brother's former wife) was illegitimate.

In 1527, Henry announced that he was having pangs of conscience about his marriage—that he had married in contradiction to a passage in the book of Leviticus. That Henry should have been plagued by conscience is indisputable, but the notion that his conscience was troubled by the legitimacy of his marriage could not be taken seriously. By 1527, Henry had conducted so many affairs and one-night stands that historians have found it virtually impossible to catalog them all. It is unlikely that Henry VIII had gone a single day in a decade without breaking the sixth or ninth commandments.

---

[68] Carroll, 109.

Nevertheless, Wolsey presented Henry's annulment case to Pope Clement VII in 1527. But at that moment, Clement VII had much greater worries than the lustful ambitions of a royal philanderer.[69] The Protestant Revolt was sweeping across Europe and threatening to decapitate the Roman Catholic Church. In the spring of that year, thousands of soldiers sacked Rome during the Italian wars. The pope escaped, but Spanish and German forces burnt churches, tortured and murdered priests, desecrated the Eucharist, and raped women. As an eyewitness phrased it, "Hell itself was a more beautiful sight to behold."[70] In the melee, the pope was taken prisoner. Henry's demand for annulment reached the pope shortly after his escape.

Rather than give an immediate and authoritative declaration as to the validity of the marriage, Clement VII authorized a marriage tribunal to determine its status. Although the pope reserved authority regarding the final verdict, the pope appointed two cardinals to oversee the proceedings: Wolsey and Cardinal Lorenzo Campeggio. Wolsey was happy with the choice of Campeggio—at least initially. Wolsey's actions regarding the case were predictable from the beginning, but Campeggio was another story. Campeggio was born in Milan in 1464, became a famous attorney, was married in the year 1500, and the marriage was blessed with three children.[71] After the death of his wife in 1510, Campeggio was ordained and became

---

[69] Carroll, 116.

[70] Hook, *The Sack of Rome*, xiii.

[71] Mattingly, *Catherine of Aragon*, 254. Some historians claim that Campeggio had five children, but Mattingly writes that he had three.

a cardinal in 1517. If Wolsey had been expecting a show trial, he was sadly mistaken. Because Lorenzo Campeggio not only believed in the sacrament of Matrimony but had experienced the love and graces of that great sacrament, which—in profound ways fully known only to God alone—still flowed through him.

But the trial took many months to convene—in some measure, by papal design. The pope had desperately hoped that Henry and Catherine would be reconciled, so he tried to delay the opening of the tribunal. But Anne was growing impatient and refused any further sexual relations with Henry until she was crowned the new queen. Henry was getting desperate, illustrated by the fact that, without the knowledge of Cardinal Wolsey, Henry sent a message to the pope asking for his permission to commit bigamy with Anne Boleyn.[72] As Warren Carroll puts it, in all papal history, "there has not been a more brazenly shameless request of the Vicar of Christ."[73] Even Wolsey, who often put his political aspirations over his priestly duties, was shocked at this request when he heard about it.

Henry's insistence on marrying Anne Boleyn raised another rather significant issue. If an impediment of affinity were created by Catherine's sexual relations with Henry's brother, a similar impediment would exist—even if Henry's arguments of affinity were affirmed—with Anne Boleyn. After all, Henry had conducted a lengthy affair with Anne's sister Mary. If Henry proved the impediment, that same impediment would have prevented him from marrying

[72] Mattingly, 244.
[73] Carroll, *The Cleaving of Christendom,* 117.

Anne.[74] Sadly, Henry would have faced similar impediments with ladies throughout his kingdom.

Nevertheless, on June 18, 1529, the most important annulment case in Church history—before or since—commenced. As we shall see, what followed that trial was an age of martyrs. It is said that divorce is hardest on children. But in the case of King Henry VIII's failed marriage, it proved harder on churchmen and statesmen. Henry's attempted annulment to his wife, Catherine of Aragon, ended in an alimony of bloodshed.

Matrimony on Trial

Catherine's legal defense team members were either appointed or required to be approved by Henry's legal team. To call that a *conflict of interest* would be a radical understatement. Another conflict existed—the trial was taking place in England, where Henry possessed the authority to execute those subjects he deemed disloyal, potentially including Catherine's attorneys. As it turned out, this was no unfounded worry. Catherine was aware of these injustices, so she appeared personally—and quite unexpectedly—during the opening court session to appeal her case to Rome, where a fair trial could take place. But her appeal was denied, and the case came to full session three days later.[75]

But if Catherine's court entrance on June 18 had been dramatic, it was far overshadowed by her appearance on June 21. The queen was called into the courtroom which was already filled with dignitaries. The seating arrangement

---

[74] Mattingly, *Catherine of Aragon*, 244.

[75] DeParmiter, *The King's Great Matter*, 99.

spoke volumes: King Henry was perched on a royal throne, sitting above everyone else the room, including the cardinals, court officers, numerous bishops, including the archbishop of Canterbury. A chair was reserved for Catherine, placed beneath Henry's.[76] But Catherine—shocking the assemblage—proceeded to walk past her designated seat and knelt at the feet of her husband and offered a powerful testimony:

> I beseech you for all the loves that hath been between us, and for the love of God, let me have justice and right, take of me some pity and compassion, for I am a poor woman, and a stranger, born out of your dominion, I have here no assured friend and much less indifferent counsel. I flee to you, as to the head of justice within this realm. . . .
>
> I take God and all the world to witness that I have been to you a true, humble, and obedient wife, ever comfortable to your will and pleasure . . . , being always well pleased and contented with all the things wherein you had any delight or dalliance, whether it were little or much.
>
> . . . This twenty years or more I have been your true wife, and by me ye have had divers children, although it hath pleased God to call them from this world. . . .
>
> And when ye had me at the first, I take God to be my judge, I was a true maid, without touch of man. And whether it be true or no, I put it to your conscience. . . .

[76] Mattingly, *Catherine of Aragon,* 271.

> I humbly require you to spare the extremity of this new court. . . . And if ye will not, to God I commit my cause.[77]

Catherine then rose, curtsied to her royal husband, and—disregarding repeated orders from the bench to return to the courtroom—exited.[78]

Modern sensibilities might be more scornful of Catherine's speech than congratulatory: after all, Henry was a lustful fornicator who was unworthy of Catherine's respect. No one, however, was more aware of that fact, or more personally effected by that reality, than Catherine. But that perspective misses the crucial point here: future actions do not invalidate a marriage. And although a husband or wife may turn their marriage into a veritable hell, the marriage was made in heaven and remains indissoluble. Just as God not only creates us but maintains us in existence even if we reject Him, so also with Matrimony. Catherine was not merely standing up for *her* marriage; she was standing up for *marriage*. Catherine recognized her duty as a lawful wife was to help her husband get to heaven, despite his vicious fornications that threatened to damn him to hell. As historian Garrett Mattingly put it, Catherine "was fighting the devil and all his minions for her husband's soul."[79] From the perspective of the theological virtue of charity, Catherine's actions were painfully heroic. And when we discuss the martyrs and heroes created in Henry's wake, we should begin that discussion with Catherine.

---

[77] Mattingly, 272–73.
[78] Mattingly, 273.
[79] Mattingly, 277.

Notwithstanding Catherine's impassioned speech, Henry stood firmly and again referenced his troubled conscience to the court—an absurdity that should have insulted everyone's intelligence and sense of decency. But just four days after Catherine's fiery speech, an event illustrated that morality was not a concern of the English bishops, except one: Bishop John Fisher. Fisher was ordained at the age of twenty-two and was promoted to bishop by thirty-three. By his mid-forties, he was appointed as chancellor of Cambridge University and bishop of Rochester, England. Fisher had been close to the Tudors; in fact, Fisher had been an academic tutor to the future Henry VIII many years prior, and delivered the funeral oration for Henry VII.[80] Fisher was known throughout the country as an outspoken critic of Martin Luther and his theology. Fisher wrote extensive critiques of Luther's theology. A man of letters and virtues, he was almost universally regarded as one of England's most learned and holy men.

Bishop John Fisher was also Catherine's most trusted lawyer in court. Though Catherine stated that she had no "assured friend" in court, Fisher would prove to be her friend. The sanctity of her marriage was the hill that Fisher was willing to die on; six years later, it was the hill that Fisher *did* die on.

When Fisher arrived in court on the morning of June 25, William Warham, the archbishop of Canterbury, read off a list of those bishops in England who agreed with Henry's theological assessment of his annulment. To Fisher's surprise,

---

[80] *The Catholic Encyclopedia*, s.v. "St. John Fisher"; Mayor, *The English Works of John Fisher*, 268.

Warham listed Fisher's name and showed that Fisher's seal was attached to the letter. Fisher informed Warham that it was a forgery. At this point, two things had become clear: first, every bishop in England except Fisher was on Henry's side; second, the court was obscenely fraudulent. Forging a signature by the defendant's attorney destroyed any potential credibility; two weeks later, Compeggio adjourned the proceedings to present the case to Rome.[81] But in arguing Catherine's case, Fisher had already made enemies with Henry.

In October, Cardinal Wolsey was arrested on trumped-up charges of insubordination to the king and replaced as chancellor by Thomas More.

Henry's chief argument in favor of his annulment—at least initially—was that the pope's dispensation had not been done properly. He and his attorneys took great lengths to parse the exact language of the papal dispensation made decades prior. On this matter, Cardinal Campeggio had raised a point in 1528 that would have easily quelled Henry's scruples: the reigning pope, Clement VII, could simply issue a new dispensation with language pleasing to Henry and proceed to bless and confirm their marriage.[82] Of course, Henry was not interested in that proposition, and neither was Anne Boleyn, through whose eyes Henry now saw the world. Boleyn's vision—or blindness—was not good news for England or the Catholic faith. As Charles V's imperial ambassador to England noted, Anne Boleyn was "more Lutheran than Luther himself."[83]

---

[81] Carroll, *The Cleaving of Christendom,* 125.

[82] Coates, *The King's Great Matter*, loc. 923 of 3076, Kindle.

[83] DeParmiter, *The King's Great Matter,* 19. From an original letter

After the marriage tribunal—the legatine court—was halted, Thomas Cromwell, a man who had been an assistant to Cardinal Wolsey, emerged and gained the ear of Henry. Cromwell's suggestion to Henry was simple: since the papacy will not deem your marriage invalid, turn around and deem the papacy invalid. Declare yourself the head of the Church of England and make your own rulings regarding your marriage.[84] Henry liked the idea.

In 1532, William Warham died, and Henry appointed Thomas Cranmer as archbishop of Canterbury in 1533. Henry wanted a Lutheran in the position, and Cranmer was the perfect choice in that regard. Cranmer argued that Henry's marriage was none of Rome's business. Henry liked that logic and finally married Anne Boleyn—who was pregnant with Henry's child—in January of 1533. Henry didn't bother waiting for his marriage to be annulled to Catherine before his marriage to Anne. Four months after his bigamous marriage to Anne, Cranmer—as promised—annulled Henry's marriage to Catherine.[85] Cranmer had officially gone rogue. After he heard of Cranmer's annulment farce, Pope Clement VII excommunicated Cranmer and threatened Henry with excommunication if he refused to recognize his marriage with Catherine.

In one of the last official acts of his papacy, Pope Clement VII affirmed the validity of Henry and Catherine's marriage. But by then, the Catholic king had lost his faith and was about to take it out on his Catholic subjects. It must

---

from Eustace Chapuys to Charles V dated March 6, 1532.

[84] Carroll, *The Cleaving of Christendom*, 127.

[85] Carroll, 135–40.

be said that Pope Clement brought much of these troubles on himself and the Church. Catherine of Aragon had possessed a papal bull declaring her marriage valid since her wedding day. Clement VII's disastrous delay in affirming the validity of one marriage resulted in threatening or damaging millions of souls. Warren Carroll, whose intense love for the papacy is evident in his writings, writes, "It would have been better for the Church, in fact, if Clement VII had died during the first year of his pontificate."[86] Because of his delay, the Catholic Church was devastated in England.

It was about to intensify.

The English Martyrs

During the annulment ordeal outlined above, the majority of England staunchly opposed Henry's affair, divorce, and remarriage. Even if their king turned his back on his valid marriage, his people would not: the British people firmly remained on Catherine's side. By extension, they detested Anne Boleyn and were not shy to say so. Boleyn was commonly referred to as a "whore" (and much worse) throughout the country, even to her face.[87] Priests openly preached against Anne, and Henry's divorce proceedings.[88] Eventually martyred, the secular priest Thomas Abell wrote a book descriptively entitled "Invicta Veritas: An Answer to the Determinations of the Most Famous Universities, that no manner of law it may be lawful for King Henry to be

---

[86] Carroll, 144.

[87] Bruce, *Anne Boleyn*, 125; Ives, *Anne Boleyn*, 249.

[88] Ives, *Anne Boleyn*, 249.

divorced from the Queen's grace, his lawful and very wife."[89] Abell was imprisoned with the charge of encouraging Catherine to remain steadfast against Henry's "divorce and separation."[90] Abell was eventually executed by Henry VIII in 1540 (and later beatified by Pope Leo XIII).

Stinging criticisms often came from the pulpit during Mass. Henry and his cronies responded by having Anne's name read instead of Catherine's during the liturgical prayers. Some prelates budged and agreed. But congregations, composed mainly of recipients of the sacrament of Matrimony, voted with their feet. On Easter Sunday of 1533, the friars at Saint Paul's Cross prayed for Anne as queen. Upon hearing the name "Anne," nearly every single member of the congregation stood up and walked out in the middle of Mass.[91] This was not an isolated incident; in the coming weeks, it came to be routine. Despite the sheriff's warnings, some parish priests refused to say Anne's name during Mass, despite the king's orders.[92] Historian James Clark notes that the Benedictines at Oxford were not only "vocal critics of the divorce" but "lampooned" Henry and his phony marriage to Anne in "their seasonal skit in December."[93] But like the devil himself, tyrants do not enjoy being mocked. And before all else, Henry was a tyrant.

Although Henry had been one of the greatest friends of the Roman Catholic Church—indeed to many Roman Catholics—he was intent on becoming her biggest enemy. His

---

89 Camm, *The Lives of the English Martyrs*, 464.

90 Camm, 466.

91 Friedmann, *Anne Boleyn*, 196.

92 Friedmann, 196.

93 Clark, *The Dissolution of the Monasteries*, loc. 4601 of 20889, Kindle.

faux-annulment, divorce, and marriage to Anne Boleyn had unleashed his dark side. He had murdered his conscience, and he was intent on murdering the conscience of his Catholic subjects. In 1534, Henry's Parliament passed the First Act of Succession and the acts of Supremacy. Collectively, these acts made it treason for anyone to even *speak* about the unlawfulness of his annulment or criticize his marriage to Anne Boleyn. Such speech was punishable by "imprisonment of their bodies at the king's will," and the forfeiture of all personal property.[94] If the offenses occurred in writing, it was considered a capital crime of "high treason," punishable by the "pains of death."[95] The First Supremacy Act rejected the authority of the reigning pope and the papacy.[96] If a British subject hoped to simply avoid speaking about the topics of Henry's annulment, that was not an option; the Second Act of Succession demanded the Oath be taken by "every subject."[97] If anyone refused to take the oath, he was be deemed guilty of "high treason," which carried capital punishment.[98] Of course, no Catholic could take the oath in good conscience. Denying the papacy's rights would constitute an act of *schism*; denying the permanence of marriage would constitute an act of *heresy*—both of which are objectively grave (mortal) matters.

(Let's ponder this for a moment. It is a thesis of this book that the Church and the sacrament of Matrimony rise and fall together; to weaken Matrimony is to weaken the Church, and

---

94 Gee, *Documents Illustrative of English Church History*, 240–41.
95 Gee, 239.
96 Carroll, *The Cleaving of Christendom*, 142.
97 Gee, *Documents Illustrative of English Church History*, 246.
98 Gee, 239.

vice versa. But whether faithful Catholics hold that observation, we must recognize that the Church's enemies seemed to accept that thesis. Henry, Cromwell, and Cranmer certainly did; after all, the insidious intent of the oath was not random. In one single oath, Catholic subjects were mandated to deny the permanence of Matrimony *and* the authority of Rome.)

To clarify what the acts and requirement to take the oath meant in practice: a British official could knock on the door of a Catholic, demand he take the Oath of Supremacy, and if he refused, he could be taken to prison for any length of time—or simply executed—as the king saw fit. In hundreds of cases, that is precisely what happened. And many of those Catholic doors were those of monasteries. What ensued foreshadowed the twentieth-century tactics of the Gestapo, except that Hitler never demanded that German citizens affirm the sanctity of his relationship with Eva Braun.

In the several years that followed, martyrdom became common—by gruesome means—and much of this was focused on convents and monasteries. Orchestrated by Henry himself and collectively known as the *Dissolution of the Monasteries*, Henry sent his "royal commissioners" to go through England and demand the monks take the oath—or die.[99] The years that followed saw unspeakable violence toward prelates, nuns, and laymen—along with the closure of nearly all religious orders in the nation. Historian J. J. Scarisbrick estimates that Henry "wiped about a thousand religious houses off the face of his native land and of those areas of Ireland under his influence."[100] James Clark writes,

---

[99] Clark, *The Dissolution of the Monasteries*, loc. 5751 of 20889.
[100] Scarisbrick, *Henry VIII*, 498.

"In precisely four years, from March 1536, each one of the kingdom's 850 religious houses, monasteries and mendicant convents for men and women . . . had been closed."[101] The process began in April of 1535, and Henry began with the religious orders that had been most critical of his divorce proceedings, particularly the Carthusians.[102] Henry seemed to believe that if the Carthusians fell in their defense of marriage, that would create a domino effect throughout England. But the Carthusians were not about to back down.

After their show trial (at which Cromwell threatened the jurors to find a guilty verdict or else be killed), three Carthusians monks were sentenced to be hanged, then drawn and quartered. On May 4, 1535, these monks were tied up and dragged behind horses for three miles to the place of their execution at Tyburn. One of these men was Father John Houghton. Bloody and beaten, Houghton was offered one final chance to take Henry's oath. Father Houghton declined. Instead, he hugged his executioner and stated, "I call Almighty God to witness, and I beseech all here present to attest for me on the dreadful day of my judgment, that, being about to die in public, I declare that I have refused to comply with the will of His Majesty the King. . . . Our holy Mother the Church has decreed and enjoined otherwise than the king and Parliament have decreed. I am therefore bound in conscience, and am ready and willing to suffer every kind of torture rather than to deny a doctrine of the Church."[103]

---

[101] Clark, *The Dissolution of the Monasteries*, loc. 139 of 20889.
[102] Scarisbrick, *Henry VIII*, 321.
[103] Hendricks, *The London Charterhouse*, 152–53.

Houghton was then hung, but he was cut down before death. Instead, the executioners laid him on the ground, ripped off his habit, cut his body open, removed his entrails and his heart, and threw them into a fire. Somewhere in the process, Houghton died. The other monks with Houghton were all offered a pardon if they took the oath. But none of the martyrs would renounce what the Catholic Church had, in Houghton's words, "decreed and enjoined."

Each man refused to take the oath.

Each man was drawn and quartered.[104]

Each man was later canonized.

Henry had hoped that the remaining Carthusians would buckle for fear of execution, but they did not. On June 19, 1535, four more Carthusians were martyred at Tyburn. Henry's wave of terror also witnessed the execution of Benedictines, Franciscans, and Augustinians.[105] It was an age of martyrs.

There was an eyewitness to these grisly scenes of martyrdom. That witness was Sir Thomas More himself. More had been sent to the prison of the Tower of London on April 17, 1534, for refusing to take Henry's oath. More's prison cell overlooked this ghastly scene, which he watched with his beloved daughter Margaret (Meg) Roper. As he watched the men accept martyrdom, he said to her, "Lo, dost thou not see, Meg, that these blessed fathers be now as cheerfully going to their deaths as bridegrooms to their marriage."[106] More's analogy to Matrimony was a powerfully suitable choice of phrasing.

---

[104] Houghton, *Houghton Ancestors,* loc. 629, Kindle.

[105] Camm, *The Lives of the English Martyrs*, 269, 274, 327.

[106] Reynolds, *The Field is Won*, 336.

More had served as Henry's chancellor since 1529 and the downfall of Cardinal Wolsey, but he resigned in 1532 as he found it impossible to support Henry's divorce and anti-papal posture. For More, the issue was simple: The marriage of Henry and Catherine was valid, and no man—whether king, bishop, or pope—could put that marriage asunder. For marriage is ultimately contracted in heaven, not on earth. More attempted to live in relative seclusion after his resignation but refused to attend the coronation of Anne Boleyn. His absence at that event, along with his prior objections to Henry VIII, led More's enemies to force him to sign the Act of Succession several weeks after it was passed. Refusing, More was sent to the Tower of London. In July of the following year, More was charged with treason. At that trial, as Pope Saint John Paul II later observed, Thomas More "made an impassioned defence of his own convictions on the indissolubility of marriage."[107] More was convicted of high treason and beheaded on July 6, 1535.

Thomas More died in defense of Matrimony.

More's last words were reported to be, "I die the king's good servant. But God's first."[108] And he spoke accurately, for a good servant reminds his king when he is in error and danger of his soul. Good bishops act likewise, which brings us back to Catherine's defense attorney. More's friend and prison-mate, Bishop John Fisher, was sent to the Tower of London only nine days after More. Fisher was the only bishop who refused to sign the oath to his eternal glory and

---

[107] John Paul II, "Apostolic Letter issued Motu Proprio Proclaiming Saint Thomas More Patron of Statesmen and Politicians."
[108] Reynolds, *The Field is Won,* 377.

to his fellow bishops' perpetual shame. Very likely, Henry had wanted his childhood tutor dead the moment he saw Fisher at Catherine's lawyer's table. While Thomas More had been quieter—though unwaveringly faithful to Church teaching—in matters of Henry's divorce proceedings, Fisher had delivered powerful sermons denouncing Henry's divorce and affirming Matrimony. Fisher had publicly likened Henry VIII to Herod.[109] While it was not surprising that Fisher was sent to prison, it was nevertheless heroic; after all, he not only had to stand against his king but also had to stand against his fellow bishops. Before his execution, some of his last words illustrated that he knew precisely why he was being martyred. Biographer Robert Conrad writes, "Fisher prepared calmly for his execution, he dressed in his finest clothes and told his servant that this was his marriage day, and it behooved him 'to dress for the solemnity of the marriage.'"[110] These words were proper for a man who died in defense of Matrimony.

John Fisher recognized the inseparable link between Matrimony and the Catholic Church. To defend one is to defend the other. One cannot be put asunder without putting the other asunder—a fact about which the devil and his enemies seem fully aware.

Conclusion

This chapter is not intended as a biography of Henry VIII or any other characters mentioned herein; instead, it highlights the notion that marriage is worth fighting for and dying for. But it is important to mention a few final biographical details.

---

[109] Fraser, *The Wives of Henry VIII*, 210.

[110] Conrad, *John Fisher and Thomas More*, loc. 50 of 2669, Kindle.

Catherine of Aragon died in January of 1536 at the age of fifty. Catherine was born a princess and proved a princess to the end. Though the exact cause of her death is unknown, she was sick enough to sense that she would die in early January. On January 7, she received Anointing of the Sick and Holy Communion, and she dictated one final letter to Henry, forgiving him, writing, "For my part, I pardon you everything, and I wish and devoutly pray God that will pardon you also."[111] When Henry heard the news about Catherine's death, he threw a party at Greenwich.[112]

If Anne had been happy about Catherine's death, her happiness would not last long. Just four months later, Anne Boleyn was beheaded by order of Henry—with a bit of help from Thomas Cromwell—in 1536. Anne had been unable to grant Henry happiness or a male heir, and that carried a death sentence from the bloodthirsty tyrant.

Henry, the man of such delicate "conscience," was married four more times. And British schoolchildren over the years have memorized the fates of the six wives in order: "divorced, beheaded, died . . . divorced, beheaded, survived."[113]

Divorced: Catherine of Aragon
Beheaded: Anne Boleyn
Died: Jane Seymour
Divorced: Anne of Cleves
Beheaded: Catherine Howard
Survived: Catherine Parr

---

[111] Mattingly, *Catherine of Aragon*, 410.
[112] Mattingly, 411.
[113] Fraser, *The Wives of Henry VIII*, 13.

Henry VIII died in 1547 at the age of fifty-five. He showed a touch of remorse before his death, but it was more wistful than conciliatory. Decades earlier, Henry had drawn and quartered his conscience. Henry, the man who had devoted so much energy to attacking the sacrament of Matrimony, died without the final sacraments.

We live in an age in which annulment and divorce are standard practices. The viewpoint would have been unthinkable to the likes of More and Fisher and John Houghton, who understood that in protecting Matrimony to the death, they were protecting the Church, the Bride of Christ. Even a weakened Clement VII was willing to suffer the loss of a kingdom than betray a marriage. For mere earthly kingdoms are made on earth, but marriage is made and sustained in heaven. The saints died for this belief. And although no one knew it at the time, the assault against marriage was only beginning.

3

Searching for John Fisher: The Counter-Revolution to Protestantism from the Council of Trent to Humanae Vitae

"Christian sacramental marriage bridges creation and redemption."

—Matthew Levering, *Engaging the Doctrine of Marriage*

THE PREVIOUS CHAPTER briefly referenced the Protestants' role in putting marriage asunder as personified in King Henry VIII's divorce. This chapter will more fully analyze Protestantism's poisonous influence on Christian marriage. Historian Warren Carroll claimed that, although historians use the term "Protestant Reformation," it had all the ingredients of a revolution.[114] The goal was never to reform but to replace the Catholic Church. The Protestant Revolutionaries no more reformed the Catholic Church than Lenin sought

[114] Warren Carroll was my history professor at Christendom College and this comment was made in his history class lecture.

to reform the Russian monarchy. Their revolution took dead aim at Matrimony and profoundly devastated Christian marriage. Nevertheless, the revolutionaries would not have the last word because Pope Paul III responded by calling a council to clarify the Church's teaching on Matrimony. That council would occur in the northeast Italian town of Trent, marking the beginning of heroic Catholic defense of marriage for hundreds of years.

The Edicts of Constantine

To understand the revolutionary character of Protestantism's view of marriage, it is helpful to look back to Rome in the years before the reign of Constantine. Before the year 331, divorce was so common in Rome that, as Roman historian Susan Treggiari notes, "most of our information on [Roman] marriage comes from our information on divorce."[115] We might say that marriage was contractual, but it constituted the feeblest and flimsiest of contracts. Marriage required both husband and wife for ratification; however, divorce only required one party. A husband or wife could simply walk away from the marriage for any reason or no reason at all. Further, nothing official—whether in print or even verbally—was even needed to finalize a divorce: a man could simply leave his house and remarry, thus signaling a divorce.[116]

In 331, however, Emperor Constantine issued a law that revoked unilateral divorce except on grounds such as

---

[115] Treggiari, "Divorce Roman Style," 33; Witte, *From Sacrament to Contract*, loc. 29, Kindle.

[116] Treggiari, "Divorce Roman Style," 32-37.

adultery, violence, and sorcery.[117] In doing so, Constantine—who had granted strong legal recognition to Christianity with the Edict of Milan in 313—strengthened the legal status of marriage. Though he may not have phrased it such, Constantine understood that marriage was vital to the life of both the Church and the state. Essentially, Constantine recognized the rights of Christian marriage within newly-Christian Rome.

The benefits of that recognition were numerous, beginning with the following.

First, it recognized the irreplacable importance of stable marriage to society. Constantine was certainly familiar with the writings of the famous first-century Roman Stoic philosopher Musonius Rufus, who had observed that stable marriage was essential to society. In the eyes of Musonius, each marriage not only served a person's own interest but also "the interest of his neighbour" and "the common good."[118] Musonius concluded that "whoever destroys human marriage destroys the home, the city, and the whole human race."[119] Constantine recognized that the protection of marriage and the family is the foundational protection of society. For a married couple with children, divorce is not something that occurs exclusively between a husband and wife; instead, it

---

[117] Sary, "The Changes of the Rules of Divorce in the Christian Roman Empire," unnumbered page. As this text notes, Constantine also lists "sepulcrorum dissolutor" (literally: "breaker of tombs," but might be understood as grave robbing) as grounds for unilateral divorce. Apparently, grave robbing was common enough in ancient Rome to warrant an official mention.

[118] "Musonius Rufus | Lectures | 14."

[119] Witte, *From Sacrament to Contract*, 21. "Musonius Rufus | Lectures | 14."

occurs among a family—the basic unit of society. Society is damaged when the family is damaged; likewise, society is strengthened when the family is supported. Hence, a society ought to foster, nourish, and protect marriage, and the children produced within marriage. This was not a novel idea; Aristotle made the same point seven centuries prior.[120] But Constantine granted this idea the power of law. The Edict of Milan in 313 and his decree of 331 further recognized primacy of the Church regarding Christian marriage.

Constantine's recognition of the primacy of the Church over the state in marriage endured for centuries, and the civil laws in many Catholic countries reflected that primacy.[121] As impossible as it may seem through the lens of modern times, it is nevertheless true: century after century, the civil laws of many heavily-Catholic countries incorporated the fundamental Christian beliefs in the indissolubility of Matrimony. The legalization of divorce in these countries is recent. For instance, divorce was illegal in Portugal until 1910. When divorce was legalized in Portugal, Pope Saint Pius X decried that decision in the encyclical *Iamdudum* (On the Law of Separation in Portugal).[122] Three decades later, Portugal reinstated the prohibition of Catholics to divorce.[123] In Italy, divorce was legalized in 1970, and in Malta, as recently as 2011.[124] In fact, Spain did not even permit civil authorities to involve themselves in Matrimony;

---

[120] Witte, *From Sacrament to Contract*, 29.
[121] Westermarck, *A Short History of Marriage*, 290–91.
[122] Pope Pius X, *Iamdudum*.
[123] Taborda, "Getting a Divorce in Portugal."
[124] *AN ACT to amend the Civil Code, Cap. 16, and Act XIV of 2011*, Malta, https://parlament.mt/media/109826/bill-182-civil-code.pdf.

for several centuries, marriage laws fell within the exclusive domain of the Church.[125]

But while the predominantly Catholic nations were defending the sacramentality and indissolubility of marriage in the Middle Ages, a rogue group of Christians was about to attack it. They were led by a renegade priest. His name was Martin Luther.

Luther's Revolution against Matrimony

Along with one, Catholic, and apostolic, holiness is a mark of the Catholic Church. The *Catechism* explains that the Church is "unfailingly holy" because "Christ gave himself up for her so as to sanctify her."[126] Among the individual members of the Church, however, "perfect holiness is something yet to be acquired."[127] The Church is holy but has unholy—even terribly sinful—members. Therefore, the Church can find herself in need of reform.

Many saints have found the Church in need of reform, so they helped reform it. Saint Francis of Assisi saw clergy engaging in scandalous luxury; thus, he urged detachment. Saint Catherine of Siena witnessed the pope abandon Rome for Avignon, so she urged him to return to Rome. The list would include many others, such as Saint Athanasius, Saint Bernard of Clairvaux, Pope Paul III, Saint Teresa of Avila, and Pope Saint Pius X. These men and women successfully influenced the discipline and practice of the holy Faith. What they did not do was attempt to change dogma and

[125] Walton, *The Civil Law in Spain and Spanish America*, 44.
[126] *CCC* 823.
[127] *CCC* 825.

doctrine. Thus, the lives of these Catholic reformers provide a clear distinction: the insistence to change dogma is not reform of the Church; it is a revolution against it. In short, though the Catholic Church often needs reform, her doctrines and dogmas are irreformable.

Though anti-Catholic literature often overstates and invents stories of corruption, it is nevertheless true that in the early sixteenth century, the Catholic Church stood in desperate need of reform. For instance, priests were buying church offices, prelates were promoting unqualified friends and family to ecclesiastical positions, members of the clergy—men completely unfit for the priestly office—were openly living lives of debauchery. And problems sometimes went all the way to the top. Perhaps the most glaring example of this was Rodrigo Borgia, who became Pope Alexander VI. Before his elevation to the papacy, Borgia scandalously fathered at least four children with his mistress (or mistresses). To make matters worse, Pope Alexander VI granted his daughter Lucrezia Borgia political power in the Vatican.[128] The lack of sanctity in the highest ecclesiastical echelons created a vacuum and fomented a revolution. The Church desperately needed a man or woman who loved the Catholic Church enough to help reform it.

Luther was not that reformer, although he is often viewed as a hero by historians who exhibit a bias against the Catholic Church. Rodney Stark, author of *Bearing False Witness: Debunking Centuries of Anti-Catholic History*, notes that "some of the most malignant contributions to anti-Catholic

[128] Gregorovius, *Lucrezia Borgia*, loc. 12, Kindle; Carroll, *The Cleaving of Christendom*, 9.

history have been made by alienated Catholics, many of whom are seminary dropouts, former priests, or ex-nuns."[129] Thus, it comes as no surprise that many modern historians—with an occasional exception—are generally sympathetic to Luther and to the Protestant Reformation.[130] Often with minimal reference to actual theology or Christianity, the historical stance can be reduced to: Luther-right/ Catholics-wrong. This is why history has deemed Luther's actions not as the Protestant Rebellion but as the Protestant Reformation.

If there had been a moment in which Martin Luther only sought genuine reform, it did not last long. Luther engaged in a wholesale rejection of Catholic doctrine. As historian and biographer Charles Beard notes, Luther "first attacked the abuses connected with the sale of indulgences, and then was led on, step by step, to an assault upon the whole position of the Church. . . . The Protestant Reformation was thus, in its essence, doctrinal."[131]

One of the most significant doctrinal Lutheran revolutions concerned the nature of Matrimony. Luther: (1) denied that marriage was a sacrament, (2) claimed that marriage did not demand fidelity, (3) denied that marriage was indissoluble, (4) urged divorce and concubinage, and (5) insisted not only that marriage should be governed by civil authorities but that the civil government should have police powers regarding marriage, up to and including capital punishment.

---

[129] Stark, *Bearing False Witness*, loc. 72 of 5661, Kindle.
[130] Stark, *Bearing False Witness,* loc. 106. Regarding the exception, see Thomson, "Martin Luther."
[131] Beard, *Martin Luther and the Reformation,* 1–2.

Individually, any of these was revolutionary; together, they constituted an outright war on Christian marriage.

Sacrament

Luther argued that he found nothing in Sacred Scripture to support the hypothesis that Matrimony was a sacrament. He claimed that the Catholic Church had misunderstood, or intentionally perverted, the language of Ephesians 5:32.[132] As John Witte explains, Luther blamed Saint Jerome for a bad translation: "Jerome had just misunderstood it a millennium earlier when he translated the Greek word *mystērion* as the Latin word *sacramentum* and included that in the standard Latin translation of the Bible, the Vulgate. The Catholic Church has gotten it wrong ever since."[133] Further, Luther decided that the book of Tobias—the book that was so beautiful in its explanation of God's providence in marriage—should not be part of the Scriptural canon. Luther simply threw it out. Luther's theological stance meant, in practice, that virtually every Christian bride and groom over the course of fifteen hundred years had misunderstood their matrimonial calling as a sacramental vocation.

Like many aspects of the Catholic faith, the sacraments underwent a development of doctrine over the centuries. Part of this development included concluding the exact number of sacraments. It was not until the twelfth century that the Catholic Church formally established seven, and only seven, sacraments.[134] (If that seems odd—the idea that Catholics

---

[132] Witte, *From Sacrament to Contract*, 131.
[133] Witte, *From Sacrament to Contract*, 131. For a detailed discussion of this topic, see Baker, "J. Ratzinger 'On the Meaning of Sacrament.'"
[134] Levering, *Engaging the Doctrine of Marriage*, 186.

were unsure about the exact number of sacraments—consider that the official canon of the New Testament was not pronounced until 382.) But as to whether Matrimony was a sacrament was not even a topic for much argument. From the time of the apostles, Matrimony has been broadly deemed an indissoluble union—notably expressed by early Fathers of the Church, popes, church councils, and the actions of Christians themselves.[135] The earliest Christian men and women deemed marriage a sacrament—even if their notion was expressed in different terminology. The Church Fathers, especially Saint Augustine, also taught the sacramentality of Matrimony. It certainly had a scriptural basis: Peter Elliott notes that Jesus's teaching in Matthew 19:3–9 and Mark 10:2–12 provide "the definitive revelation which raises Marriage to the level of a sacrament."[136] Again, for fifteen hundred years, Christian couples in the lands of Christendom had unceasingly considered Matrimony an indissoluble bond.

Martin Luther's comment that marriage was merely "a figure or symbol . . . in Christ and the Church" was not only revolutionary but at odds with fifteen centuries of Christian practice.[137] Considering this fact perhaps gives a person added appreciation of Newman's observation: "To be deep in history is to cease to be a Protestant."[138] Newman continues, "And this utter incongruity between Protestantism and

---

[135] "What the Early Church Believed: Marriage."; Grappone, "Divorce and Remarriage in the Early Church."

[136] Elliott, *What God Has Joined*, 21.

[137] Luther, *Works of Martin Luther*, 285.

[138] Newman, *An Essay on the Development of Christian Doctrine*, loc. 3, Kindle.

historical Christianity is a plain fact, whether the latter be regarded in its earlier or in its later centuries."[139]

Divorceable, Dissolvable, Unfaithful

Luther denied Matrimony not only as a sacrament but as a spiritual reality. In Luther's words, "marriage is an outward, bodily thing, like any other worldly undertaking."[140] Luther's vision of marriage did not even rise to the level of a stable contractual undertaking; rather, he viewed it as inherently breakable. Though Luther did see value in marriage and, ideally, thought that it should be permanent, Luther allowed and even encouraged divorce for not only bilateral reasons but unilateral ones.[141] Like some other civil contracts, a couple could simply terminate the marriage for any reason, but a husband or wife also could divorce on the grounds of infidelity or even lack of sexual satisfaction within his or her marriage.

Luther's view of sexual fidelity within marriage was shocking. Luther bluntly recommends that forlorn husbands should seek other sexual partners: "One finds many a stubborn wife like that who will not give in, and who cares not a whit whether her husband falls into the sin of unchastity ten times over. Here it is time for the husband to say, 'If you will not, another will; the maid will come if the wife will not.'"[142] For Luther, a wife's refusal to engage in conjugal acts with her husband—even on a temporary basis—amounted to the

[139] Newman, loc. 3, Kindle.
[140] Lull, *Martin Luther's Basic Theological Writings*, 152.
[141] Witte, *From Sacrament to Contract*, 132.
[142] Lull, *Martin Luther's Basic Theological Writings,* 156; Witte, *From Sacrament to Contract*, 132.

cessation of the marriage. Luther writes that if the able wife refuses conjugal union, it "dissolves the marriage."[143]

State Power over Marriage

While Luther espoused bizarre theological theories regarding marriage, his civil application toward marriage was even more bizarre. Luther objected to any involvement of the Catholic Church regarding marriage; nevertheless, he knew that men and women were still going to choose marriage. In Luther's grand plan, the Catholic Church would no longer have any authority over marriage; rather, the state would have supreme control over marriage. He was not simply theorizing: as states formally adopted civil Protestantism, that control over marriage was enacted. As John Witte explains, "Political leaders—long envious of the church's lucrative jurisdiction over marriage and inspired by the new Protestant teachings—were quick to establish new civil marriage statutes."[144]

In addition to statutes permitting easy divorce, Luther recommended several other marriage statutes—some of which involved capital punishment. Luther recommended the death penalty for adulterers: "The temporal sword and government should therefore still put adulterers to death."[145] Among the Protestant "reformers," this was not an uncommon opinion. German reformer Martin Bucer also called for capital punishment for adulterers.[146] Luther also recommended the death penalty for wives who refuse

---

[143] Lull, *Martin Luther's Basic Theological Writings,* 156.
[144] Witte, *From Sacrament to Contract,* 114.
[145] Lull, *Martin Luther's Basic Theological Writings,* 155.
[146] Hall, "Martin Bucer in England," 156.

to have sexual relations with their husbands. He writes, "When one resists the other and refuses the conjugal duty she is robbing the other of the body she had bestowed upon him. . . . For this reason the civil government must compel the wife, or put her to death."[147] Once marriage became a governmental function, the government could use its police powers to enforce it. Violations of marriage were met with criminal penalties. Such was Luther's so-called "reform" of Matrimony. As this illustrates, Luther's degradation of marriage as a sacrament had both theological and societal ramifications.

The Response of Trent

As necessity is the paradoxical mother of invention, heresy often serves as the mother of theology. In church history, a particular truth about the Faith is commonly believed well before it is defined; sometimes, formal definitions from Rome only occur in times of public challenge. For instance, the assumption of Mary was commonly held by the faithful for fifteen centuries, yet it was only defined in the nineteenth century when the belief came under attack. Something similar happened with Matrimony. Catholics commonly held Matrimony as a sacrament, yet the Church did not formally and officially declare it as a sacrament during all those years.

Why not?

Simply put, there was no need; virtually no one denied it. No one, that is, until Luther. Thus, the Council of Trent was convened to reform the Catholic Church and condemn Protestantism.

---

[147] Lull, *Martin Luther's Basic Theological Writings,* 156.

The first meeting of the Council of Trent took place on December 18, 1545. Though the Council of Trent was called, in considerable measure, to condemn the propositions of Martin Luther, he did not live long enough to see those anathemas. Exactly two months after that first meeting at Trent, Luther died in his bed. But the Protestants no longer required Luther to continue the revolution; as Hubert Jedin points out, the Protestant Revolt was no longer "the affair of one man."[148] The rejection of the one, true Faith had spread throughout Europe. The Council of Trent fathers had their work cut out for them.

The council took too long to be convened. By the time of the first meeting at Trent, Luther had already spread his poisonous theology for three long decades. Pope Clement VII, who was indecisive and delayed affirming the validity of Henry VIII's first marriage, refused to call a council.[149] Along with his delayed response to Henry VIII's marriage validity, Clement's reticence proved damaging. Francisco de Vitoria, the famous theologian and founding theology chair at the University of Salamanca, surveyed the potential damage of refusing to call a Church council: "Ever since the Popes began to fear a Council, the Church has been without one and will remain without one, to the detriment and utter ruin of religion."[150] Vitoria, a man not given to hyperbole, illustrates the gravity.

The council's delay also had immediate repercussions, specifically regarding Matrimony. In light of Henry VIII's scandalous actions—and the even more scandalous actions of

---

[148] Jedin, *A History of the Council of Trent,* vol. 2, 208.
[149] Jedin, *A History of the Council of Trent,* vol. 1, 284–86.
[150] Jedin, 287.

the Catholic bishops who sided with Henry in this matter—Matrimony needed to be reaffirmed through the weight of a council. The vital importance of a church council was recognized by both friends and enemies of the Church. Jedin writes, "Henry VIII fought the Council everywhere and by every means for he saw it as the greatest danger to his crown and realm."[151] But even Henry VIII did not prove weighty enough to halt a council. In 1536, two years into his pontificate, Pope Paul III issued a bull calling for a council.

Although there were numerous delays, the Council of Trent convened in 1545. An entire decade had passed since John Fisher was martyred in defense of Matrimony. Those Catholics who had been praying and fasting for the Church, perhaps searching for the next John Fisher, were not disappointed with the council's powerful pronouncements regarding marriage. Guided by the Holy Spirit, the Catholic Church championed Matrimony at the Council of Trent. While Luther had denied marriage as a sacrament, the council document affirms the sacramentality of Matrimony. It states, "Since therefore matrimony in the evangelical law surpasses in grace through Christ the ancient marriages, our holy Fathers, the councils, and the tradition of the universal Church, have with good reason always taught that it is to be numbered among the sacraments of the New Law."[152] The council doctrine notes the damage that occurs when the sacrament of Matrimony is questioned by those "ungodly men" who "have not only formed false ideas concerning this

[151] Jedin, 307.
[152] Schroeder, *Canons and Decrees of the Council of Trent*, loc. 4148 of 6821, Kindle.

venerable sacrament" but caused "great harm to the faithful of Christ."[153] The first canon regarding Matrimony restated the Church's position and condemned the contrary: "If anyone says that matrimony is not truly and properly one of the seven sacraments of the evangelical law, instituted by Christ the Lord, but has been devised by men in the Church and does not confer grace, let him be anathema."[154]

Luther had claimed that adultery could dissolve Matrimony. The seventh canon condemned this position in detail: "If anyone says that the Church errs in that she taught and teaches that in accordance with evangelical and apostolic doctrine the bond of matrimony cannot be dissolved by reason of adultery on the part of one of the parties, and that both, or even the innocent party who gave no occasion for adultery, cannot contract another marriage during the lifetime of the other, and that he is guilty of adultery who, having put away the adulteress, shall marry another, and she also who, having put away the adulterer, shall marry another, let him be anathema."[155]

Luther had claimed that the state, not the Church, should govern marriage. The Twelfth Canon condemned that position also: "If anyone says that matrimonial causes do not belong to ecclesiastical judges, let him be anathema."[156] Thus, the sacrament of Matrimony is the domain of the Church, not the state.

---

[153] Schroeder, loc. 4150.
[154] Schroeder, loc. 4154.
[155] Schroeder, loc. 4169.
[156] Schroeder, loc. 4182.

For good measure, Trent's third canon regarding Matrimony squarely aimed at King Henry VIII's decades-prior argument about his marriage to Catherine of Aragon. It reads, "If anyone says that only those degrees of consanguinity and affinity which are expressed in Leviticus can hinder matrimony from being contracted and dissolve it when contracted, and that the Church cannot dispense in some of them or declare that others hinder and dissolve it, let him be anathema."[157] (One can only wonder how the world might be different if Pope Clement VII had officially pronounced these words years earlier to Henry VIII.) Also, for good measure, Trent reaffirmed the Canon of Sacred Scripture. Luther had jettisoned the book of Tobias from the Bible, which constituted an attack on the Providential nature of marriage. The Council of Trent reaffirmed the book of Tobias and the other books that Luther had discarded.

The Council of Trent not only restated and defined doctrines concerning the indissoluble nature of Matrimony; the council documents painstakingly illustrate the profound damage caused by rejecting that doctrine. The Church stood firm in her defense of Matrimony. But it would not be the last time the Church stood up to a massive Protestant assault on marriage. Four centuries after Trent, it would happen again. And like Henry VIII's revolt, it began at a castle in England.

---

[157] Schroeder, loc. 4161.

Lambeth v. *Casti Connubii*

Following from marriage's primary purpose, the Catholic Church has consistently taught that contraception a sin. A married couple can undoubtedly engage in legitimate sexual union in infertile times and stages of elderliness when fertility is impossible without miraculous intercession (as in the case of Sarah, who was ninety when she conceived Isaac). But even elderly couples, irrespective of age, cannot willfully use methods and devices which prevent conception. To do so would constitute a grave sin and deny the nature of marriage itself. Positively, every sexual act must be open to life. Any endorsement of contraception strikes at the heart of Christian marriage. Sadly, that is precisely what happened in the Anglican Church in the 1930s.

To understand the issue, we need to take a brief glimpse of Anglicanism along with a bit of history and geography. In 1867, the Anglican archbishop of Canterbury[158] called a meeting for the Anglican bishops and archbishops of the world. It was held at a castle in Lambeth, a borough of London. Though it was merely termed the Lambeth *Conference*, it might appear to Catholics as a church council.[159] After all, it was a meeting intended to convene all the Anglican bishops and issue an "encyclical" concerning the Anglican beliefs and guidelines for moral action.[160] Though the Anglicans do not claim authority for the conference as the Catholic Church recognizes her divine magisterial authority, the

[158] Reginald Cardinal Pole served as the final Catholic archbishop of Canterbury until 1558. See Mann, "The Man Who Was Almost Pope."
[159] Stephenson, *The First Lambeth Conference*, 1–2.
[160] Stephenson, 326.

Lambeth Conference had always carried enormous weight for Anglicans.

Anglicanism influences the whole of Protestantism. Since Anglicanism is identified as the "Church of England," it is easy to understate its influence by considering it a geographically-specific and geographically-confined religion. But it is not. One must understand that the Church of England is the church of the United Kingdom, and the kingdom is vast. England's colonization of foreign lands has amounted to a *de facto* proselytization of Anglicanism. To illustrate that fact, consider that there are currently more Anglicans in Nigeria than in England; there are twice as many Anglicans in Uganda as in Australia, a nation that flies the British flag; there are almost ten times more Anglicans in Sudan than in New Zealand.[161] England colonized vastly. Thus, when we say that the Lambeth Conference carries weight, it is essential to understand that its influence on Anglicans is global. While the Lambeth Conference may not have intended to speak for Protestants worldwide, it is nevertheless heard and respected in quarters outside Anglicanism. Thus, the Anglican view of contraception is enormously influential in the world.

In 1908, the Lambeth Conference met and issued a clear resolution against contraception. It stated, "The Conference regards with alarm the growing practice of the artificial restriction of the family, and earnestly calls upon all Christian people to discountenance the use of all artificial means of restriction as *demoralising to character* and *hostile*

[161] World Atlas, "Countries with the Largest Anglican Populations."

to national welfare."[162] They restated their position at their following meeting in 1920, but even more strongly. Resolution 68 read, "We utter an emphatic warning against the use of unnatural means for the avoidance of conception, together with the grave dangers—*physical, moral and religious*—thereby incurred, and against the evils with which the extension of such use *threatens the race*. . . . We steadfastly uphold what must always be regarded as the governing considerations of Christian marriage. One is the *primary purpose for which marriage exists*, namely the continuation of the race through the gift and heritage of children."[163] Resolution 70 continued the same stance: "The Conference urges the importance of enlisting the help of all high-principled men and women . . . in *bringing pressure* to bear upon authorities both national and local, *for removing such incentives to vice* as . . . the open or secret sale of contraceptives."[164] To this point in time, the Lambeth Conference had made not one but numerous distinct arguments against contraception. In addition to condemning contraception as mortally damaging on both a personal and societal level, contraception turned a blind eye toward the "primary purpose" of marriage. In reference to marriage, the Lambeth document was making a timeless argument here about the nature of marriage. Contraception was viewed as an attack on marriage, independent of time and place.

In 1930, a mere ten years following this series of bold statements about contraception, the Lambeth Conference

[162] Website of Anglican Communion, Resolution 41, emphasis added.
[163] Website of Anglican Communion, Resolution 68, emphasis added.
[164] Website of Anglican Communion, Resolution 70, emphasis added.

changed its position. But the word "changed" is an understatement. If the Anglican leaders had sought to steer the ship in 1908 and 1920, they turned exactly one hundred and eighty degrees in 1930.[165] Resolution 15 read:

> Where there is clearly felt moral obligation to limit or avoid parenthood, the method must be decided on Christian principles. The primary and obvious method is complete abstinence from intercourse (as far as may be necessary) in a life of discipline and self-control lived in the power of the Holy Spirit. Nevertheless in those cases where there is such a clearly felt moral obligation to limit or avoid parenthood, and where there is a morally sound reason for avoiding complete abstinence, the Conference agrees that other methods may be used, provided that this is done in the light of the same Christian principles. The Conference records its strong condemnation of the use of any methods of conception control from motives of selfishness, luxury, or mere convenience.[166]

This official statement that contraception must be done "in the light of . . . Christian principles" is an exercise in the fallacy of question-begging—that is, it assumes the legitimacy of contraception in its premise in order to draw a conclusion that conception is allowable. For instance, it would make no less sense to say, "Adultery must be done in the light of Christian principles." Actions that are disallowed by natural law cannot be done "in the light of Christian

---

[165] Clancy, *The Hunt for Red October*, loc. 387, Kindle.
[166] Website of Anglican Communion, Resolution 15.

principles." Logic aside, this endorsement of contraception was the first of its kind in the whole of Christianity.[167] And its influence, for reasons outlined above, was vast. It created a domino effect; as Michael Pakaluk notes, the Federal Council of Churches in America "passed a similar resolution" shortly after.[168] Indeed, Christian denominations quickly aligned with the 1930 version of Anglicanism. The whole of Christianity seemed on the verge of changing its position on marriage.

But if the world had hoped the Catholic Church would somehow change its teaching on Matrimony, it was a vain hope. Before the year 1930 ended, Pope Pius XI countered with the encyclical *Casti Connubii*, which John Noonan rightly describes as "a small summa on Christian marriage."[169] While the Protestant world was denying marriage, Pius XI affirmed it, assuring the world that the Church's teaching on marriage was defined and unchangeable. Pius XI emphasized the *indissolubility* of Christian marriage and its divine origin. In diametric contrast to Luther, Pius points out that Matrimony "is not subject to any civil power."[170] Though Mosaic Law had begrudgingly allowed divorce, Matrimony—now raised to a sacrament—had no such allowance. Pius explained that "Christ, by virtue of His supreme legislative power, recalled this concession . . . and restored the primeval law in its integrity by those words which must never be forgotten, 'What God hath joined together let no man

[167] Pakaluk, "Lambeth, 90 Years Later."
[168] Pakaluk, "Lambeth, 90 Years Later."
[169] Noonan, *Contraception*, 506.
[170] Pius XI, *Casti Connubii*.

put asunder.'"[171] The "second blessing of matrimony," Pius explains, "is the blessing of conjugal honor which consists in the *mutual fidelity* of the spouses in fulfilling the marriage contract, so that what belongs to one of the parties by reason of this contract sanctioned by divine law, may not be denied to him or permitted to any third person."[172] Further, he reminded the faithful that Matrimony is a *sacrament*. Whereas Luther had denied Matrimony's sacramentality, Pope Leo used the word "sacrament" over forty-five times in reference to Matrimony.

Pius XI reiterates the constant teaching of the Church, quoting the recent Code of Canon Law: "The primary end of marriage is the procreation and the education of children."[173] He further states that children are the primary *blessing* of marriage: "Thus amongst the blessings of marriage, the child holds the first place."[174] He clarifies the meaning of education by explaining: "Christian parents must also understand that they are destined not only to propagate and preserve the human race on earth . . . but children who are to become members of the Church of Christ, to raise up fellow citizens of the Saints, and members of God's household."[175] The goal of a Catholic husband and wife is not only to bring children into the world but to educate them in religious truth and, ultimately, lead them to eternal happiness. Pondering the importance of that duty helps illustrate why contraception is so mortally wrong. Contraception intentionally obstructs

[171] Pius XI, *Casti Connubii.*
[172] Pius XI, *Casti Connubii*, emphasis added.
[173] Pius XI, *Casti Connubii.*
[174] Pius XI, *Casti Connubii.*
[175] Pius XI, *Casti Connubii.*

the primary end of marriage. It is a willful rejection of God's creation and grace.

Pius XI explained that the prohibition against contraception was permanent teaching rooted in divine law. And on this teaching, the Church would never surrender. He writes, "Since, therefore, the conjugal act is destined primarily by nature for the begetting of children, those who in exercising it deliberately frustrate its natural power and purpose sin against nature and commit a deed which is shameful and intrinsically vicious."[176] Pope Pius continued, "Any use whatsoever of matrimony exercised in such a way that the act is deliberately frustrated in its natural power to generate life is an offense against the law of God and of nature, and those who indulge in such are branded with the guilt of a grave sin."[177]

Pope Pius further explains that the sin of contraception injures not only the primary purpose of marriage but the unitive ends as well: "Every sin committed as regards the offspring becomes in some way a sin against conjugal faith, since both these blessings are essentially connected."[178] In 1965, *Gaudium et Spes* made the same connection, stating, "By their very nature, the institution of matrimony itself and conjugal love are ordained for the procreation and education of children, and find in them their ultimate crown."[179] Three years later, in stark contrast to Protestant denominations throughout the world, Pope Paul VI would make this

---

[176] Pius XI, *Casti Connubii.*
[177] Pius XI, *Casti Connubii.*
[178] Pius XI, *Casti Connubii.*
[179] *Gaudium et Spes.*

same connection in *Humanae Vitae*, observing, "A man who grows accustomed to the use of contraceptive methods may forget the reverence due to a woman, and, disregarding her physical and emotional equilibrium, reduce her to being a mere instrument for the satisfaction of his own desires, no longer considering her as his partner whom he should surround with care and affection."[180]

Conclusion

Martin Luther did more to damage the sacrament of Matrimony than anyone since the serpent. Almost from its first moments of existence, Protestantism had challenged the Catholic Church and her doctrine of Matrimony. But the Church stood firm. For over four hundred years, the Church stood firm in defense of the sacrament of Matrimony, its primary purpose, and its goods. In her notion of the sacramentality of Matrimony and rejection of contraception, the Church stood virtually alone against almost every non-Catholic form of Christianity. The Church was definitive and decisive against nearly all its assailants in matters of marriage. But beginning in earnest in the 1950s and 1960s, quiet dissent within the Church was growing loud and boisterous. And something else was happening simultaneously: the outside world was about to launch a major offense against marriage.

[180] Paul VI, *Humanae Vitae.*

4

The Assault from Without: Society's War against Marriage

"There is no plague more dangerous than an enemy in the family circle."

—Boethius

THE FOLLOWING CHAPTERS will illustrate that ecclesiastical failures to protect Matrimony over the past six decades have contributed to marriage's demise. We might term this an assault from *within*. Notwithstanding that fact, however, we must also recognize that there has been an assault on marriage from *without*. And though one could easily argue that many outside factors have hurt marriage, three stand out in particular: pornography, feminism, and the rejection of fatherhood. In his *Commentary on the Lord's Prayer*, Saint Thomas Aquinas says that a human's temptations arise from the flesh, the world, and the devil.[181] The large-scale enticements against marriage follow that exact alignment. Pornography, primarily in men, is a temptation of the flesh; feminism, primarily in women, is a temptation of the world; the denial of fatherhood, in its reflection of God the Father, can be seen as

[181] Aquinas, "The Catechetical Instructions of St. Thomas."

a temptation of the devil. And because millions of men and women have succumbed to these temptations, marriage has been decimated. If we are going to have a serious discussion about marriage, we need to make this recognition. It is not within this book's scope to comprehensively address these three subjects; instead, the focus is simply on how these three things have damaged marriage in recent decades.

The Temptation of the Flesh: Pornography

December 1, 1953.

On that date, the first issue of *Playboy* magazine hit the newsstands. A smiling Marilyn Monroe adorned the cover. A caption on the front cover read: "FIRST TIME in any magazine, FULL COLOR, the famous MARILYN MONROE NUDE." Lest the red block letters promising nudity failed to convey the magazine's intended audience, the cover read under the title: ENTERTAINMENT FOR MEN. Price: fifty cents. The magazine's publisher, Hugh Hefner, was worried that it might not sell, but his fears were quickly dispelled. The magazine sold fifty thousand copies.[182] That front cover contained a microcosm of the world of pornography.

Hefner's choice of the cover model for his premiere issue was apropos for all the most insidious reasons. Norma Jean Mortenson, whom the world would come to know under the alias of Marilyn Monroe, had an unspeakably brutal childhood. Norma Jean's single mother was clinically insane, so when little Norma Jean was not at an orphanage, she was shuffled off to multiple foster homes, where she was repeatedly

[182] McLaughlin, "A Comprehensive History of the Rise and Fall of *Playboy* Magazine."

sexually abused. She turned to drugs and alcohol in search of escape. As historian Paul Johnson put it, "It would be hard to imagine a more depressing and hostile background than the one which encompassed Monroe, composed as it was . . . of severe mental illness, syphilis, alcoholism, divorce, illegitimacy, and desertion."[183] By the time Marilyn Monroe appeared on *Playboy*'s cover, she had been abused, raped, deserted, and sexually used by some of the most influential men in her life. And for the price of two quarters and a conscience, men worldwide could now lust after her body. Like so many of her acquaintances, these men ignored—or conveniently forgot—that she had a soul. Less than a decade after appearing on *Playboy*'s cover, Norma Jean lay dead after a barbiturate overdose. Monroe's biography—from its aspects of broken homes, sexual abuse, alcoholism, drug use, and violence—might appear unique. But according to many former "playmates," it is not unique at all.

Playboy's first foray in 1953 was certainly not the first time pornography appeared in human history; the ancient hedonists evidence that sad fact. Nor was *Playboy* the first instance of pornography in America: pornographic movies were produced almost simultaneously with the invention of moving pictures. What *Playboy was* able to do, however, was to promote pornography as acceptable, healthy, and masculine. In 1953, pornography was primarily looked down upon, but month after month—issue after issue—Hefner's empire slowly chipped away at that shame. Suddenly, "dirty pictures" were no longer considered dirty. They were cool. And if you disagreed, you were uncool.

---

[183] Johnson, *Heroes*, loc. 4007 of 5720, Kindle.

It is essential to recognize that *Playboy* was not merely graphic pornography—although it certainly was that. But in the pages of the issues of the early 1960s, Hefner preached the adoption of a new moral code, called, simply enough, "The Playboy Philosophy."[184] Of course, it bore no relation to philosophy in the ancient Greek sense of the word—Philos (love) + Sophia (wisdom)—but it proffered Hugh Hefner's vision of history, humanity, and recommended way of life. It also mocked and libeled Christianity.

Among Hefner's critiques of Christianity, he writes, "It is certainly true that incest and Oedipal fears played a major role in the early history of Christendom."[185] Here's an ironic statement from the publisher of a men's magazine: "The medieval Church was obsessed with sex to an extreme degree. . . . 'Sexual issues dominated its thinking in a manner which we should regard as entirely pathological.'"[186] "Since it was the intent of the Church to reduce sexual opportunity to the minimum, it recognized divorce for a limited number of reasons, including barrenness."[187] Hefner even insinuates that chastity leads to devil worship, claiming, "It is undoubtedly true that in a period of such extreme sexual repression some devil worship really did exist."[188] Hefner claims that the Catholic Church murdered a vast number of people accused of witchcraft: "No one knows the total number of human beings exterminated in this manner and estimates range from a conservative few hundred thousand to several

[184] Hefner, *The Playboy Philosophy*.
[185] Hefner, 99.
[186] Hefner, 102.
[187] Hefner, 106.
[188] Hefner, 109.

million."[189] Nearly all of Hefner's historical points could be easily dismissed with a little research, but which of his readers—caught up in his private onanistic fantasy—would bother with doing such research? But its ongoing message was clear: it's not pornography that's the problem; it's Christianity. *You want to practice chastity? Fine. You want to adhere to a Catholic moral code with all its talk about monogamy in marriage? Fine. But you're stupid because you're missing what all these girls have to offer. And if you insist on monogamy, don't be surprised if you find yourself worshiping the devil one day.*

The Playboy Philosophy is the sort of manuscript one might expect to find hidden under a mattress in an asylum, but that did not stop otherwise-serious critics from claiming it was genius. Shockingly, *Playboy* was widely hailed as great literature. In the 1970s, men often claimed they read *Playboy* "for the articles." And there was a certain genius in it, if only a serpentine one: the text of the magazine matched the pictures. Both were rooted in lies and deceit, and many men bought in to both. While *Playboy* photoshopped the body, it also photoshopped the mind. And its sphere of influence was massive. By 1972, *Playboy* was selling over seven million issues per month.[190] That was enough copies for one in every ten American men, ages fifteen to seventy-five, to have his own copy.[191] *Playboy* had not only a foothold into the minds and hearts of American men; it had a stranglehold.

---

[189] Hefner, 112.

[190] *Encyclopaedia Britannica Online*, s.v. "Playboy," accessed October 20, 2022.

[191] PopulationPyramid.net, "United States of America, 1972."

Pornography addiction, a largely unknown illness to almost all previous generations, became widespread. But something else was occurring: *Playboy* was becoming a victim of its material success. American men didn't want to be associated with "porn," but they still wanted to view the pages of *Playboy*, so they simply claimed that *Playboy* wasn't pornography in the first place.[192] Of course, it's a ridiculous argument. *Merriam-Webster* defines pornography as "the depiction of erotic behavior (as in pictures or writing) intended to cause sexual excitement."[193] Sexual excitement is the explicit goal of the magazine. Thus, in philosophical terms, *Playboy* did not lack porn-*ness*. To argue that it did lack the nature of pornography, however, meant that pornography now only referred to the "harder stuff." Of course, once a society defines pornography down, the "harder stuff" draws closer to acceptability. And that is exactly what happened. Especially with the advent of the internet, hard-core pornography became mainstream, widespread, and grappling in its addictive nature.

Even neurologists are beginning to discover how extensive pornography's damage can be. As Dr. Norman Doidge, author of *The Brain That Changes Itself* writes:

> Pornography, by offering an endless harem of sexual objects, hyper-activates the appetitive system. Porn viewers develop new maps in their brains, based on the photos and videos they see. Because it is a use-it-or-lose-it brain, when we develop a map area, we long

[192] Paul, *Pornified*, 5.
[193] *Merriam-Webster*, s.v. "pornography," accessed October 20, 2022, https://www.merriam-webster.com/dictionary/pornography.

> to keep it activated. Just as our muscles become impatient for exercise if we've been sitting all day, so too our senses hunger to be stimulated. The men at their computers [addicted to] looking at porn [are] uncannily like the rats in the cages of the NIH, pressing the bar to get a shot of dopamine or its equivalent. Though they [don't] know it, they [have] been seduced into pornographic training sessions that [meet] all the conditions required for plastic change of brain maps.[194]

Hugh Hefner deemed himself a philosopher, but considering the neurological effects of pornography, Hefner bore more resemblance to a drug dealer.

The prevalence of pornography has created several distinct attacks on marriage.

First, and most statistically apparent, divorce. Numerous studies have indicated that pornography by one or both partners leads to divorce. One study determined that the use of pornography can double the likelihood of divorce.[195] A poll taken at a 2003 conference of the *American Academy of Matrimonial Lawyers* revealed that "56% of the divorce cases involved one party having an obsessive interest in pornographic websites."[196] In fact, law firms are beginning to specialize in representing clients seeking divorces on the grounds of pornography addiction. And they seem to have no shortage of clients.

---

[194] Doidge, *The Brain That Changes Itself,* 108, in Layden, *The Social Costs of Pornography*, loc. 272 of 1170, Kindle.
[195] Perry, "Till Porn Do Us Part?"
[196] Layden, *The Social Costs of Pornography,* loc. 330.

Second, unhappy marriages. Though pornography causes many couples to separate and divorce, some marriages can withstand it—but it causes significant suffering for husband and wife. As the authors of *The Social Costs of Pornography* write, "In North American and Western European culture, wives generally seek marital relationships founded upon mutual respect, honesty, shared power, and romantic love. Pornography as depicted on the internet enshrines the opposite: relationships based on disrespect, detachment, promiscuity, and often abuse."[197]

Quite often, porn-addicted husbands begin to demand that their wives sexually behave like the female actresses, thus preferring histrionic depravity, lust, and violence over what should be a beautiful expression of love, friendship, and marital intimacy.[198] In many cases, marital intimacy will cease altogether, as porn-addicted husbands lose all romantic interest in their wives in favor of electronic stimuli.[199] The brains of some men have become so re-wired that they become virtually incapable of having a human relationship of any kind, much less an intimate one. In its addictive and destructive nature, pornography addiction is similar to alcohol addiction. Yet, in some ways, it is considerably worse. The porn addict is not watching "actors" and "actresses" in any common understanding of that term; he is willingly viewing unwilling participants appearing onscreen as a product of human trafficking and drugs. As the *Victims of Trafficking and Violence Protection Act of 2000* pointed out,

---

[197] Layden, loc. 324.
[198] Paul, *Pornified,* 230.
[199] Paul, 230–32.

> At least 700,000 persons annually, primarily women and children, are trafficked within or across international borders.
>
> . . . Many of these persons are trafficked into the international sex trade, often by force, fraud, or coercion. The sex industry has rapidly expanded over the past several decades. It involves sexual exploitation of persons, predominantly women and girls, involving activities related to prostitution, pornography, sex tourism, and other commercial sexual services.[200]

The porn addict is not watching *simulated* acts: he or she is watching *actual* rape, *actual* violence, and *actual* grave sins against the fifth, sixth, and ninth commandments. How could viewing such material—especially habitual viewing—not be devastating to a marriage? Pornography often involves human trafficking: that much is well-documented. But we need to consider that pornography is not only the trafficking of the body; it is the trafficking of the soul.

Third, the overall reluctance to commit to marriage. It is often said that pornography is "widespread." But that term fails to convey its pervasive and invasive nature. A nonprofit organization called Fight the New Drug has assembled some statistics that give us a more tangible insight. According to their research, "porn sites receive more website traffic in the U.S. than Twitter, Instagram, TikTok, Netflix, Pinterest, and Zoom *combined*."[201] "In 2019, 12,500 gigabytes of porn

[200] Victims of Trafficking and Violence Protection Act of 2000, H.R. 3224, 106th Cong., 2000. https://www.govinfo.gov/content/pkg/BILLS-106hr3244enr/pdf/BILLS-106hr3244enr.pdf.

[201] "How Many People are on Porn Sites Right Now? (Hint: It's a

were uploaded to the site every minute—enough to fill the memories of every smartphone in the world."[202] In that same year, the contents of one porn site were viewed for over 5.8 billion hours. Fight the New Drug states, "That's equal to almost 665 centuries of content consumed in 1 year, on just one porn site."[203] Simply put, the world has never seen a pandemic like this—nothing even comes close. If pornography were alcohol, it would not be sold by the liter; it would be sold in fifty-gallon drums.

For the scope and purposes of this book, we can note that many of those viewers are young adults approaching marrying age. But after enough hours, days, and years of viewing pornography and thousands of men and women in sexual situations, the idea of monogamous marriage can seem unattainable and undesirable. It can also become physically impossible. As neurology studies pornography's effects on the mind, medical researchers note its impact on the body. After years of overstimulation by pornography, the male body can reach a point where it can no longer perform the monogamous marital act. Simply, the body and mind become bored. Monogamous actions no more stimulate the porn addict than a cocaine junkie feels a rush after a sip of decaf coffee.

One last point before moving on to the subject of feminism. The goal of this section is not to induce hopelessness but rather to investigate what has happened to marriage in the past decades. Any comprehensive discussion of the

---

Lot.)," emphasis added.

[202] "How Many People are on Porn Sites Right Now? (Hint: It's a Lot.)"

[203] "How Many People are on Porn Sites Right Now? (Hint: It's a Lot.)"

downfall of marriage must discuss the influence of pornography. It may be unpleasant to discuss, but it is untruthful to avoid. It is also dangerous, for at this moment, pornography poses a devastating threat to marriage.

The Temptation of the World: Feminism

While pornography was producing an increasing distaste for marriage among American men, a simultaneous movement was fostering a similar distaste in women: feminism.

In his book *Intellectuals*, Paul Johnson notes the irony that Karl Marx is revered as an economist who uniquely understood the plight of the industrial worker. Why ironic? Because, as Johnson notes, "Marx never set foot in a mill, factory, mine or other industrial workplace in the whole of his life."[204] Johnson also notes that Marx had significant "hostility" toward those "who had such experience" of factory conditions.[205] With its admixture of ignorance about marriage and hostility toward those who practice it, modern feminism is often plagued with the same problem. Many feminist "experts" on marriage have little experience with marriage, and to the extent that they do, they tend to despise marriage.

One of the chief problems when discussing feminism is that the word itself is remarkably ambiguous. One person might use the word "feminism" to reference a set of beliefs completely aligned with the Catholic faith; another person might use the same word to reference a movement aligned with witchcraft. But just as communism might be better described as *Marxism-Leninism* (since Karl Marx and

---

[204] Johnson, *Intellectuals*, 60.
[205] Johnson, 60.

Vladimir Lenin were the theory's chief contributors), the American feminism of the 1960s might be defined, however awkwardly, as Beauvoir-Friedan-Steinemism (in reference to Simone de Beauvoir, Betty Friedan, and Gloria Steinem).

Born in 1908 in Paris, Simone de Beauvoir was raised Catholic but rejected her faith altogether, opting for the religion of atheism in her teen years. She carried on a decades-long affair—although by no means an exclusive one—with Jean-Paul Sartre and was extraordinarily promiscuous with both men and women. Her anti-marriage comments could fill a book; indeed, she *did* fill a book with such statements. Her 1949 book is a meandering jeremiad against marriage, including passages such as this: "Man has succeeded in enslaving woman. . . . Since the rise of chivalric love it is commonplace that marriage kills love. . . . The marriage rites were originally intended to protect man against woman; she becomes his property. But all that we possess possesses us in turn, and marriage is a form of servitude for a man also. He is taken in the snare set by nature: because he desired a fresh young girl, he has to support a heavy matron or a desiccated hag for life. The dainty jewel intended to decorate his existence becomes a hateful burden."[206]

In her autobiography, Beauvoir admits, "It is true that I despised marriage."[207] In 1984, a book of interviews was released, with the following quotes: "Being a mother these days is real slavery. . . . If a woman wants a child in spite of everything, it would be better to have one without getting

[206] Beauvoir, *The Second Sex,* 187.
[207] Beauvoir, *The Prime of Life*, 34.

married, because marriage is really the biggest trap of all."[208] She also stated, "I believe that marriage is dangerous for a woman."[209] Moreover, she did not seem to believe that raising children at home should even have state sanction: in 1975, Beauvoir stated to another famous feminist, "No woman should be authorized to stay at home to raise her children. Society should be totally different. Women should not have that choice, precisely because if there is such a choice, too many women will make that one."[210] Of course, even though she was carrying on an affair with a celebrity chain-smoking French existentialist, Beauvoir was hardly in a position to enact legislation that would force women out of the home. What she really needed was a discipline who could organize a political structure that would do so. Her words quoted above, "No woman should be authorized to stay home," were publicly spoken to a woman named Betty Friedan.

Beauvoir greatly influenced Betty Friedan. Friedan achieved relative stardom upon publishing her 1963 book, *The Feminine Mystique*. While Beauvoir had written what she probably considered a general and philosophical critique of marriage, Friedan was more specific about her comment about American housewifery in particular. Friedan writes what she thinks is *really* going on inside American homes: "Each suburban wife struggled with it alone. As she made the beds, shopped for groceries, matched slipcover material, ate peanut butter sandwiches with her children, chauffeured Cub Scouts and Brownies, lay beside her husband at

[208] Schwarzer, *Simone de Beauvoir Today*, 73.
[209] Schwarzer, 42.
[210] Beauvoir, "Sex, Society, and the Female Dilemma."

night—she was afraid to ask even of herself the silent question—'Is this all?'"[211]

There's a hubris in claiming to speak for "each" wife that marriage and motherhood are cul-de-sacs to happiness, yet that was Friedan's opening salvo. The observation that *some* women feel unfulfilled in their lives could hardly be considered insightful. But Friedan's argument went well beyond that. Friedan's thesis was essentially that the drudgery of being a wife and mother was *inherently* unfulfilling to the point of despair, alcoholism, and suicide; this unfulfillment could only be addressed by work outside the home.

The book was a big hit, quickly achieving bestseller status. Friedan's biographer, David Horowitz, writes, "As much as any book written in the middle of the twentieth century, *The Feminine Mystique* helped transform the course of America's political and social history. Historians view its publication as marking the beginning of the modern women's movement."[212] Kathleen Parker, author of *Save the Males*, notes that Friedan's book was almost immediately influential and widespread, observing, "By the mid-sixties, following Betty Friedan's assertion that women were miserable and it was men's fault, the culture generally tilted toward women finding fulfillment beyond the confines of home."[213] Parker summarizes the Friedan worldview: "If home was a prison, men were the wardens."[214] But it was worse than that. While Beauvoir had compared the life of a housewife to slavery—

---

[211] Friedan, *The Feminine Mystique*, 11.
[212] Horowitz, *Betty Friedan*, 4.
[213] Parker, *Save the Males*, loc. 40, Kindle.
[214] Parker, loc. 40.

which was offensive in its own right—Friedan repeatedly drew comparisons between the life of a housewife and life inside a Nazi "concentration camp."[215]

But beyond the book itself, *The Feminine Mystique* was a springboard to political power. Three years after its publication, Friedan became the founding president of the *National Organization for Women* (NOW), a group that would become extraordinarily powerful for decades. In 1969, Friedan helped found the *National Association for the Repeal of Abortion Laws* (NARAL), which not only wielded legislative power but also influenced Justice Harry Blackmun in his *Roe v. Wade* majority decision.

By the time her book was published, Friedan had already been married for about fifteen years, so one naturally wonders what Friedan's marriage was like, especially with the concentration camp comparison. In her 2000 book *Life So Far*, Friedan describes her husband as a man who regularly beat her after they both engaged in bouts of heavy drinking. She writes:

> But for reasons that are still unclear to me, I still wasn't considering divorce. I didn't confront Carl. That's the reason I've always been uneasy, politically, about the battered wife issue because I knew from personal experience that it wasn't that simple. . . . I think if I had made it clear to Carl that I would leave him if he didn't stop hitting me, he probably would have stopped. But I didn't. . . .

[215] Friedan, *The Feminine Mystique,* 294–98.

> Was Carl really a vicious wife-beater? Or, taunting himself as he must have when my fame became just too much, did the slightest hint of taunt from me, when we were both drinking as much as we were drinking then every night. . . . Looking back on it now, I was so into what we would surely call denial. . . . I taunted him into finally beating up on me and giving me those black eyes. . . .
>
> And so, despite the concern of my friend Milton Carrow, who had seen Carl smack me around in the car, despite the support and concern of my shrink, who was worried about permanent damage to my face if I let it go on (I still have some scar tissue), . . . the marriage continued.[216]

(Carl Friedan quickly denied those charges, claiming, "I am the innocent victim of a drive-by shooting by a reckless driver savagely aiming at the whole male gender."[217])

Simply judging by Friedan's own assessment above, she suffered terrible physical abuse, admitted to being a heavy drinker, and conceded that she needed ongoing psychological help. That is terribly sad in many ways, but it's important to remember that Friedan viewed American marriages as much like her own—in some respects, akin to a "concentration camp." When considering Betty Friedan's own assessment of herself and her marriage, a question naturally arises: What gives her the right to claim that her marriage was a microcosm of American marriage? For that

---

[216] Friedan, *Life So Far*, 166.
[217] Blackman, "Books: The Friedan Mystique."

matter, what makes Betty Friedan an expert on American marriage generally?

After Betty Friedan, Gloria Steinem was perhaps the most famous feminist in American history. Steinem was a journalist whose work appeared in influential papers and magazines such as *Show* and *Esquire*.[218] Steinem's breakthrough assignment was working as a Playboy "bunny" and then writing an exposé about the working conditions in Hefner's club. Generally considered very pretty, Gloria Steinem appealed to an audience of younger women who identified with her. She rode that stardom to found *Ms.* magazine in 1972. While Hefner could also muster 50,000 copies of the premiere issue of *Playboy*, Steinem beat that number sixfold, with the premiere issue highlighting women who had aborted their babies. *Ms.* magazine eventually garnered three million readers per month.[219]

Steinem was ten years old when her parents divorced and was not married until she was sixty-six. Nevertheless, Steinem was routinely hailed as an expert on marriage, or more specifically, why marriage is bad. One of her most commonly attributed quotes was, "The surest way to be alone is to get married."

One might wonder: Why single out feminism here? Even if feminism is a temptation of the world, isn't it just a subheading of materialism—of greed? In a word, no. Materialism might reject the good of marriage, but that is because it loves wealth inordinately, not because it detests marriage. Materialism does not regard marriage and family

---

[218] Stern, *Gloria Steinem*, 137–38.
[219] Foussianes, "The True Story of *Ms.* Magazine."

as the sworn enemy, but feminism often does—and does so proudly. In 1973, an anthology of contemporary feminist writings was released. Consisting of forty-five recent essays, the book exhibits a collective antipathy toward marriage and traditional family and a desire to abolish both institutions. An essay by Sheila Cronan, cofounder of a feminist group called Redstockings, wrote, "Since marriage constitutes slavery for women, it is clear that the Women's Movement must concentrate on attacking this institution. Freedom for women cannot be won without the abolition of marriage."[220] Bonnie Kreps, a leader of the Canadian feminist movement, writes that "we must fight the institutionalization of the oppression of women—especially the institution of marriage."[221] In an essay by a group simply named "THE FEMINISTS" (in caps, lest we miss the point), reads, "Marriage and the family must be eliminated."[222]

The Footnote of Fatherhood

Many scientific fields—economics, psychology, medicine and wellness, criminology—have analyzed fatherhood and confirmed its benefits.[223] Often, a seemingly unrelated field will view fatherhood through its lens and discover even more benefits. In 1981, for instance, a book called *The Secret Life of the Unborn Child* was released by Dr. Thomas Verny. After years

---

[220] Koedt, *Radical Feminism*, 219.
[221] Koedt, 239.
[222] Koedt, 376.
[223] Flynn, "Data Show Benefits Of Fathers"; "Family Engagement," Early Childhood Learning and Knowledge Center.

of research, Verny concluded that a father can have a beneficial impact even while the child is in the womb: "Our latest studies indicate that . . . how a man feels about his wife and unborn child is one of the single most important factors in determining the success of a pregnancy."[224] As Verny argues, a father's beneficial influence can be immediate in time and importance.

It takes blindness of metaphysical proportions to deny the value of fatherhood; nevertheless, beginning in earnest in the 1960s, the feminist view of fatherhood was broadly accepted—with little objection from the experts. As Paul Raeburn writes, "Psychologists and other social scientists, who should have been leading the charge to change prevailing views of fatherhood, instead contributed to the devaluation of fathers. . . .Fathers could hardly assert their importance when they were repeatedly being told they were irrelevant, except as the providers of the family income."[225] People are inclined to leave when they are not wanted; prior to that, they are unlikely to agree to fatherhood in the first place. An attack on fatherhood is a frontal attack on marriage itself, for marriage cannot be attacked without attacking fatherhood, nor can fatherhood be attacked without attacking marriage. They rise together, and—as the world has increasingly witnessed since the 1960s—they fall together.

For those who accept the fallacies of Friedanist feminism, it is a logical consequence that fatherhood should be dismissed as meaningless, at best. As an author and university teacher, Camille Paglia has remained one of the most recognized and lauded feminists from the 1990s to the present day. Though

---

[224] Verny, *The Secret Life of the Unborn Child*, 13.
[225] Raeburn, *Do Fathers Matter?*, loc. 8–9, Kindle.

she favors legalized prostitution, abortion, pornography, and hallucinatory narcotics, political conservatives often hail Paglia as an insightful genius. Conversely, she is often criticized by other feminists who consider her a traitor to their cause. Why? Because these feminists consider Paglia overly favorable toward men. That assessment speaks volumes, especially concerning Paglia's written statements about men. In her 1990 breakthrough book *Sexual Personae*, Paglia writes, "Conception is a pinpoint in time . . . from which the male slides back uselessly. The pregnant woman is daemonically, devilishly complete. As an ontological entity, she needs nothing and no one."[226] In the world of modern feminism, simply calling fathers "useless" is simply not enough. Instead, feminists are expected to chuckle and applaud every time they hear Gloria Steinem repeat her favorite quip, "Women need men like a fish need a bicycle."[227] The stance is summarized in a 2010 column in *The Atlantic*: "The bad news for Dad is that despite common perception, there's nothing objectively essential about his contribution."[228] In the feminist worldview in which men are extraneous, fatherhood is considered an anachronism.

But this *irrelevant-father* outlook has not been confined to pseudo-scientific tracts, clickbait articles, and abortion rallies. From the late 1960s onward, the feminist viewpoint that *fathers are useless* was exhibited in legislative acts, judicial bodies, and cultural mores. Beginning in 1969, unilateral divorce laws began sweeping the nation, meaning that a wife and mother could simply walk away from her family or take

---

[226] Paglia, *Sexual Personae*, 12.
[227] "Happy 80th Birthday Gloria Steinem: 8 of Her Funniest Quips."
[228] Paul, "Are Fathers Necessary?"

her children away from her husband.[229] As of 2018, mothers were granted legal custody of their children in 80 percent of cases in America.[230] Four times out of five, a judge considered the mother the more suitable parent. This amounts to the legal system telling fathers that their lives don't particularly matter—at least to their children. Fathers are but a footnote to a shaky former marriage contract that is no more.

The entertainment culture only reinforces this anti-father view. In his book *Hollywood vs. America*, Michael Medved illustrates that fathers in the 1960s were generally portrayed as wise and virtuous men, but it changed over the following decades. In 1963—the year Friedan's book was released—shows included the likes of *The Dick Van Dyke Show*, *The Andy Griffith Show*, *My Three Sons*, and *Ozzie and Harriett*. Each of these shows featured caring, intelligent fathers who believed in justice. *Andy Griffith* and *My Three Sons* featured single fathers lovingly raising their sons. But as the years went by, men were increasingly portrayed as stupid, promiscuous, and violent. If a movie had a father in it, he was likelier to be a sadist than a saint. The only salvation for many cinematic families was getting rid of the father. Medved proves numerous cases of this same anti-father subgenre. As Medved writes, "Hollywood's current fascination with the most disastrous, bizarre, and destructive family situations goes well beyond the normal tendency to focus on dramatic, real-life difficulties, and amounts to a stacked deck against the very institution of marriage."[231]

---

[229] Venker, *The Flipside of Feminism*, loc. 158, Kindle.
[230] Grall, "Custodial Mothers and Fathers and Their Child Support: 2017."
[231] Medved, *Hollywood vs. America*, loc. 127, Kindle.

Raeburn notes, "Our failure to acknowledge fathers' importance is now reflected in the shape of the American family. Fathers are disappearing. Fewer American fathers are participating in the lives of their children now than at any time since the United States began keeping records."[232]

The rejection of fatherhood has devastated marriage.

Conclusion

The primary purpose of marriage is the procreation and upbringing of children, but pornography, feminism, and the denial of fatherhood stand in firm opposition to achieving those purposes. In terms of those social factors that have wounded marriages—whether they are existing marriages, failed marriages, or marriages that never came to fruition—the above is not an exhaustive list. Sadly, numerous headings and even subheadings could be added. To name a few: the use of *artificial contraception*, if not addressed in the previous chapter, would appear here. *Macroeconomic conditions* that have negatively affected the traditional family could certainly appear here, as could the push for same-sex marriage. True to the thesis of this book, however, it must be stressed: while some of the leadership of the Church has failed to nourish marriage—or much worse—there are pre-ecclesiastical cultural influences. That concession made, we can now address the problems specific to Church leadership.

---

[232] Raeburn, *Do Fathers Matter?*, 13.

5

The Assault from Within: A Crisis of Confidence

"It is extremely interesting how people react to the telling of the truth."

—William F. Buckley,
God and Man at Yale

THE WORD "ENCYCLICAL" arrives in English from the Greek word for *circle*: *egkyklios*, signifying that an encyclical is meant to circle the earth—that all the faithful hear it.[233] From the moment of its release on July 25, 1968, *Humanae Vitae* seemed to accomplish that. Upon its release, the words "Humane Vitae" were frequently on the lips of Catholics, many of whom were shouting. Known in English as "On the Regulation of Birth," Pope Paul VI's encyclical condemned the use of contraception. For that reason, it was met with furious clerical opposition. Influential prelates openly rejected its dogmatic teaching that dated back to apostolic times. In such opposition, these dissenting prelates directly

[233] *The Catholic Encyclopedia*, s.v. "Encyclical"; dict.com, s.v. "εγκύκλιος," accessed October 21, 2022, https://www.dict.com/greek-english/egkyklios.

attacked Matrimony. Whereas the attack on marriage had occurred mainly outside the Church to this point in history, the rejection of *Humanae Vitae* signaled that a fifth column of churchmen would henceforth join the world's battle against marriage from within. But it was only the beginning of a larger ecclesiastical war that occurred on many fronts—and that war was reflective of the contemporary conflict in Southeast Asia.

Six months before *Humanae Vitae*'s release, in January of 1968, the communist forces of Ho Chi Minh began to launch a coordinated series of military attacks against South Vietnam. Named the "Tet Offensive," in reference to the "Tet" new year celebration, the goal was less military than psychological. It was hoped that a major series of attacks would break America's will, causing American leaders to withdraw military support for South Vietnam.[234] In that respect, the offensive was successful. On February 27, 1968, the nationally famous and well-respected CBS news anchor Walter Kronkite announced to his television audience that the Vietnam War was unwinnable and that it was time for America to withdraw.[235] Kronkite's broadcast shifted public opinion; although the war continued for several more years, Vietnam was lost.[236] The Tet Offensive had proven decisive.

---

[234] Burke, *The Tet Offensive*, 8.

[235] Burke, 177.

[236] Dr. Warren Carroll, founder of Christendom College and holder of a PhD in History from Columbia University, was my history professor at Christendom. In a class lecture, Carroll expressed that the Tet Offensive did not make the war unwinnable; rather, it was Kronkite's statement on CBS that made the Vietnam War unwinnable. Kronkite's pontification significantly decreased popular support for the war.

Tragically, the dissent to *Humanae Vitae* was only the first battle in what amounted to a clerical Tet Offensive against marriage. In the ensuing decades, the primary purpose of marriage was denied, as was the sacramental nature of marriage, the indissolubility of marriage, and the fidelity of marriage. Though they could not overturn *Humanae Vitae*, the revolutionaries began to wage a battle over the Code of Canon Law.

A Culture of Dissent

The two generations between *Casti Connubii* and *Humanae Vitae* witnessed the march of communism. In 1946, Winston Churchill argued that "an iron curtain" of Soviet communist domination had "descended across the Continent" of Europe.[237] After his famous "Iron Curtain" speech, Churchill was criticized for his histrionics and overstatement. But the following twenty years proved his words an understatement—for communism's hunger for power was not satiated with the mere morsel of Eastern Europe. Following its Trotskyite belief in "permanent revolution," communism's march included Stalin's attempted starvation of Berlin, the Korean War, Ho Chi Minh's war on South Vietnam, and Mao's bloodthirsty Cultural Revolution. To illustrate communism's foothold in the world, Republican presidential candidate Barry Goldwater produced a map in 1964 that showed the officially communist countries in deep red and the "countries actively promoting the communist cause" in a lighter shade of red.[238]

---

[237] Churchill, "The Sinews of Peace."
[238] Ridgway, "The Record."

Although Goldwater had not shaded the United States of America, he certainly could have.

As William F. Buckley had pointed out in 1951 in his book *God and Man at Yale*, Buckley's Ivy League alma mater promoted atheistic socialism in the classroom. But Yale was only a microcosm of American colleges and universities. The chief economics texts in American colleges advocated Marxist systems.[239] As Paul Craig Roberts—former assistant secretary of the Treasury in the Reagan Administration—points out, economics professors were afraid not to endorse Soviet Marxism. Robert writes that the economists were often in error, but teaching Marxist economics was not about being correct; it was about fitting in. Speaking of teaching objective error regarding Soviet economics, Roberts writes, "Economists could make such errors with impunity without any adverse effect on their careers, because a positive attitude toward central planning was considered a sign of sophistication. It was more important not to be considered anticommunist than to know what one was talking about."[240]

Even if they wanted to oppose Marxism in the classroom, American professors were afraid to do so, lest they be fired; students parroted their professors regarding Marxism, lest they fail their courses. Marxism could not win a war of economic truth since its theses and conclusions contradict a panorama of historical data. However, the academic skirmish was not fought on the battlefield of ideas but ideology. Of course, college graduates with teaching degrees and

---

[239] Barringer, "The Mainstreaming of Marxism in U.S. Colleges."
[240] Roberts, "My Time With Soviet Economics."

certificates were hired in elementary schools, where they promulgated their Marxist notions to younger generations.[241]

There has also been significant testimony about the direct infiltration of Marxism within the seminaries. Bella Dodd, one of the most prolific Communist Party members in the Western hemisphere, reconverted to the Catholic Faith under the tutelage of Bishop Fulton Sheen. As her spiritual advisor, Sheen instructed Dodd to tell the world the truth about communism. As part of that mission, Dodd testified to her communist activities in front of the United States Congress. During a speech in Texas in the 1960s, Dodd claimed that in her communist years—following Josef Stalin's directive—helped place twelve hundred men in Catholic seminaries over the years.[242] Though it is often popular to casually dismiss her claims as outlandish, one should note that Dodd had the backing of Bishop Fulton Sheen and Alice von Hildebrand.[243] We might further note that her claims are consistent with the culture of dissent that followed in seminaries and religious orders; that is, if Dodd did not place communists in seminaries, how do we explain the decimation of the seminaries? Whence the widespread rejection of doctrine? Even if one dismisses all those reports, it is undeniable that many Catholic seminarians were products of Marxist college educations.[244] That is an essential point because Marxism is a religion of dissent from God and from the Catholic Church. This explains why communism in power has singled out the

[241] Nicholas, *The Devil and Bella Dodd*, 22, 238.
[242] Nicholas, 262–66.
[243] Nicholas, 262–66, 273.
[244] Kevin Symonds, "Rethinking Bella Dodd and Infiltration of the Catholic Priesthood."

Catholic Church for unique atrocity and ferocity. As Marx considered the family the first form of alienation, Marxism is dissent from marriage. And by 1968, communism was entrenched in American academic establishments. Even if one tried to do so, there was little chance of navigating around it.

Marxism was gaining a foothold in the Catholic Church, but dissent and the denial of doctrine went deeper. This sad fact was illustrated in October 1966 when, shortly after the close of the Second Vatican Council, a new catechism was released. Originally written in Dutch and named *De Nieuwe Katechismus* (*A New Catechism*), it was often referred to as the "Dutch Catechism." The text was written in considerable measure by the Belgian priest Edward Schillebeeckx, a professor of dogmatic theology who was a significant influence at the sessions of Vatican II.[245] It was signed by the bishops of Holland, who had grandiose aspirations for the widespread acceptance of their catechism.[246] Their wildest aspirations were realized: the book sold 400,000 copies in Holland in its first year, which was enough for about one in every thirty Hollanders to own a copy for himself.[247] But that was only the beginning, as it was quickly translated to many other languages.[248] As an article in *Time* magazine put it, "What was written for the Dutch is apparently destined to

[245] Wrenn, *Catechisms and Controversies*, 142. Regarding the influence of Schillebeeckx, see Wiltgen, *The Rhine Flows into the Tiber*, 23, 35, 58.
[246] Ratzinger, "The Dutch Catechism."
[247] PopulationPyramid.net, Netherlands, 1966, accessed October 21, 2022, https://www.populationpyramid.net/netherlands/1966/.
[248] "Roman Catholics: Catechism in Dutch."

instruct the world."[249] That was a chilling statement because the Dutch Catechism was filled with heresy.

The Dutch Catechism denied—or at least permitted denial of—the virgin birth, the existence of angels, original sin, the satisfaction of Christ's redemption, the Real Presence in the Eucharist, infallibility, and more.[250] As to the subject of contraception, the catechism not only endorses the practice but argues that the Church lacks the authority even to judge the use of contraception: "It is advisable in such matters also to approach a doctor who can take all the varying circumstances into account and after due discussion can decide what is medically the best for each particular case. The last word lies with the conscience, not with the doctor or the confessor."[251] (To the authors of the Dutch Catechism, the duty to properly form one's conscience was apparently not a factor in the discussion of contraceptives.)

How could the Dutch Catechism endorse contraception in light of *Casti Connubii* and all that had come before it? The answer to that question provides insight not only on this particular issue but much more broadly. The writers of the Dutch Catechism fancied their text to be the veritable catechism of the Second Vatican Council; simultaneously, they opined that all theology must be viewed through the lens of that council. Keeping those factors in mind, they argued that Vatican II had not condemned contraception; therefore, the Second Vatican Council allowed it. It states,

---

[249] "Roman Catholics: Catechism in Dutch."

[250] Congregation for the Doctrine of the Faith, "Declaration of the Commission of Cardinals on the 'New Catechism.'"

[251] Smyth, *A New Catechism*, 403.

"The Second Vatican Council did not speak of any of these concrete methods as such in the relevant chapter of the constitution on the Church in the Modern World. This is a different standpoint than that taken under Pope Pius XI, some thirty years ago, which his successor also maintained. We can sense here a clear development in the Church, a development which is also going on outside the Church."

Their essential argument was that since *Vatican II didn't mention contraception, it was therefore allowed.* By that same logic, plenty of things would be allowed. After all, Vatican II was also silent on the issues of insider stock trading, burglary, and currency counterfeiting. It is not the job of a council—whether it is Vatican II or the Council of Florence—to restate every doctrinal definition and every prohibition of the Decalogue. It would often be highly imprudent to do so, mainly because it would make the impression that definitions and prohibitions require restatement, as opposed to the principle of *Roma locuta est; causa finita est* (Rome has spoken; the case is closed).

Moreover, the catechism's concept of *development of doctrine* is bizarre in the extreme, as though the development of doctrine can contradict irreformable teaching that has come before it, as though silence on an issue constitutes a development of doctrine, and as though the development of doctrine can occur "outside the Church." Their argument that *silence equaled consent* is both logically and theologically fallacious. The catechism's authors were in clear and present dissent.

Shortly after its publication, a group of Dutch Catholics appealed to Pope Paul VI to censure the catechism.[252] Pope Paul VI picked a few theologians to examine the Dutch Catechism, meet with the authors of the catechism, and illustrate to the Dutch bishops where their catechism was in error. When that meeting took place, Pope Paul's representatives could not sway the Dutch. As Monsignor Michael Wrenn phrases it, "The Dutch side proved to be absolutely adamant in insisting that what had been written in the Dutch Catechism to stand."[253] After that meeting, Pope Paul VI established a group of cardinals to assemble a written list of the catechism's errors and omissions. Again, the catechism's authors rejected Rome's insistence on changing the catechism—even distributing a document as to why Rome's changes were "unacceptable."[254]

The Vatican went public with the cardinals' findings. The Congregation for the Doctrine of the Faith cited all these problems with the Dutch Catechism in a document called "Declaration of the Commission of Cardinals on the 'New Catechism.'"[255] Begrudgingly, the publishers added the text of the cardinals' concerns, but only as an insert in the back of the book—sending a message that the doctrinal objections to Rome were an incidental nuisance to an otherwise spectacular catechism. As Monsignor Wrenn writes, "The text of the Dutch Catechism itself, however, was never corrected, as had been directed by the commis-

[252] Wrenn, *Catechisms and Controversies*, 141.
[253] Wrenn, 142.
[254] Wrenn, 143.
[255] Congregation for the Doctrine of the Faith, "Declaration of the Commission of Cardinals on the New Catechism."

sion of cardinals. The era of setting aside and ignoring authority in the Church and doing one's own thing instead had begun."[256] (As it turned out, that era lasted quite some time. Not only did the Dutch Catechism sell millions of copies in many languages, but smaller catechisms and catechetical programs worldwide used the Dutch Catechism as a template.) It is clear that though *Humanae Vitae* is often believed to be a document that fomented dissent, many of those who dissented from *Humanae Vitae* were already dissenting from *Casti Connubii*, Tradition, and Scripture. It would be much more accurate to say that *Humanae Vitae* was released into a culture of dissent within the Catholic Church.

Falling Like Lightning: The Rejection of *Humanae Vitae*

When *Humanae Vitae* was officially released, a ragtag army of dissent was quickly formed among priests, bishops, and Catholic professors. The earliest and most famous dissent came from a Catholic priest who was a theology professor at the Catholic University of America. His name was Rev. Charles Curran. And his dissent did not take months, weeks, or even days. Instead, it was a matter of hours. With the endorsement and assistance of Bernard Haring, a Redemptorist priest and German moral theology teacher, Curran issued a dissent on the same day of *Humanae Vitae*'s issuance in America. Father Curran was not acting alone in his dissent; he was leading a parade. Eighty-seven theologians and professors signed the

[256] Wrenn, *Catechisms and Controversies*, 144.

document.[257] It was eventually signed by more than six hundred influential theologians and professors.

Curran and his followers claimed, or at least feigned, a need to issue an immediate dissent that argued that *Humanae Vitae* did not contain infallible teaching. Since he organized a press conference to accompany his statement of conflict, he certainly wished to call the press's attention. But why the rush? By writing it and organizing signers so quickly, Curran risked a criticism that neither he nor the other signers had bothered to read it. In his memoir, Curran acknowledges, "Critics claimed that we had issued our statement before reading the encyclical."[258] But that's not a particularly relevant criticism: maybe they had read it; perhaps they hadn't. Here is a better question: What did *Humanae Vitae* claim that *Casti Connubii* had not claimed? Based on the lightning-fast response of the dissenters, one might think that *Humanae Vitae* radically changed prior teaching. But it did no such thing. *Humanae Vitae* may have been a beautiful document with some charming prose, but it changed absolutely nothing in Catholic teaching. In judicial terms, *Humanae Vitae* was not an overturn of *Casti Connubii*; it was a concurring opinion. But it was the concurrence that so angered Curran and his followers. They were desperately hoping for an overturn.

How and why might they have rationally expected an overturn?

To answer that question, we need to look back five years. In the spring of 1963, Pope John XXIII established a six-member papal commission to investigate the question

---

[257] Curran, *Loyal Dissent*, 51.
[258] Curran, 52.

of birth regulation within marriage. John XXIII died in the summer of that year, but Pope Paul VI kept the commission in place, even doubling the size of the commission to twelve members. Although the commission was somewhat secretive, Pope Paul VI did announce that such a commission was in place and that he was awaiting their findings; however, he reiterated in 1964 that *Casti Connubii*'s prohibition on contraception was still in place.[259] The commission did not officially report its majority opinion until 1966.

Before we discuss the finding of the 1966 commission, we must address an obvious question: Considering its paramount importance, why wasn't *Humanae Vitae* a conciliar document of Vatican II rather than an encyclical issued three years after the council's close? Pope Paul VI had hoped that the Second Vatican Council would issue a conciliar document on marriage along with other conciliar documents such as *Guadium et Spes*. A preparatory schema (a preliminary document that is presented to a church council for discussion and modification) on marriage had already been written. The schema—titled *De castitate, virginitate, matrimonio, familia*—arrived on July 13, 1962, and reaffirmed the primary purpose of marriage as the procreation and education of children.[260] Tragically, as Fernando Vittorino Joannes, author of *The Bitter Pill: Worldwide Reaction to the Encyclical Humanae Vitae*, tells us, "The schema was never discussed."[261]

---

[259] Joannes, *The Bitter Pill*, 18–19.
[260] Joannes, 17.
[261] Joannes, 18.

Nevertheless, the issue of marital ethics and primary purpose was raised at the Second Vatican Council—and not only presented but hotly debated. One of the overriding themes of the Second Vatican Council was dialoguing with the modern world, and some council fathers were concerned that if the Church refused to recognize the potential goods of bioscience regarding marital ethics, it might seem anti-science. At a conciliar session in late October of 1964, the Belgian cardinal Leo Suenens stated, "I beg you, my brothers; let us avoid a new Galileo case; one is enough for the Church."[262] But Suenens's argument was confusing the ability to do something with whether or not it should be done; that is, methods and devices can prevent conception, but that fact alone provides no ethical insight into whether they ought to be used. The point was that the Church had condemned such methods and devices numerous times—a fact that Cardinal Alfredo Ottaviani made in response. Ottaviani stated, "I am surprised by what was said in the Council yesterday, putting in doubt the teaching up to now on the principles of married life. Does not this way of looking at the question put in doubt maybe the inerrancy of the Church? Or in past centuries was the Holy Spirit not in the Church to illuminate minds on this point of doctrine?"[263] Largely because of the heated debate, Pope Paul VI tabled the discussion, and Vatican II did not mention contraception.[264]

One year after the council's close, however, the papal commission on contraception was finally ready to report its

[262] Joannes, 20.
[263] Joannes, 22.
[264] Joannes, 22.

findings and opinions to Pope Paul VI. In this discussion, it should be emphasized that—in a similar sense that an amicus brief has no binding authority on a Supreme Court decision—the commission's findings had no binding power whatsoever. The commission only existed at the pleasure of Pope Paul VI, who was free to disband or reject some or all of its findings. That fact was made even more apparent when an oddity occurred: the commission came back with not one single report but a report by the majority of its members and another by a minority. The reports fundamentally disagreed. Something else added to the intrigue. The commission's reports were intended to be confidential, for the eyes of Pope Paul VI only. Yet the Vatican had leaks, and *The National Catholic Reporter* obtained copies of the reports, even printing them in full on its pages.

The majority report was titled the *Schema for a Document on Responsible Parenthood*. The document acknowledged changes in "new bodies of knowledge in biology, psychology, sexuality and demography," illustrating the need for parenthood that was "responsible"—a term the document mentioned twelve times.[265] The authors noted that "the magisterium itself is in evolution" and that "a further step in the doctrinal evolution, which it seems now should be developed, is founded . . . on a better, deeper and more correct understanding of conjugal life and of the conjugal act when these other changes occur."[266] Leaving aside the theologically troubling term "doctrinal evolution," this statement was insulting to Catholic married couples—as though husbands

---

[265] "Pontifical Commission on Birth Control – Final Report (1966)."
[266] "Pontifical Commission on Birth Control – Final Report (1966)."

and wives throughout the ages had an imperfect understanding of the "conjugal act," that can only now be viewed more correctly through the lens of demographics.

The majority document conceded that "marriage and conjugal love are by their nature ordained toward the begetting and educating of children," but—and this is primarily where the document contradicted prior teaching—not every conjugal act must be open to life.[267] It stated, "The morality of sexual acts between married people takes its meaning first of all and specifically from the ordering of their actions in a fruitful married life, that is one which is practiced with responsible, generous and prudent parenthood. *It does not then depend upon the direct fecundity of each and every particular act.* Moreover, the morality of every marital act depends upon the requirements of mutual love in all its aspects."[268]

The majority's document was revolutionary in three main ways. First, it allowed contraception. The argument was that couples must *generally* be open to life, but not any *particular* sexual act required openness to life. Second, not only did it *permit* contraception, but it urged that "responsible" parenthood might *necessitate* contraception. Third, by saying that *every marital act depends on love* but that *not every act must be open to life, they argued* that love and procreation are separable realities. The marital act is, by nature, simultaneously unifying and procreative, but the authors denied this nature.

A counter-document, issued by a minority of the members of the commission, moved past the majority's smokescreen

---

[267] "Pontifical Commission on Birth Control – Final Report (1966)."
[268] "Pontifical Commission on Birth Control – Final Report (1966)," emphasis added.

of "biology, psychology, sexuality and demography" to arrive at the heart of the matter, stating, "The central question to which the Church must now respond is this: *Is contraception always seriously evil?* All other questions discussed are reduced in the final analysis to this simple and central question."[269]

To answer this question, the minority document proceeded to do something that the majority had failed to do in four years of deliberation: define *contraception*. They write, "Contraception is understood by the Church as any marriage right in the exercise of which the act is deprived of its natural power for the procreation of life through the industry of men."[270] They further explained that there are those things that are "intrinsically evil," which means those things "which never can be justified by any motive or any circumstance."[271]

Did the Church view contraception as one of those intrinsically evil things? She most certainly did, they explained. Contraception violates natural law; as such, it "is not evil because it is prohibited, but it is prohibited because it is evil."[272] That contraception is always seriously evil has been maintained "in the whole history of teaching on the question."[273] They produced a mountain of evidence to support their case. The Roman curia had made official pronouncements against contraception nineteen times from 1816 through 1929, *Casti Connubii* had condemned contraception as a "grave sin" in 1930. Pius XII's 1951 *Allocution to Midwives* had con-

[269] "Conservative Position."
[270] "Conservative Position."
[271] "Conservative Position."
[272] "Conservative Position."
[273] "Conservative Position."

demned contraception as a violation of both natural law and divine law. Pius XII continued to condemn contraception in other addresses to various groups over a span of eighteen years. Pope John XXIII's *Mater et Magistra* of 1961 again condemned contraception. They wrote, "The teaching of the Church in this matter is absolutely constant. . . . For in answer to this question there has never been any variation and scarcely any evolution in this teaching. The ways of formulating and explaining this teaching have evolved, but not the doctrine itself."[274] The minority noted that some people had argued that since *Casti Connubii* was not irreformable teaching, contraception might still be allowed. The minority countered this position, pointing out that *Casti Connubii* was not the origin of teaching against contraception; it was simply one document in a long line of documents that issued the same condemnation: "The teaching of the Church in this matter would have its own validity and truth even if *Casti Connubii* had never been written." The minority explained, "The Church cannot change her answer because this answer is true. . . . The Church cannot substantially err in teaching doctrine which is most serious in its import for faith and morals."[275] Moreover, the minority explained that it is clearly within the authority of the Church to pronounce judgment on contraception. The minority's document was a potent response and was all the things the majority's document was not: clear and precise, well-researched, and logically argued.

From a theological point of view, Pope Paul VI could not officially change Church teaching; the Holy Spirit would

[274] "Conservative Position."
[275] "Conservative Position."

prevent him from doing so. Yet, from a human point of view—that is, a view unfamiliar with the concept of inerrancy and papal infallibility—the dissenters hoped Pope Paul VI could overturn the church teaching. Of course, Pope Paul VI did no such thing; he affirmed all those teachings that had come before him. Most notably to this discussion, Pope Paul VI wrote, "The Church, nevertheless, in urging men to the observance of the precepts of the natural law, which it interprets by its constant doctrine, teaches that each and every marital act must of necessity retain its intrinsic relationship to the procreation of human life."[276]

Just as Paul VI affirmed prior teaching, the dissenters opposed all the prior teachings on the matter. And they came out of the woodwork to do so. Other prelates wanted to join in Curran's dissent; such is the nature of parades. Prelates from all around the world openly voiced dissent. Some of the conflicts took the form of rallies and sit-ins—a popular political expression in the 1960s. In November of 1968, a conference of the American Catholic bishops met in Washington, DC. The event occurred after the cardinal of Washington, DC, had censured forty-one priests. *Time* magazine reported that "130 priests burst into the lobby of the Washington Hilton hotel, where the bishops met, to stage a sit-in" to protest the reprimanding.[277]

To argue that contraception is morally valid—beyond that, to claim that the use of contraception is somehow beneficial to Matrimony—is to betray the sacrament of Matrimony. It is to deny that which is integral to

[276] Paul VI, *Humanae Vitae*.

[277] "Religion: Catholic Freedom v. Authority."

marriage. To be sure, many laymen also rejected *Humanae Vitae*. The same *Time* magazine article referenced above notes that during the same bishops meeting in DC, over one hundred laymen carried on a pro-contraception demonstration in the hotel lobby, singing—among other things—the Impossible Dream.[278] Perhaps they viewed *Humanae Vitae* as an "unrightable wrong." Certainly, the number of laymen who used contraception was growing larger. But it's worth noting that they did so with the full and express approval of many prelates, some of whom held positions of great power and prestige in the church and the university classrooms. The dissenting battle for contraception was a battle against marriage. And it was led by prominent prelates.

Before moving on from the topic of contraception, one more point should be made here because it strengthens the traditional argument against contraception. In 1981, Pope John Paul II issued the encyclical *Familiaris Consortio*, denouncing contraception. Contraception violates the primary end of marriage; for obvious reasons, that has been the focus of ecclesiastical condemnation. But John Paul added a further argument: contraception also violates spousal love. He writes, "When couples, by means of recourse to contraception, separate these two meanings that God the Creator has inscribed in the being of man and woman . . . they act as 'arbiters' of the divine plan and they 'manipulate' and degrade human sexuality—and with it themselves and their married partner—by altering its value of 'total' self-giving. . . . This leads not only to a positive refusal to be open to life but also

---

[278] "Religion: Catholic Freedom v. Authority."

to a falsification of the inner truth of conjugal love, which is called upon to give itself in personal totality."[279]

While the dissenters were attempting to chip away at the Church's condemnation against contraception, Pope John Paul II was strengthening that condemnation.

The Redefinition of Marriage?

By 1968, it was clear that the dissenters had lost the battle to overturn the traditional teachings of the Church on contraception. The dissenters had big hopes for overturning Casti Connubii, but their hopes were dashed: Humanae Vitae was an official reality. But ever since the Garden of Eden, the war against marriage has been conducted on many battlefronts and battlefields. And a new one was emerging: the campaign to redefine marriage itself. And the object would not be an encyclical like Humanae Vitae; it would be the upcoming Code of Canon Law.

To understand this battle, it helps to look at canon law's nature and history. Canon law professor Archbishop Cicognoni defines canon law as "the body of laws made by the lawful ecclesiastical authority for the government of the Church."[280] He further clarifies that "the lawful ecclesiastical authority for the Universal Church is the Supreme Pontiff."[281] By her apostolic authority, the Church has both power and duty to promulgate ecclesiastical laws and regulations binding on the faithful.[282] And although the earliest

---

[279] John Paul II, *Familiaris Consortio*.
[280] Cicognani, *Canon Law*, 43.
[281] Cicognani, 43.
[282] Van de Wiel, *History of Canon Law*, 16.

Code of Canon Law was promulgated in 1917, ecclesiastical laws date back to the very dawn of the Church, when the body of these laws were known as the *ius canonicum*.[283] The purpose of canon law is primarily disciplinary, but that discipline should reflect doctrine, dogma, and the truth of Christianity. Let's use the following example. That Christ died on a Friday is a doctrine of the Faith. The Church's prohibition of eating meat on Fridays—a sacrificial act—reflects that doctrine. That said, while the doctrine cannot change, the Church has the authority to modify that discipline. Over the centuries, canon law has differed in some respect and expression, and that expression can take the subtle form of emphasis. Since the Code of Canon Law is a governing document for the Roman Catholic Church,[284] its importance is obvious.

On January 25, 1959, Pope John XXIII announced that a new Code of Canon Law was necessary to update the Code of Canon Law of 1917. Four years later, he formed a forty-member pontifical commission to assist with writing the new code. Pope Paul VI added new members, and eventually, the number of consultants grew to one hundred and eighty, composed of laymen and clergy.[285]

During the next twenty-four years, a problem festered within certain quarters of both laity and clergy—namely, a dispute over the primary purpose of Matrimony. For some time, there had been a growing sentiment among some prominent Catholics that, although the procreation and

---

[283] Van de Wiel, 12–13.

[284] The Eastern Catholic Church has its own Code of Canon Law.

[285] Van de Weil, *History of Canon Law*, 173.

education of children was an end of marriage, marital love and unity should not be subordinated to that end. In other words, there was a growing push to present these ends as co-equal. In his 1978 book *Annulment or Divorce?*, William H. Marshner brilliantly explains the problem in historical and philosophical detail. Marshner traces the issue back to Herbert Doms, author of the 1935 book *The Meaning of Marriage*. Marshner notes that Doms "wanted to get rid of the very terms 'primary' and 'secondary end' of marriage."[286] Marshner could have traced this argument back even further to Ferdinand Probst, a nineteenth-century German doctor of theology who wrote about such matters in 1850. Probst had wandered even further from the traditional teaching of primary end. In his book *Katholische Moraltheologie*, Probst wrote, "In the conjugal act alone this sharing finds its highest expression. By it the principal end of marriage becomes other [than procreation], to wit, precisely the sharing of the undivided life of the spouses."[287] The famous theologian Dietrich von Hildebrand was also referenced as part of this discussion. Von Hildebrand made the argument that while marriage's "primary end" is procreation and education of children, the "primary purpose" of marriage is the loving union between the husband and wife.[288] It's a cryptic argument, especially from the perspective of Aristotelian metaphysics, yet—and justice dictates that we highlight—von Hildebrand did affirm traditional

[286] Marshner, *Annulment or Divorce?,* 38.
[287] Probst, *Katholische Moraltheologie,* II, 180, in Noonan, *Contraception*, 494.
[288] Levering, *Engaging the Doctrine of Marriage*, 157.

teaching that the primary end of marriage is procreation and education of children.[289] Nevertheless, the confusion and denial about the primary purpose of marriage were becoming widespread. Pope Pius XII, alarmed by the error, promulgated an official pronouncement to affirm the traditional primary marriage end. That proclamation came in the form of a decree of the Holy Office, April 1, 1944, which stated:

> Certain publications concerning the purposes of matrimony, and their interrelationship and order, have come forth within these last years which either assert that the primary purpose of matrimony is not the generation of offspring, or that the secondary purposes are not subordinate to the primary purpose, but are independent of it.
>
> In these works different primary purposes of marriage are designated by other writers, as for example: the complement and personal perfection of the spouses through a complete mutual participation in life and action; mutual love and union of spouses to be nurtured and perfected by the psychic and bodily surrender of one's own person; and many other such things.
>
> In the same writings a sense is sometimes attributed to words in the current documents of the Church (as for example, primary, secondary purpose), which does not agree with these words according to the common usage by theologians.

289 Levering, 157.

> This revolutionary way of thinking and speaking aims to foster errors and uncertainties, to avoid which the Most Eminent and Very Reverend Fathers of this supreme Sacred Congregation, charged with the guarding of matters of faith and morals, in a plenary session, on Wednesday, the 28th of March, 1944, when the question was proposed to them "Whether the opinion of certain recent persons can be admitted, who either deny that the primary purpose of matrimony is the generation and raising of offspring, or teach that the secondary purposes are not essentially subordinate to the primary purpose, but are equally first and independent," have decreed that the answer must be: In the negative.[290]

In short, the procreation and education of children is the primary end of marriage—and a Catholic may not hold a position otherwise. *Roma locuta est.* Rome had spoken, again—echoing century after century of what Rome had previously taught. *Causa finita est.* The case is closed.

To reiterate an essential point made earlier in this chapter: official teachings of faith and morals do not require restatement for validity. Like milk, doctrinal teaching nourishes the faithful; unlike milk, however, doctrinal teaching has no expiration date. Pope Pius XII did not have to issue a statement like the one above (although he was certainly free to do so) to affirm the teaching. Similarly, even if no pope ever again refers to the doctrine of the Immaculate Conception, the doctrine stands and cannot be overturned. The Church

[290] DeFerrari, *Denzinger*, 624–25.

is not required to restate the totality of her beliefs every time she makes a public statement or proclamation.

The same principle is true for individuals. A Catholic must accept all the defined truths of the Catholic faith, but he is not required to recite the *Summa Theologica* whenever he is introduced to a stranger. Nor is it fair to suspect that man of doubting the Virgin Birth because he failed to mention it at a business luncheon. This example might seem comical, but that is precisely the logic that dissenters often employ. In the mind of a dissenter, any failure to restate teaching hints—or positively screams—at a change in doctrine. In the mind of a dissenter—as the entire history of Modernism illustrates—moral teachings are all in flux anyway. Sure, the logic goes, same-sex marriage is outlawed by the Church, but the Church will eventually change her teaching on that, so let's front run the inevitable. Order the invitations! Just as Cardinal Richelieu famously quipped that "treason is only a matter of dates," many dissenters have the same attitude toward doctrine.

It is essential to keep this principle of *Roma locuta est; causa finita est* in mind as we move forward—not only for this present discussion of Canon Law but to recognize the nature of dissent.

Returning to our discussion of canon law, we take a look at the 1917 Code of Canon Law, which identified the primary end of marriage: "The primary end of marriage is the procreation and education of children; the secondary [end] is mutual support and a remedy for concupiscence."[291] Not

[291] Peters, *The 1917 or Pio-Benedictine Code of Canon Law,* Canon 1013.1.

only is that crystal clear, but it restates the teaching of the Church for two thousand years. However, the 1983 Code of Canon Law fails to identify a primary end. It reads, "The matrimonial covenant, by which a man and a woman establish between themselves a partnership of the whole of life and which is ordered by its nature to the good of the spouses and the procreation and education of offspring, has been raised by Christ the Lord to the dignity of a sacrament between the baptized."[292] Especially in light of 1983's contraceptive culture into which the Code was released, it could certainly be argued that the Code *should have* restated the primary end teaching. Further, canon law is a legal text, and, as such, it should have legal clarity. As Marshner phrased it, "Canon law requires a minimum definition. . . . Failure to appreciate this point reflects a blunder not so much in the understanding of marriage as in the understanding of law itself."[293] Marshner's distinction here is crucial: while this section of the Code might be legally sloppy, it does not contradict prior teaching. Instead, the Code emphasizes marital love between one man and one woman. But *emphasis* is not *end.*

The Second Vatican Council's *Gaudium et Spes*, which the Code of Canon Law echoed, had done the same thing: emphasized marital love without identifying the primary end. Was there a logic to that emphasis and that omission? Marshner provides one, beginning with pointing to the fact that *Gaudium et Spes* was a pastoral document rather than a dogmatic constitution. As such, it identified its audience as

---

[292] Peters, Canon 1055.1.

[293] Marshner, *Annulment or Divorce?*, 28.

"the whole of humanity."[294] Marshner notes that "the whole of humanity" includes those unfamiliar with the concepts of *finis operis* [end of the act]. If the document had simply discussed the primary end rather than emphasized love, it would have seemed callous to the intended audience. Marshner writes, "Do you know what it sounds like to the man in the street, to say that procreation is the 'primary end' of marriage? It sounds like this: 'Yes, sir, that's the Roman Catholic Church for you. The Pope don't give a damn if you love each other, you just gotta keep havin' kids.'"[295] Marshner notes this was a constant harangue against the Church for many years leading up to the 1960s. "That is why," he writes, "there is no technical terminology in *Gaudium et Spes*."[296] Recognizing the objection that *Gaudium et Spes* redefined marriage, Marshner points out that the document did no such thing.[297]

Just as those who claimed that Vatican II had redefined marriage, canon lawyers and others came forward to argue that the 1983 Code also changed marriage. A person grows in appreciation of Aristotle's definition of virtue—a mean between two extremes—when he considers that many traditionalists and liberals claimed that the Church had redefined marriage. Both groups had to ignore what the text *said* and attempt to define what the text nefariously *meant*. On the liberal/dissenter side, not only was there a perceived "spirit of Vatican II," but a perceived *spirit of canon law*. And

[294] Marshner, *Annulment or Divorce?*, 28; *Gaudium et Spes*.
[295] Marshner, *Annulment or Divorce?*, 46.
[296] Marshner, 46.
[297] Marshner, 46.

although the traditional Catholics may have had the noblest of intentions, the position that marriage had been redefined by either Vatican II or the 1983 Code of Canon Law is simply wrong on its face.

All this said, the Code of Canon Law should have not only restated but should have championed the primary purpose. The problem with the Code was not that it redefined the primary purpose of marriage but that it did not define marriage at all—and it should have. While *Gaudium et Spes* had a pastoral purpose, the Code had a legal one. Although the teaching indeed remained in place without the necessity for restatement, both prudence and jurisprudence called for restatement. The Code's pontifical commission consultants could have easily predicted the ensuing dissent.

Dissenters historically search for real or imagined loopholes to support their cases. Granted, when dissenters imagine silence to be a development of doctrine, the parody stage has been passed. But the prudential acts must consider this and leave as little room as possible for dissent.

Communicable Dissent

When prelates are loudly voicing dissent, it is not a merely personal matter but rather a public one that affects hundreds, thousands, or millions of souls. In America, which has recently grown progressively hyper-focused on politics, this problem also relates directly to Catholic politicians. Some Catholics who hold office gleefully vote in favor of abortion one day and receive Holy Communion the next. The Church has two main legal remedies, but bishops have proven extremely reticent to use them: *first,* denying the sacraments; *second*, formal excommunication. And because the Church leadership has proven largely unwilling to employ these sanctions, souls have been put in immediate and grave jeopardy.

The refusal to excommunicate has also specifically harmed Matrimony.

The case of the aforementioned Rev. Charles Curran provides an example. Earlier in this chapter, we discussed Curran's 1968 actions of openly dissenting from *Humanae Vitae* and calling a news conference to highlight that dissent. Let's pick up the story from there. One might have guessed that Curran's actions would result in his termination; after all, here was a Catholic priest openly dissenting from Rome on teaching that dated back to apostolic times. To add to those blinding optics, Curran not only taught at *a* Catholic university in America but *the* Catholic University of America. Further, Catholic University was not governed by a group of laymen; instead, all of Catholic University's board members were bishops.[298] Due to that board composition, it would be logical to believe that Catholic University's professors and classes reflected the beliefs and the will of the bishops in America. Curran's actions should have resulted in his termination even if he were a professor of mathematics, much less a theology professor of sexual ethics.

Sadly, that is not what happened.

In 1967, the CUA board dismissed Curran, but after a student strike over his dismissal, Curran was rehired. Rev. Peter M. Mitchell writes, "The CUA board of trustees hoped for an end to controversy and a restoration of stability when

[298] Mitchell, *The Coup at Catholic University*, 16.

they decided to reinstate Curran to his teaching position. Such a hope for an end to their troubles, however, could not have been more completely misplaced."[299] Rather than fire, censure, or even discourage Curran from teaching error, his rehiring emboldened other dissenters. Mitchell continues, "The dissenting professors became fully confident that they could teach at CUA in open disagreement with the Magisterium and that the American bishops would not and could not effectively do anything about it."[300] And so, Curran taught at Catholic University for another eighteen years—infecting another generation with heresy and dissent. As Curran cast an ever-widening net of dissenting opinions both in and out of the classroom, he not only grew in the admiration of the students but also of an adoring, dissenting public. He wrote articles, made speeches, and gave television interviews that mocked official Church teaching on matters of sexual ethics. In 1986, *The Washington Post* ran a story noting that Curran was "the most controversial Roman Catholic priest in the world today" and "one of the nation's most influential theologians."[301] Sadly, the *Washington Post* was correct.

By 1986, the Vatican had finally had enough of Curran's heresies. In July, Curran received an official letter from Cardinal Ratzinger, prefect for the Congregation for the Doctrine of the Faith (CDF). The letter amounted to a canonical cease and desist order. It read: "The purpose of this letter is to inform you that the Congregation has confirmed its position that one who dissents from the Magisterium as you

[299] Mitchell, 19.
[300] Mitchell, 19.
[301] Romano, "The Convictions of Father Curran."

do is not suitable nor eligible to teach Catholic theology."[302] The document cataloged Curran's insistent errors, many of which were directly related to marriage: "right to public dissent from the ordinary Magisterium, the indissolubility of consummated sacramental marriage, abortion, euthanasia, masturbation, artificial contraception, premarital intercourse and homosexual acts."[303] The letter of the CDF eventually resulted in Curran's termination from Catholic University. Indeed, some celebrated the CDF's letter and Curran's dismissal as a victory. Curran had done incalculable damage to the Church.

Charles Curran should have been forbidden from teaching at Catholic University (or any university calling itself Catholic) back in 1967, but certainly no later than 1968. Yet he was not suspended until 1986. That delay was tragic to the Catholic faithful. Imagine a store owner whose establishment has been robbed nightly for eighteen years but no prosecution is ever demanded. After a point, it would seem that the store owner does not particularly care about his store. But even this analogy is weak: the store owner is only losing things of material value. The Church was losing souls or leaving them in mortal danger.

When Charles Curran was finally reprimanded, many defenders argued that he was being singled out unfairly. His defenders had a point, but for all the wrong reasons. Many other famous and outspoken heretics and dissenters were never censured. Bernard Haring, the famous German theologian friend of Curran's, maintained his support for

[302] Ratzinger, "Letter to Father Charles Curran."
[303] Ratzinger, "Letter to Father Charles Curran."

sterilization and contraception and referred to marriage indissolubility as guilty of creating "cruel hardships on the young."[304] Schillebeeckx, whose heretical catechism was the most widespread "Catholic" catechism for thirty years, was investigated by the CDF on three major occasions. By that point, not only was his theology of marriage devastatingly erroneous, but so were many other areas of his writing. The Congregation for the Doctrine of the Faith wrote that "it has found in your work many statements which cause great bewilderment; some of these statements have to do with principles of methodology, . . . others still with dogmatic theology."[305] But his writings were never condemned. More recently, in 2017, Father James Martin expressed that Catholics should "reverence" homosexual marriage.[306] That directly attacks the doctrine that marriage is between one man and one woman.[307] Two years later, Father Martin enjoyed a private audience—and widely covered photo-op—with Pope Francis.[308] This list could refer to hundreds of other prelates in the same period. We might say that Rome has been *reluctant* to condemn heretics, but there comes the point where reluctance becomes outright refusal. Even assuming the best and most noble intentions on the part of Church leaders in this matter, it

---

[304] Thevathasan, "Bernard Häring and his Medical Ethics."

[305] Schoof, *The Schillebeeckx Case*, 19.

[306] Stoelker, "Building a Bridge Between the Catholic Church and the LGBT Community."

[307] Peters, "Fr. James Martin, S.J., and accusations of heresy."

[308] O'Connell, "Pope Francis meets with Father James Martin in private audience."

is nevertheless the case: the failure to censure or criticize heretics has caused incalculable damage to the Church.

The truth is that any open *dissent* from official teaching on marriage, any heresy regarding marriage, is an *attack* on marriage. Perhaps surprising, at least initially, is that so many dissenters and heretics take aim at marriage. Regardless of the particular heresy that made him or her famous, it is the rare heretic who follows Church teaching on marriage. What prominent dissenter or heretic of the past one hundred years—or for that matter, in the entire history of the Catholic Church since apostolic times—*affirmed* the Church teachings on marriage? One struggles to think of a case. On the other hand, think of those who denied the teachings on marriage: the Gnostics, the Manicheans, the Albigensians, the Modernists, Martin Luther, King Henry VIII, John Calvin, Charles Curran, Edward Schillebeeckx, and countless others. It goes without saying that the refusal to discipline prelates on this matter is also an attack on marriage.

Conclusion

Since the 1940s, well-known prelates have questioned or flatly denied the primary purpose of marriage, the secondary goods of marriage, the official teachings on contraception and sterilization, the indissolubility of marriage, and the prohibition on divorce. To understand how we got here—the *here* being a time when the number of marriages has fallen by 50 percent in a single generation—we must look not only at the heresies and dissent of the renegade prelates but at the failure to act against those heresies. The bishops of the Catholic Church have the three-fold duty to teach, sanctify, and govern. But if there is a failure to govern—which includes the willingness to address heresy and dissent adequately—it becomes challenging to teach or sanctify. Heresy often proves louder than the teaching, and because of that, people find little need for sanctification. At present, they find little need for marriage at all. If premarital sex is deemed acceptable and the good of children is denied, why choose Matrimony? If indissolubility is rejected, what need is there for even remaining in one's present marriage? It prompts a prior question: Was it ever a marriage in the first place? And if so, who stands ready to affirm it? This is a question we'll address in the next chapter.

6

Wine into Water: The Scandal of Annulments

"If among the evils of divorce exists the danger of making the celebration of matrimony less serious and demanding to the point that today among many young people it has lost its due consideration, we must also fear that judgments of declaration of matrimonial nullity, if they were to multiply as easy and hasty pronouncements, would add to the same existential and psychological perspective."[309]

—Pope John Paul II,
Address to the Roman Rota, 1991

It's a phrase often uttered: "Annulments are Catholic divorce." When we Catholics hear those words, we might feel the urge to explain the crucial difference between the two. And to be sure, there is a crucial difference. A *divorce* is a civil matter that seeks to terminate a marriage contract; in legal terms, it dissolves a partnership. Better termed as a "finding of nullity," an *annulment* is the formal ecclesiastical pronouncement that a marriage—once considered

[309] John Paul II, "Address of John Paul II to the Tribunal of the Roman Rota."

valid—never existed in the first place. How could that happen? The general answer is that a marriage can have *impediments*—things that impede or prevent a marriage's confection. Jesus mentions one in Matthew 19:9: an incestuous union. If a brother and sister marry each other, for instance—even though both parties may have been unaware of the blood relationship at the time—the marriage has an impediment. There are others, including impediments pertaining to *age* (a boy of eleven years, for instance, is not eligible to marry), a *vow* (a priest under a vow of celibacy cannot be married), *impotence* (the consummation of the marriage is impossible), *abduction* (a man cannot marry a woman he has kidnapped), and *simulation of consent* (a groom adamantly refuses to have children). There can also be a lack of *canonical form related* to the following circumstances. *First,* if a baptized Catholic man married a baptized Episcopalian woman at her church, and the man had not obtained a dispensation from his bishop, that marriage would lack *form*. *Second*, if a marriage between two baptized Catholics were performed secretly (as in the movie *Braveheart*), that marriage would lack form.[310]

Since her earliest days, the Church's ecclesiastical law—currently expressed in the Code of Canon Law of 1983—has cited impediments to marriage. As the guardian of the sacraments, the Catholic Church can add, subtract, modify, or dispense with certain impediments. Notwithstanding

[310] To ensure that this does not spoil the movie for Catholic viewers, William Wallace's secret marriage to Marion Braidfute would have been both valid and legal. Before the Council of Trent, secret marriages (those without witnesses) were canonically allowed.

that ability, most of the rules regarding impediments have been those of fine-tuning rather than overhaul. For example, clandestine marriages were once allowed, but following the Council of Trent, they are forbidden. For another example, the minimum age for Matrimony today is sixteen for males and fourteen for females; in the previous code of 1917, the required ages were fourteen and twelve, respectively. There have not been significant changes regarding impediments for several main reasons. *First,* the nature of the sacrament of Matrimony has not changed since its institution by Jesus: marriage has not become *less* indissoluble, for instance. *Second,* the nature of free will has remained unchanged. Man did not suddenly become an irrational creature who is unable to consent to marriage. *Third,* the Church recognizes the natural right to marriage. Because there is a natural right to marriage, the Church would not and cannot mandate a list of impediments so challenging to overcome that they disallow that right. Even on an individual basis, a priest cannot refuse marriage between an eligible man and an eligible woman without grave and explicit reason. The Church loves marriage, and she imposes only those vital impediments—and even those impediments are sometimes easily dispensed on a case-by-case basis.

The Catholic Church did not *create* marriage; rather, God created marriage prior to founding His Church. In fact, marriage is part of God's primordial design for humanity; that is, it dates back to the very origin of creation. As Peter Elliott explains, "Marriage is found within the divine act of creation."[311] Further, marriage is not only primordial in *time*

---

[311] Elliott, *What God Has Joined*, 7.

but also primordial in essence because of its reflection of the Trinity. As Pope Saint John Paul II explains, "In the light of the New Testament it is possible to discern how *the primordial model of the family is to be sought in God himself.*"[312] Why point this out? Because it is important to understand that men and women have a natural right to marriage—a natural law right that precedes ecclesiastical law. When the Church blocks a marriage, She decides in conformity with the nature of marriage. Her impediments do not reflect arbitrary rules, but instead realities reflecting the nature of marriage. Thus, the powers of the Catholic Church regarding marriage are limited by divine design. The Church did not establish marriage; she cannot abolish marriage. For all her authority, the Church cannot put any marriage asunder, for she lacks the ontological ability to do so.

Another important clarification is necessary here: annulments *per se* are not an invention of modern times despite some critics. As we will see, the Church has long recognized that findings of nullity are an essential component in sacramental guardianship. The problem concerning annulments is not their novelty but rather their ubiquity. In terms of their occurrence, annual annulment numbers have rivaled those of marriage ceremonies. But findings of nullity were rare prior to the Protestant Revolution. In a 1941 address, Pope Pius XII summarized the Church's position on annulments, "As regards declarations of nullity of marriages, everyone knows that the Church is rather wary and disinclined to favor them. Indeed, if the tranquillity, stability, and security of human intercourse in general demand that contracts be not lightly

[312] John Paul II, *Gratissimam Sane.*

set aside, this is still more true of a contract of such importance as marriage, whose firmness and stability are necessary for the common welfare of human society as well as for the private good of the parties and the children, and whose sacramental dignity forbids that it be lightly exposed to the danger of profanation."[313] That was in 1941. And then came 1970, and annulments became commonplace.

This chapter will examine how things changed so rapidly and profoundly regarding annulments, as the numbers will illustrate. Disturbing as the numbers may be, the statistics mask an underlying problem: a deep reluctance toward marriage. The faithful are taking note, if only by osmosis, that marriage is not being taken seriously in the Church. If marriage is simply a contract that awaits the inevitable discovery of its invalidity, why bother marrying in the first place? There is an unfortunate and devastating logic to that question.

The current annulment practices and procedures in America—which began fifty years ago—presents a clear and ongoing threat to the sacrament of Matrimony. It is not the contention in this chapter that annulments are improper, per se; after all, the Church has processed cases of nullity for many centuries. But just as the temptation exists for judicial activism in the administration of civil law, so does that same temptation within the administration of canon law.[314] The problem is not the law; the problem is the activism. In civil law, judicial activists impose standards, regulations,

---

[313] John Paul II, "Address of John Paul II to the Tribunal of the Roman Rota." John Paul here quotes Pope Pius XII, October 3, 1941.
[314] Vasoli, *What God Has Joined Together*, 59. Vasoli uses the term "judicial adventurism."

and burdens that surpass both letter and spirit of constitutional and statutory law—focusing on penumbras and emanations rather than text or intention of the lawgiver. But even though many tribunals may have the noblest motives and desires, they can exhibit a similar judicial activism that serves neither justice, charity, nor truth. Tribunalists (those who serve on marriage tribunals) and canonists (those who practice canon law) must not commit the logical and theological fallacy of moving the goalposts when it comes to validity. That is, tribunals must not begin to impose a difficult hurdle for marriage validity, especially regarding matters of maturity and consent. Tribunalists, laity, and parish priests should promote and defend Canon 1060: "Marriage possesses the favor of law; therefore, in a case of doubt, the validity of a marriage must be upheld until the contrary is proven." Canon 1060 is not a whimsical suggestion; it is a promulgated statutory law signed into power by the pope. It is judicial activism that does not scrupulously adhere to Canon 1060. All Catholics are bound to agree that no valid marriage should ever be found null.

The annulment process is in vital need of reform; thus, it would help to begin this discussion by illustrating how the Church dealt with annulment abuses of the past.

The First Defender of the Bond

After the death of Pope Clement XII in 1740, a conclave of fifty-four cardinals convened a few days later in Rome. It was all very standard, except for one thing: the cardinals could not agree about whom to elect. Various factions of cardinals seemed unwavering in support of their particular candidate, so three compromises were discussed. One of them was an Italian cardinal, well-regarded for his academic brilliance. His name was Prospero Lambertini. During the debate, Cardinal Lambertini arose and stated, "If you wish to elect a saint, choose Gotti; a statesman, Aldobrandini; an honest man, elect me."[315] The conclave chose honesty, and Lambertini took the name Pope Benedict XIV. The new pope turned out to be not only honest but a saint and statesman as well. He also proved to be a hero of Matrimony at a time when the Church desperately needed that hero.

Two centuries prior, the divorce of Henry VIII rocked Christendom. Some of the damage, such as the English schism itself, was clear and immediate. But some of the fallout was more subtle and took years to unravel; in this category, we can include annulments. Before Henry's phony annulment, few lay Catholics were familiar with the canonical process of nullity. After all, why would they be? Just as most Catholics in the twenty-first century are unaware that ordinations can be annulled, most Catholics in the early sixteenth century were probably ignorant—and much more importantly, *disinterested*—that marriages could be found null. But Henry had opened Pandora's Box, and "nullity" was added to common parlance.

Following Henry's divorce, an increasing number of Catholics in some European nations and dioceses filed for annulments. It is difficult to arrive at accurate numbers in this regard, but the numbers were high enough to alarm Pope Benedict XIV. Worse, the pope was angry that many of these annulments were granted by local ecclesiastical bodies,

---

[315] *The Catholic Encyclopedia*, s.v. "Pope Benedict XIV."

which seemed lax, even eager, to grant them. Thus, very early in his papacy, Pope Benedict XIV issued a widespread reform of the process as spelled out in 1741's *Dei Miseratione*. In that document, the pope highlighted the problem, using some emphatic verbiage:

> We have heard that in some ecclesiastical curias too many judges with imprudent facility, rashness and lack of prudential judgment have issued sentences in favor of the nullity of marriage and have given spouses the ability to marry again with others. . . .
>
> These clearly unprepared judges afflicted by the condition of human nature like our first Parent . . . ought to in some way be admonished lest they precipitously and with audacity break the sacred and perpetual bond of marriage.[316]

Pope Benedict explained that some judges were not even bothering with the basic legal process of discovery before issuing their findings of nullity. In some cases, only the spouse who sought nullity would appear before the judge, and the judges passed the sentence without even hearing from the other spouse member involved.[317] The glaring problem, as Reverend Smith points out in *Elements of Ecclesiastical Law*, is that "it happened that the party demanding the annulment of the marriage easily obtained a sentence of nullity, and was thus enabled to remarry."[318] This is an offense to justice on the level of basic jurisprudence, to say nothing of

---

316 "Origins of the Defender of the Bond."
317 Smith, *Elements of Ecclesiastical Law*, 391.
318 Smith, 391.

sacramental integrity. (Imagine admitting only a plaintiff's testimony in a civil suit before rendering judgment.) Based on the pope's verbiage, he also had reason to believe that the judges were taking bribes offered by those seeking annulments. Pope Benedict XIV had promised honesty—a quality that this entire process lacked. He needed to find honest men, so he devised a plan to protect marriage.

As part of his reforms of 1741, Pope Benedict XIV established the position of *matrimonii defensor*. In English, the position was known as the defender of Matrimony or defender of marriage. Pope Benedict mandated that *every diocese on earth* have a defender of marriage appointed by the local bishop. Further, although the *individual* office holder of defender could be changed, the *position* of defender itself was permanent. Moreover, he was not simply an observer; quite the contrary. Smith notes that the defender of Matrimony was "strictly bound to be present at all the proceedings of the case," and that "all proceedings of such causes of nullity are null and void if the defender of the marriage is not properly cited to act in the case."[319] He not only acted as a defender of the marriage but also acted as a court official who maintained both right and duty to examine all pertinent "documents and testimony."[320] The defender was required to repeatedly swear "an oath to fulfil his duties faithfully" not just as a ceremony in which he achieved the position but "every time he acts in a cause."[321] Sent into a system that had

[319] Smith, 392.
[320] Smith, 393.
[321] Smith, 393.

grown corrupt, the defenders were essentially the untouchables of a prior age.

But Pope Benedict XIV's reforms involved both the establishment of the defender of Matrimony and the procedure for finding nullity. If the court came to a ruling of nullity, the defender was required to file an automatic appeal. With Benedict's reforms, this means that a marriage could not be decided null unless it was found to be null twice—*at least.* The defender had the authority to appeal even after two cases—even to Rome directly.[322] Even beyond that, there was another legal qualification. As Reverend Smith clarifies: "However, it must be observed that even when the marriage has been . . . twice declared invalid, and the parties have remarried, it is allowed at any time afterwards, no matter how many years have elapsed, to produce new proofs (i.e., proofs which have been either *newly* discovered or were not submitted in the former trials, either because of collusion, ignorance, etc.) in the ecclesiastical court to show that the marriage was valid. For matrimonial causes of nullity, *never* become *res judicatae.*"[323]

Looking at his reforms and the authority and powers granted to the defenders of Matrimony, it is clear that Pope Benedict XIV viewed Matrimony as the primordial sacrament: to protect it is to protect the Church herself.

Many Catholics are altogether unfamiliar with Pope Benedict XIV, but his name deserves mention, along with Saint Thomas More and Saint John Fisher, as a valiant protector of marriage. Two hundred years after their martyrdoms, marriage

---

[322] Smith, 393.
[323] Smith, 394.

was in crisis, and Pope Benedict XIV served as marriage's hero. However, two centuries after Pope Benedict's death in 1758, the Church would find herself in the throes of an annulment crisis again. This time, it would happen in America.

The Fire Begins

On June 23, 1970, *The New York Times* ran a short news piece that was awkwardly crammed on the bottom of page 43: the obituary page. The headline read in caps: "ANNULMENT CHANGES BACKED BY VATICAN."[324] Had a Catholic historian written the headline, it might have been headlined: BENEDICTINE REFORMS ABOLISHED. As the *Times* noted, the Vatican had granted permission to the American bishops to make changes that were "designed to speed the granting of annulments of marriages involving Catholics."[325] That was a superlative understatement. Known as the American Procedural Norms (APN), the changes went into effect on July 1 of that year.[326]

There were three major changes.

First, a single judge could now decide a case. Before 1970, marriage tribunals were required to have a minimum of three judges. Under APN, a single judge could arrive at a finding of nullity. This amounted to a concentration of power that gave rise to alarm; as Lord Acton observed, "absolute power corrupts absolutely." Even so, Rome had only allowed a case to have a single judge—rather than a multi-member

---

[324] "Annulment Changes Backed by Vatican."

[325] "Annulment Changes Backed by Vatican."

[326] Vasoli, *What God Has Joined Together*, 27; Marshner, *Annulment or Divorce?*, 10.

tribunal—for "a grave reason."[327] But given an inch, tribunals took a mile. In his book *What God Has Joined Together*, Robert Vasoli notes that "single-judge tribunals were the (virtually ironclad) rule rather than the exception."[328] In the eyes of many tribunalists, every reason appeared "grave."[329]

Second, the mandatory appeal of a finding of nullity—the appeal that Pope Benedict XIV had deemed so vital—was dropped. The system allowed for appeal but was neither mandatory nor practical in many cases. Beyond that, Vasoli speculates that many respondents were not even informed of their right to appeal an annulment finding.[330] And without a required and automatic appeal, tribunal judges had little worry of even being second-guessed.[331] In practice, the new rule was: one and done.

Third, the required evidence to *prove* invalidity was drastically lessened. Before 1970, judges required "moral certitude" that a marriage was null before declaring it null. Moral certitude might be likened to a term more familiar to Americans as "beyond a reasonable doubt." In criminal law, a person is presumed innocent *unless* and *until* proven guilty "beyond a reasonable doubt." That standard nears 100 percent certainty. Why require such a high standard? Because sending innocent people to prison on flimsy evidence devastates their lives and destroys the integrity of a society. We can contrast this with civil law, in which the standard is lessened to a "preponderance of the evidence"—that is, any evidence over 50 percent. A jury must only be 51 percent sure in

---

[327] Vasoli, *What God Has Joined Together*, 27.
[328] Vasoli, 27.
[329] Vasoli, 27.
[330] Vasoli, 27.
[331] Godfrey-Howell, *Consensual Incapacity to Marry*, loc. 93, Kindle.

a civil case for a plaintiff or defendant to win the case. In other words, the jury might adequately arrive at a verdict, even though they are 49 percent in doubt about that verdict. Returning now to the annulment reform, the judges only needed the "'prevailing weight' of evidence" to determine that a marriage was null.[332] Though this change was visually unseen, it was perhaps the most staggering.

In sum, with the new changes, one judge could declare a marriage null with only 51 percent certainty that he was correct in a case that was unlikely to be appealed. Pope Benedict XIV must have rolled over in his grave.

These radical changes naturally lead to the question: Why these drastic changes? What was so broken that required such a desperate and immediate fix? Where did the Vatican get the idea for such sweeping reforms to the annulment process? And if the process prior to the tribunal system was so flawed, why was America singled out? In other words, why weren't these norms adopted universally in all nations? To address those questions, we must examine the actions of the Canon Law Society of America (CLSA).

Formed in 1939, the CLSA had become an influential organization in the Catholic Church in America by 1970. To understand *why*, consider the following. The Catholic Church operates a system of ecclesiastical law called *canon law*, a comprehensive body of regulations for church governance. It includes—among many other things—the administration of the sacraments, procedures for removing a priest from his clerical duties, and finding a marriage null. Canon law is serious matter, and those who work in the field of

[332] "Annulment Changes Backed by Vatican."

canon law have responsibilities that would make angels quiver. It is also difficult to attain: only a few academic institutions in the world have the pontifical authority required to confer the postgraduate degree. Prior to 1970, only one school in the United States was even authorized to confer a canon law degree: Catholic University. But if one nevertheless wished to pursue a career in canon law, he would need to devote at least two years of his life to obtaining the lesser degree of Licentiate of Canon Law (JCL), or three years to get the Doctorate of Canon Law (JCD). As with any degree, he would also need the time and the financial wherewithal to achieve such degrees. For these reasons and more, canon law is plagued with an extrinsic problem: canon lawyers are an extreme rarity. Considering the powerful influence of just one canon lawyer, he or she wields significant power in Church matters. Now consider the amount of power wielded by an organization of canon lawyers that, without a competitor, constitutes a monopoly. It gets even more monopolistic when considering that *The Jurist*, the official magazine of the CLSA, was published by the Catholic University of America. It speaks volumes that Charles Curran—the most famous dissenter of the twentieth century—contributed to *The Jurist*. The power and influence of the CLSA on the practice of canon law in America was staggering. That was true in 1969. That is still true today. Though it might seem more logical to compare the CLSA to the American Bar Association (ABA), it is more similar in some respects to the American Medical Association (AMA). The AMA's medical recommendations are deemed so authoritative that disagreement with the AMA's pronouncements would be widely viewed as quackery.

In 1969, the CLSA petitioned the American bishops to petition the Vatican for the abovementioned changes.[333] The prior year, there were 338 annulments in America. In 1970, the first year of APN, that number exponentially skyrocketed to 5,403—an increase of sixteen-fold.[334] (Little did anyone fully realize it at the time, the tribunals were only getting warmed up: by 1991, the number of annulments increased another eleven-fold.)

But alarming numbers were not exclusive to America: due in no small measure to the Dutch Catechism anti-catechesis, the Church in Holland was granting annulments in droves. The Dutch were brazen in their actions, which amounted to a wholesale denial of Church doctrine on marriage. By the end of 1971, Rome had seen enough heresy from the Dutch—again. Cardinal Staffa, the prefect of the Apostolic Signatura, wrote a powerful letter to the Dutch cardinal Alfrink. Like the United States Supreme Court, the Apostolic Signatura is the highest court of canon law in the Catholic Church. The prefect of the Apostolic Signatura is essentially its chief justice. Thus, Staffa's letter was extraordinarily weighty and genuinely authoritative, and his observations regarding the doctrine of marriage apply not only to the Dutch but to all the Catholic faithful.

Staffa demanded immediate reform to the tribunal process in Holland and clarified that these reforms were not simply matters of procedure but involved "the very doctrine touching the

---

[333] Vasoli, *What God Has Joined Together,* 27.
[334] Kendra, "American Annulment Mills."

nature of marriage between baptized persons."[335] Staffa's letter was authoritative and clear, echoing irreformable doctrines that had existed since the infancy of the Catholic Church, focusing on six main areas. First, *indissolubility.* Dutch tribunals had presented indissolubility as "ideal" but not essential—or even *normative*—to marriage. Second, *the nature of consent.* The tribunals had presented consent—not as an *event* that occurs at the nuptial ceremony—but as an evolutionary *process* that unfolds over the years. Some tribunals viewed the wedding ceremony and vows as simply the "matrimonial debut," which begins a process that "becomes marriage progressively." Staffa points out that "this erroneous doctrine" not only "subverts the foundations of marriage law" but presents the logical problem that it becomes impossible "to establish whether a marriage is valid or not." The Dutch had claimed that Vatican II established such procedures of progressive consent; Staffa pointed out that Vatican II did no such thing. Third, *readmission to the sacraments.* Staffa condemned the Dutch practice of readmitting persons to the Eucharist who were divorced and remarried. The Dutch did not seem to have an issue with this practice in the least, primarily because—in their heretical eyes—marriage cannot ever be proven valid in the first place. In fact, the Dutch were not big fans of the word "Matrimony" but seemed to prefer terms like "the evolution of the interpersonal relationship." Fourth, *the ranking of doctrine over pastoral concerns.* Violations of the doctrine of marriage were being justified by "pastoral concerns," as though a priest could deny doctrine and still lead his parishioners to Jesus. Staffa reprimands, "The pastoral concern to which

---

[335] "Nature of Marriage (Sig. Apost., 30 Dec., 1971) Private." All quotes from this paragraph, unless otherwise noted, are from Staffa's letter.

certain Dutch judges often refer, must be called superficial. It is completely devoid of theological foundation and is more interested in remedying human situations in one way or another than in conserving revealed faith." Fifth, *happiness and validity*. Staffa condemned the idea that husbands and wives could deem their marriages invalid because they had turned out to be unhappy. Sixth, *psychological defect*. Staffa warned against overly involving "specialists in psychology" in the process, who seem eager to find mortal defects. Staffa noted a specific contradiction that was becoming more common: "the experts contradict themselves by affirming the absolute incapacity of the parties for marriage and afterwards declaring that these same persons are capable of contracting a new marriage."[336]

Staffa's letter was addressed to Cardinal Alfrink, but it could have been rightfully addressed to every wayward tribunal in America—because some Dutch errors were shared in America. Though the positions of the American canonists were more subtle and nuanced than their Dutch counterparts, many of these same errors were becoming increasingly popular in American tribunals. But it was psychological defect that American canonists latched on to, which happened in earnest in the years leading up to the 1983 Code of Canon Law issuance.

Psychobabble

The proposed and adopted changes of the APA in 1970 were not simply procedural; in large measure, they were based on a new philosophy of marriage and even man himself. Canon lawyer Catherine Godfrey-Howell references a paper

[336] See also Vasoli, *What God Has Joined Together*, 63–64.

presented at the CLSA Convention in 1968, later appearing in April 1969's *The Jurist*.[337] Authored by Rev. John T. Finnegan, JCD, the article was titled "The Capacity to Marry."[338] It is worth examining this article in detail because it represented a growing opinion among canonists and tribunalists in the late 1960s and present. As Godfrey-Howell points out, Finnegan's article was reprinted in 2016 "as if to reiterate that this perspective is still valid today."[339]

Finnegan's article centers on the idea that while men and women have "the right to marry," not all have the "capacity to marry."[340] Finnegan admits that the capacity to marry had been traditionally and typically applied to a physical inability to perform the marital act or to "intellectual defect of consent" (as in the case, for example, of a man who says the words of the vows while simultaneously planning on cheating on his wife the next day).[341] But Finnegan argues that the incapacity to marry should be much more broadly applied to psychology. Thus a man or woman could have a *psychological incapacity* to consent to marriage. And this psychological incapacity is formed by a broad mix of social, economic, and geographical factors. Finnegan writes, "*'Moral impotency' or the incapacity to marry will be more common today due to social and occupational conditions that place great stress on the making of a successful marriage.*"[342]

---

337 Godfrey-Howell, *Consensual Incapacity to Marry*, 96.
338 Finnegan, "The Capacity to Marry."
339 Godfrey-Howell, *Consensual Incapacity to Marry*, 159, n. 233.
340 Finnegan, "The Capacity to Marry," 248.
341 Finnegan, 248.
342 Finnegan, 252–53.

Let's pause for a moment here to make an essential distinction: a man either has the capacity to marry or he does not. There is no such thing, canonically, as lacking the capacity for a *successful* marriage. Further, the entire notion of "success" in this respect is objectively impossible and subjectively vague. What if "success" for my wife equals a flat stomach, a new Lexus, a pool, and a well-manicured lawn? If Finnegan's argument is taken to its logical end, my inability to provide my wife with those things constitutes my so-called "incapacity" to marry her. (As Godfrey-Howell points out, canonists would later argue that a man's incapacity to marry a *particular* woman is not necessarily an incapacity for that man to marry a *different* woman.[343]) Of course—and this is where marriage tribunals enter the picture—no one was aware of my incapacity on the day of our wedding; outwardly, it appeared that I had so much promise. My incapacity was only later discovered when an AMC Gremlin adorned my driveway rather than a Lexus convertible. Finnegan's integral linking of success with validity would become a common theme at marriage tribunals across America in the coming years.

Returning to Finnegan, he continues, "Some people do not have the personal wherewithal, or ego-strength, to undertake the contemporary experience of marriage. What we are saying here in this proposal is that marriage requires *more* of a person today than it ever did in the past. It takes more internal stamina to make a success of marriage and family life today."[344] That sort of comment gets the mind racing, hearkening back to various ages during which Christianity

[343] Godfrey-Howell, *Consensual Incapacity to Marry*, 117.
[344] Finnegan, "The Capacity to Marry," 253.

itself carried a death sentence and marriage ceremonies had to be conducted underground. But notwithstanding Finnegan's lack of conception about much of Christian history, why—in Finnegan's eyes—is marriage so much harder now? Finnegan answers this question, illustrating his overall view of marriage. He writes:

> Young couples because of the mobility of our age live in "isolated conjugal units"; the head of the household no longer works with his family finding children an occupational asset, but most likely the father works outside the home and *develops roles of aggressiveness* and *hard-line business tactics* which he is expected to repudiate when he concludes work and enters the home; the highly educated mother no longer finds the automated housekeeping chores a *challenge to her life or the realization of her true potential*; children within this context are a *genuine parental burden* because of the many years of education and effort it requires to outfit a child for responsible adulthood.[345]

Finnegan views marriage and family life as stagnant, bleak, and miserable. His view of marriage is the stuff of Betty Friedan's rants and Margaret Atwood's dystopian novels: "aggressive" fathers border on violence, and mothers are caught in a web of despair woven by their burdensome children who destroy any potential happiness the couple might otherwise have. Finnegan's view is designed to build his case against—as the article's title reminds us—the capacity to marry. His logic is that if men and women don't fully understand just

---

[345] Finnegan, 253, emphasis added.

how bad marriage can be, they are psychologically incapable of consent to such an arrangement of marriage and family life. He writes, "We must be realistic enough to admit that many will be 'morally impotent' or incapable to understand the contemporary marital experience."[346] Finnegan's comments are tantamount to saying: *In this day and age, you would have to be crazy to desire marriage. And crazy people are incapable of making psychological consent.* This became, more or less, the normative position of the CLSA. It also became the increasing viewpoint of marriage tribunals.

In an article that discusses the validity of marriage—especially one written by a Catholic priest—one might expect to see the words "grace" and "sacrament." After all, the article focused on married men and women's challenges in performing their duties as spouses and parents. How would a Catholic hope to have that conversation without once referring to God's grace, a supernatural gift given to help us achieve our duties? But the word "grace" does not appear in his article. And neither does the word "sacrament" appear. That's like discussing the Trinity without mentioning God. It is not simply that sacramentality is an added *feature* of marriage but that marriage *is* a sacrament. In the late 1980s, Cardinal Edouard Gagnon, the president of the Pontifical Council for the Family, lamented the de-emphasis of marriage's sacramentality: "All the time we have had before our eyes the most obvious truth that Marriage is a sacrament. Did we perhaps tend to avoid looking closely at the sacrament because it is

[346] Finnegan, 253.

too much of a challenge to us? . . . How far have we allowed the social sciences to displace the central reality?"[347]

But rather than focus on theological terms like "sacramentality" and "grace," Finnegan presents us with terms and concepts seemingly related to psychology: "ego-strength," "moral impotence," and "isolated conjugal units." This language epitomizes the contemporary literature of the 1960s, which was intent on using language that came to be known as "psychobabble." Psychobabble can be defined as "a form of speech or writing that uses psychological jargon, buzzwords, and esoteric language to create an impression of truth or plausibility."[348] Psychobabble was the consequence that during the late 1960s and 1970s, everyone seemed fascinated by psychoanalysis. As one trained psychoanalyst commented at the time, "virtually everyone who is touched by psychoanalysis identifies with it and soon wants to become a therapist himself."[349] Sadly, many canon lawyers were not immune to the siren song of psychoanalysis. Finnegan considers that the tribunal system of the late 1960s was "institutionally incapable of meeting the obligations of the Church and the needs of our people in a broken marriage." He continues, "Our knowledge and understanding of man has been enhanced by the advances in the behavioral sciences and has resulted in the greater appreciation of the *mystery* of man." But Vasoli points out that these so-called "advances" are vague at best: "Whenever canon lawyers speak of new departures in the behavioral sciences, they are usually referring to unspecified

[347] Elliott, *What God Has Joined*, vii–viii.

[348] *Wikipedia*, s.v., "Psychobabble," accessed October 22, 2022, https://en.wikipedia.org/wiki/Psychobabble.

[349] Rosen, *Psychobabble*, 19.

'advances' made by unspecific somebodies, in unspecified directions for reasons that are unclear."[350] Nevertheless, these "advances" somehow led to an appreciation of "the mystery of man." Sadly, that emphasis produced a substantial devaluation of the mystery of the sacrament of matrimony itself.

From the time of Finnegan's presentation in 1968, adopting psychoanalysis to the tribunal process would quickly become standard—and so would annulments. There was a direct relationship between the two because many cases used psychoanalysis to "prove" defective consent. By a wide margin, defective consent became the most prevalent reason for a finding of nullity. And it would become even more common with the Code of Canon Law issuance in 1983.

Defective Consent and Canon 1095

The 1983 Code, issued under the pontificate of Pope Saint John Paul II, contains several canons about invalidity. Among others, Canon 1098 involves malicious deceit, whereby a man or woman is tricked into marriage. Canon 1102 states, "A marriage subject to a condition about the future cannot be contracted validly (for instance, a woman agrees to marry a man with the condition that he becomes a millionaire by age thirty). Canon 1103 addresses those cases which involve force or fear (for instance, a man cannot marry a woman he has kidnapped). But while the canons are relevant, they are—*mercifully*—rarely applied. Presumably, there are few cases where a woman offers kidnapping as grounds for a tribunal hearing.

[350] Vasoli, *What God Has Joined Together*, 69.

But as far as annulments are concerned, it is canon 1095 that is most often employed—by far.[351] According to research by Vasoli in numbers obtained in the Statistical Yearbooks of the Church, between 1984 and 1994, "over 95 percent of the ordinary process decisions by American tribunals relate to defective consent."[352] Canon 1095 reads: "The following are incapable of contracting marriage: 1/ those who lack the sufficient use of reason; 2/ those who suffer from a grave defect of discretion of judgment concerning the essential matrimonial rights and duties mutually to be handed over and accepted; 3/ those who are not able to assume the essential obligations of marriage for causes of a psychic nature."[353] In one sense, there is nothing new in Canon 1095; it simply reiterates prior teaching and prior law. The difficulty with this phrasing, however, is that it is vague. As Rev. Mark Pilon writes, "The problem with the new definition is that the essential rights and obligations of marriage, which are the basis for the grounds for annulments, including the annulments based on psychological grounds, were not specified in the Code, but supposedly were left to be worked out in the Church's courts."[354] The language was vague enough to allow enterprising canonists and tribunalists to pursue major loopholes, which they did.

The *New Commentary on the Code of Canon Law*, commissioned by the CLSA, attempts to explain these terms in Canon 1095. Though canon law specifically uses the term

---

[351] Vasoli, 72.

[352] Vasoli, 25. Vasoli notes on p. 61 that the data is unavailable for the years leading up to 1984.

[353] Canon 1095.

[354] Pilon, "Streamlining Annulments."

"grave defect of discretion," the *Commentary* headlines this section with the phrase "Lack of Due Discretion."[355] Within the Catholic theological lexicon, "grave defect" and "lack" are not synonyms by any means; they are nearly antonyms. The failure to say grace before meals is a "lack," while fornication is "grave." The two simply cannot be equated, yet the *Commentary* opts to use that terminology. Nevertheless, here is its explanation of "lack of due discretion." It states:

> "A person may possess sufficient use of reason to have a rudimentary and abstract understanding of marriage and its obligations but still be incapable of consent, if he or she lacks the ability to deliberate critically about this choice in the concrete. For example, a teen-aged girl captivated by the story of Romeo and Juliet may have adequate abstract knowledge of marriage and intend a marriage with her first boyfriend like the one portrayed in Shakespeare's play, but still be unable to consent validly to the marriage because of her immature assessment of her own and her boyfriend's readiness for marriage. Canon law calls this incapacity for critical deliberation lack of maturity or discretion of judgment."[356]

Juxtaposing this explanation with Finnegan's view of married life, the CLSA establishes a fascinating dichotomy. If a young woman has Finnegan's dysphoric concept of marriage outlined above, she is considered more ready to undertake vows of Matrimony; however, if Shakespeare's fictional lovers

---

[355] Beal, *New Commentary on the Code of Canon Law*, 1299.
[356] Beal, 1299.

have influenced that same young woman's impression of marriage, she is incapable of marriage. The anecdotal observer might note that most Catholic brides smile during their wedding ceremonies, which would seem to indicate that their notion of marriage is not that of Finnegan's. Perhaps their concepts of marriage were formed by *Brides* magazine, Beach Boys songs, and Jane Austen novels. Does listening to the Beach Boys album *Pet Sounds* vanquish one's ability for critical deliberation? Does a multiple reading of *Sense and Sensibility* establish an invalidating influence also? It is difficult to see how this would constitute a lack, much less a "grave defect to consent." But if this is true, what are we to make of a man who became a priest because he was inspired by Karl Malden's priestly character in *On the Waterfront*? This sort of logic would be humorous, but for its tragedy. The *Commentary* is suggesting—nay, *stating*—that a marriage should be annulled on the grounds of an infatuation with a Shakespeare play.

Godfrey-Howell writes, "In American jurisprudence, 'due discretion' is cited in the vast majority of cases citing consensual incapacity, including those that also cite the inability to assume the essential obligations of marriage."[357] Part of the reason this is allowed to occur is because of the vagueness of the terms. Godfrey-Howell notes, "American jurisprudence proceeds without serious attention to the basics of the legal formula of consensual incapacity, and it furthermore develops in a particular manner despite challenges posed by more universal (and in some cases more authoritative) channels of scholarship."[358]

---

[357] Godfrey-Howell, *Consensual Incapacity to Marry*, 52.
[358] Godfrey-Howell, 52.

One of those more authoritative sources—in fact, the *most* authoritative source—is the Roman Rota. Regarding marriage cases, the Roman Rota is essentially the Supreme Court of canon law. Structurally, if a case receives a finding of nullity, it is possible to appeal the case to the Roman Rota. One might think that the Roman Rota confirms the vast majority of decisions of the American marriage tribunals, but that is not the case—not even close. Though he refers to a small sampling, Vasoli notes that during a decade between the mid-1980s and 1990s, "at least 92 percent of American defective consent cases reviewed by the Rota were overturned."[359] That figure is confirmed by canon lawyer Father Gerald Murray, who served on the Archdiocese of New York's tribunal. Father Murray says that "in the mid-90s," the Rota overturned "approximately 90 percent" of the nullity decisions.[360]

From the beginning of his pontificate, Pope Saint John Paul II warned marriage tribunals to avoid rebelling against the Rota's directives, to keep an unflinching focus on doctrine, and to be wary of pop psychology that obstructs the truth about both the human person and marriage itself. In a 1981 address to the Roman Rota, Pope Saint John Paul II instructed, "Indeed, *any innovation of law, substantive or procedural, that does not correspond to the jurisprudence or practice of the tribunals and dicasteries of the Holy See, is reckless.* We must be convinced that a serene, attentive, thought-out, complete, and exhaustive examination of marriage cases demands full conformity to the correct doctrine of the Church, to canon law, and to sound canonical jurisprudence,

[359] Vasoli, *What God Has Joined Together,* 62.
[360] Murray, *Calming the Storm*, 55.

which has come to maturity above all through the contribution of the Sacred Roman Rota."[361] That is, marriage tribunals have the sacred duty to view every case through the lens of the primary purpose of marriage, the indissolubility of marriage, the fidelity of marriage, the sacramentality of marriage, and—for that matter—all defined doctrine. And if they are acting against statutory canon law and the jurisprudence of the Roman Rota, they are operating in direct contravention of Rome.

Sadly, American tribunals from coast to coast repeatedly failed to heed the pope's instructions and admonitions: their reckless behavior continued.

In a 1995 address to the Rota, Pope John Paul II again highlighted the problem: "Thus it is helpful once again to call the attention of ecclesiastical tribunals to the unacceptable consequences resulting from—erroneous doctrinal approaches, which have negative repercussions on the administration of justice and, in a particular and even more serious way, on the handling of cases of marital nullity."[362]

His 1998 address to the Rota clarifies an important aspect of 1095: consent in relation to psychological health. To understand his point, we need to provide this preliminary explanation. It would be wonderful if everyone were perfectly psychologically healthy; however, that is not the case. Many people suffer from obsessive-compulsive disorders (OCD), which manifest themselves in many ways. Some people

---

[361] John Paul II, "Address of John Paul II To the Tribunal of the Roman Rota."

[362] John Paul II, "Address of His Holiness John Paul II to the Tribunal of the Roman Rota."

excessively wash their hands as though they are preparing to perform surgery. Some people obsessively count numbers by tapping on their fingers. Others obsessively worry about objectively trivial things, thinking they are serious. Some Catholics suffer from scrupulosity, which is often considered a manifestation of OCD. Even more common than OCD problems are phobias. Many—if not *most*—people suffer from irrational fears such as fear of heights (acrophobia), fear of enclosed places (claustrophobia), or fear of clowns (coulrophobia). To be sure, these are abnormalities—although nearly each of us possesses one or more psychological abnormalities. Just as it is challenging to find someone with a "perfect" body or who is emotionally flawless, it is difficult to find someone who is psychologically impeccable. But the question is this: Conceding that psychological problems can be so grave as to make marriage impossible, does *every* psychological abnormality constitute grounds for invalidity? More concretely, in reference to Canon 1095, are we prepared to deny marriage to a clown-fearing finger tapper? (This might seem like an extreme and absurd example—and it is. But it is no more ridiculous than claiming nullity for a young woman on the basis of her love for a Shakespeare play.)

Pope Saint John Paul II noted the temptation of psychologists and canonists to be expansive in their treatment of psychic abnormalities; thus, he provided an essential distinction that canon law's prohibition of marriage applies only to grave disorders.[363] He said that "for the psychologist or psychiatrist every form of psychic illness can appear contrary to normality." But if we are ready to dismiss marriages

[363] Vasoli, *What God Has Joined Together*, 78.

between any men and women who exhibit abnormalities, marriage itself is rendered nearly impossible for anyone. John Paul II says that "normality on the theoretical level can easily become a myth and on the practical level, one *ends up denying to the majority of people the possibility of giving valid consent*" (emphasis added). He stressed, "Only the most severe forms of psychopathology impair substantially the freedom of the individual." Further, he clarified that canon law—which flows from divine law—takes precedence over the ever-changing and contentious methods and views of psychology. He says, "Psychological concepts do not always correspond with canonical."[364]

Acutely aware of the fact that American tribunals were, in effect, nullifying marriages on the grounds of unhappiness, Pope John Paul II addressed this specific error again in 2004: "Then what can one say to the argument which holds that the failure of conjugal life implies the invalidity of the marriage? Unfortunately, this erroneous assertion is sometimes so forceful as to become a generalized prejudice that leads people to seek grounds for nullity as a merely formal justification of a pronouncement that is actually based on the empirical factor of matrimonial failure."[365] He said such attitudes oppose the canonical favor of marriage—the "*favor matrimonii*."[366] The failure of a marriage does not signify the absence of its validity;

---

[364] John Paul II, "Address of John Paul II to the Tribunal of the Roman Rota," January 25, 1988.
[365] John Paul II, "Address of John Paul II To the Members of the Tribunal of the Roman Rota for the Inauguration of the Judicial Year."
[366] John Paul II, "Address of John Paul II To the Members of the Tribunal of the Roman Rota for the Inauguration of the Judicial Year."

rather, it often indicates the presence of sin. As John Paul II puts it, "Valid marriage can fail because of the spouses' own misuse of freedom."[367]

Sadly, the powerful wisdom of Pope Saint John Paul II was largely ignored; couples kept seeking annulments, and American tribunals kept granting them in droves. Between 1970 and the present, the psychological incapacity to consent has become the nearly ubiquitous verdict of non-form annulment findings. Cardinal Raymond Burke served as the prefect of the Apostolic Signatura from 2008 to 2014, so he would be uniquely positioned to assess the problem. In his introduction to Godfrey-Howell's book in 2020, Cardinal Burke states:

> The so-called *psychological grounds of nullity*, that is the alleged nullity of marriage consent because of the psychic incapacity of one or both of the parties, have, in many ecclesiastical tribunals in North America, for example, almost totally *dominated the jurisprudence*. The situation became such that *reasonable people began to wonder whether any party is truly psychologically capable of giving marriage consent*. What should be one of the more difficult grounds of nullity to verify with moral certitude, that is the proof of a psychological pathology rendering a party incapable of giving marriage consent, became known as the easiest grounds by which to establish the nullity of consent.[368]

---

[367] John Paul II, "Address of John Paul II To the Members of the Tribunal of the Roman Rota for the Inauguration of the Judicial Year."
[368] Godfrey-Howell, *Consensual Incapacity to Marry*, 17, emphasis added.

Cardinal Burke's comments here illustrate not only that there exists a dominating jurisprudence of annulment but an even more significant problem: a dominating *culture* of annulment. This culture creates thoughts about annulling marriages in the minds of husbands and wives who may have otherwise never considered the possibility.

A Parish Fishing Expedition

Sacramental marriages will almost certainly undergo periods of difficulty and suffering, which is as much a commentary on life as it is on marriage. But for many marriages, trials make it stronger. The loss of a job, the loss of a house, and the loss of fortune and finances are moments that can cause a husband and wife to worry. But their love, confidence in each other, and hope in God all alleviate worry. While a husband lies in a hospital room awaiting a medical diagnosis, his wife can pray the Rosary with him, meditating on the many miracles of Jesus—in hopes that Jesus's next miracle will be his. A miscarriage can cause a husband and wife to sob quietly together unbeknownst to many in the world who will never understand their sorrow. However, there are those married couples for whom difficulty and suffering have the opposite effect: pain drives the husband and wife further apart. And, of course, many marriages lie somewhere in the middle.

Each and every marriage, especially those facing difficult times, needs the encouragement of priests, the nourishment of the sacraments, and the support of other couples in their parish. Very often, however, they never hear the word "Matrimony" mentioned during a sermon, they witness divorced and remarried parishioners receive Communion every Sunday. They pass brightly-colored brochures for annulments when they walk into church every week. Couples in good marriages might be confused or annoyed by all this, but couples in troubled marriages will be intrigued and tempted. As a man watches his wife age, the secretaries in his office seem to grow younger, and the annulment brochures grow shinier. He begins to ask himself: Did I have the right state of mind twenty-seven years ago when I took my marriage vows? After all, I was an immature twenty-one-year-old at the time; how could I have possibly understood what my life would be like? One Sunday, he doesn't walk past the brochure rack in the vestibule; this time, he stops to grab a brochure on annulments. Or perhaps he reads the Sunday bulletin, which invites all the parishioners to a weeknight presentation about annulments. Could *he* get an annulment? Thus, in legal slang, this is where the *fishing expedition* begins. And it is a fishing expedition with an exceedingly wide net because tribunals around the country seem eager to provide the bait.

For example, the Archdiocese of Chicago has over sixty "field delegates" for the marriage tribunal who help the petitioner through the annulment process. The program coordinator states that most cases concern (and this will come as no surprise at this point) "the moment of consent." He explains, "Our focus on the moment of consent is a real eye-opener for some people."[369]

No doubt.

But this process of looking back years and even decades illustrates another problem. It is a general principle of law

---

[369] Martin, "Tribunal Field delegates help people with annulment process."

that there be a *statute of limitations* on criminal prosecution. *Black's Law Dictionary* defines *statute of limitations* as "a law that bars claims after a specified period."[370] It proceeds to explain the logic behind the statute, "The purpose is to require diligent prosecution of known claims, thereby providing finality and predictability in legal affairs and ensuring that claims will be resolved while evidence is reasonably available and fresh."[371] There is, however, no statute of limitations on annulment. In practice, this means that tribunals can be assigned to investigate—if they even bother to investigate—the state of mind of a man thirty-five years prior on his wedding day. If a marriage is annullable for numerous reasons, even at a late date, this might cause a married man to fall into an abyss of curiosity about his own state: *Was I perfectly healthy psychologically back then? Did I have any feelings for any other woman in my past? Was I getting married—in some measure—because I thought it would make my parents happy?* Thoughts like these can wreak havoc on the imagination. This can cause a soul to undergo the torment of scrupulosity. And that might be more common than we think. As Dr. John Janaro observes, "The 'invalid marriage' obsession is an extremely common one among committed Christians with OCD."[372] A poor soul in this state may wonder if he can lawfully make love to his wife of thirty-five years for fear that he is not validly married—thus sinning with the marital act. The nature of annulments is such that a statute of limitations cannot be juridically applied. The problem,

---

[370] Garner, *Black's Law Dictionary*, 1179.
[371] Garner, 1179.
[372] Janaro, *Never Give Up*, loc. 26, Kindle.

however, is not the absence of a statute of limitations; the problem is combining it with an expansive notion of *consent*. And yet, American tribunals in Chicago and elsewhere are encouraging this process.

The Archdiocese of Newark has a website for those investigating annulment. The canons relevant to marriage have lists of questions to help determine if they might apply. Canon 1095.2 explains: "If one or both spouses either lacked sufficient knowledge of marriage or failed to exercise mature judgment in choosing to marry, this ground can be considered."[373] Without addressing the fact that "mature judgment" borders on impossible to define, this section contains a questionnaire to help you deduce whether you attained that mature judgment. It asks: "Did either you or your former spouse have extremely little or no dating experience before becoming engaged? . . . Did the two of you date for only a brief time? Did the two of you make immature and impulsive decisions in other areas of life (career, finances, etc.)? . . . Was your decision to marry based on some pressing issue or circumstance (for example, a pre-marital pregnancy)?"[374]

I turn to you, dear reader, and ask: Would affirmative answers to these questions annul the marriage? If you said *yes*, then congratulations. You've just annulled the marriage of Mary and Saint Joseph.

The more one investigates tribunal action, the more one realizes how it can occur that an annulment culture can damage otherwise healthy marriages. It can make a happy and holy wife begin to question her own marriage. As Cardinal

---

[373] "Selecting the Ground."
[374] "Selecting the Ground."

Burke wrote, "Reasonable people began to wonder whether *any* party is truly psychologically capable of giving marriage consent." Beyond that, her friends might begin questioning her marriage also. It is the rare adult Catholic today who does not have a friend—or numerous friends—who have received an annulment. While they may not be familiar with the annulment *process*, they are undoubtedly aware of the annulment *itself*, as well as the relative ease that the annulment occurred. This can lead to the canonical equivalent of armchair quarterbacking: *Jeff and Joan say they've been married for ten years, but Jeff is as OCD as Adrian Monk, and Joan was only nineteen when she married him. There's no way that marriage was ever valid. They should just get an annulment and move on.* In Catholic social media, Catholic armchair canonists abound. And in today's annulment culture, what marriage is *not* held in some degree of suspicion? And just to reiterate, these doubts are rarely countered by sermons focusing on the good of marriage.

The Mandate to Divorce

We began this chapter by distinguishing annulment and divorce, but let's repeat it: annulment is not divorce. Divorce is a civil matter that abolishes a legal contract; divorce recognizes that a marriage once *was*. Annulment is an ecclesiastical matter that declares that a marriage *never was*. Some find this annulment/divorce distinction very comforting and affirming. Some tribunalists, canonists, laity, priests, and bishops consider annulment a great mercy, blessing, and healing. Brochures in the back of many Catholic churches reiterate this message: annulment can be a great mercy.

That's a fascinating position when one considers what it all means. It means that the graces of the sacrament never existed because the sacrament never existed. It means that a man and woman's honeymoon in the Bahamas was the equivalent of celebrating an extravagant birthday party for a person who—as it turns out—never existed. It means that a man may never think back on making love to his "wife" without engaging in the sin of lust: conjuring such images would constitute a sin against the sixth commandment. (If she remarried, the man's intentional phantasm would also include an objective sin against the ninth commandment.) All this is referred to as a "mercy" by tribunals whose job is to decide whether a marriage ever was. True, annulment is not divorce. Divorce recognizes that marriage once *was*; annulment affirms the contrary.

But in the discussion of annulment and divorce, it is important to recognize a rather large elephant in the room, and it's a fact that many church-going Catholics are unaware of: while annulment is not divorce, the annulment process in America often *requires* a divorce. According to canon lawyer Ed Peters, "Virtually every diocesan tribunal in America requires proof of a civil divorce before accepting a canonical nullity petition."[375] You read that correctly: a person may not even get a *hearing*—not a final ruling, but an initial hearing—without a civil divorce decree. If nothing else in this book causes you alarm, that should.

At this point, citing the numerous ecclesiastical prohibitions on divorce throughout the ages would be unnecessarily tedious. Suffice it to quote the official *Catechism of the*

---

[375] Peters, *Annulments and the Catholic Church*, loc. 41, Kindle.

Catholic Church, which describes divorce as "a grave offense against the natural law," "immoral," and "a plague on society."[376] Granted, the Church does allow civil divorce in some cases: "If civil divorce remains the only possible way of ensuring certain legal rights, the care of the children, or the protection of inheritance, it can be tolerated and does not constitute a moral offense."[377] Though the *Catechism*'s verbiage is unfortunately vague (the term "certain legal rights" is ambiguous), it is clear that the *Catechism* presents divorce as the last resort.

Why then, is divorce mandatory before even receiving a hearing from a tribunal? Among canonists, there is the constant admonition that annulment is not divorce, and yet the process of annulment *requires* divorce. This hearkens back to Martin Luther's chilling insistence that marriage is primarily a civil thing. One can philosophize all he wants that this is not the case, but in practice, a diocesan tribunal will not proceed unless and until a civil court produces a document that says that marriage is ended. The diocesan tribunals of the Catholic Church will not proceed without what appears to be the state's permission. And yet, we wonder why the faithful lost sight of the sacramentality of marriage.

From there, it gets even worse.

To describe the process, let's use a fictional example of Thomas and Michelle. They are each twenty-seven years old, have been married for six years, and have a three-year-old daughter named Lilly Catherine. Michelle wants to have an annulment hearing but is told that she first needs to obtain

---

[376] *CCC* 2384, 2385.
[377] *CCC* 2383.

a divorce. From Michelle's perspective, her marriage is not valid, but that is not the perspective of Thomas. Nevertheless, Michelle asks Thomas to sign the divorce papers. Thomas informs Michelle that, in good conscience, he cannot sign such documents because of scandal. Michelle becomes incensed at Thomas and proceeds with a no-fault divorce. As one might imagine, this process does little to ameliorate an already-troubled union. But with the document firmly and finally in hand, Thomas and Michelle appear before the tribunal. At this point, two things can happen: the marriage can be found null (the statistically overwhelming likelihood), or it can be affirmed as valid. Let's examine how the divorce decree affects these two possibilities.

Thomas and Michelle wait eleven months for their tribunal hearing. During that time, they live apart. Michelle lives at their family home with her new boyfriend named Keoki, while Thomas rents a guest house by the beach for $1,500 a month. Thomas has hired a canon lawyer at the rate of $375 an hour, and Michelle has hired a canon lawyer and a civil lawyer, each charging about $300 an hour. Their savings accounts are quickly exhausted, and both husband and wife make early withdrawals of their 401k retirement plans. In eleven months, they have spent well over $100,000 in various divorce/annulment-related expenses. Finally, their case is heard.

The wife explains her grounds for annulment as she sees it. She explains that she had only dated a few men before her wedding, and after five years of marriage, she had fallen in love with Keoki, a physically-gifted bartender at her club. She explains that she did not understand, before her wedding, that men could be as muscular as Keoki, so she was unable to provide full consent on her wedding day. At the hearing, she admits that she understood marriage was permanent, that it demanded sexual fidelity, and that she was not only open to children but eager to become a mom—which she soon did. To everyone's surprise, the tribunal affirms the marriage. This leaves the couple divorced—through the mandate of the diocese—but in a valid marriage. We can hope and pray that husband and wife get together. Still, either way, the divorce mandate has devastated their marriages in numerous ways that would have been preventable without the divorce mandate.

Of course, it rarely turns out that well, and here's what is more likely would happen in Thomas and Michelle's case. The tribunal takes particular interest, not in Michelle's affirmation of permanence, fidelity, and openness to children, but in the fact that she only had limited experience with men. They also find it interesting that Michelle was civilly divorced, interpreting this to mean that the marriage was in trouble. After all, what happily-married wife would sign a divorce decree? They also note that Thomas refused to sign the decree. They can't even agree on that. Their marriage is "discovered" null. Thomas thinks about appealing the decision, but that would mean bankruptcy; after all, he had spent thousands of dollars already. There's nothing left. The divorce proved costly in ways that cannot be easily tallied on a ledger.

And the life of their daughter, Lilly Catherine, is forever altered.

Conclusion

To reiterate an earlier point, it is not the contention of this book to claim that annulments are always improper. In certain cases, justice not only *allows* annulments but *requires* them. Today, we live in a world of online dating sites, social media, and virtual relationships—in other words, a world where someone can more easily appear to be the type of person he is not. If a man maliciously defrauds a woman in order to marry her (for example, the man is a fugitive who marries her in hopes of robbing her house after the wedding), the marriage can be annulled by canon law 1098: "A person contracts invalidly who enters into a marriage deceived by malice, perpetrated to obtain consent, concerning some quality of the other partner which by its very nature can gravely disturb the partnership of conjugal life." This innocent woman has the right in justice to a speedy annulment inquiry and finding of nullity. Hopefully, she has that "marriage" annulled. But the current annulment system raises a problem for her; namely, that if she tells people she has had an annulment, others may look at her with suspicion—knowing that annulments are so easily granted to many people. It does her no favors that her case was settled in a diocesan system which statistically decided all their cases with the same verdict. Paradoxically, the annulment culture has been harmful even to those who are granted annulments on rock-solid grounds. Justice demands this system is fixed in every diocese. But to fix something is to first admit that it is broken—an admission that American bishops, tribunalists, and canonists have trouble making.

But it is broken.

The Catholic Church in America has gone from 338 annulments in 1968 to over 72,000 annulments initiated in 1989 to over 24,000 initiated in 2014—the last number being perhaps the most chilling since it reflects a massive drop in Catholic marriages.[378] Years ago, Robert Vasoli noted—as have many others—that with "just 6% of the world's Catholics," American tribunals dole out nearly 75% of the worldwide annulments.[379] The world is watching. When the American dollar is weak, tourists come to America to shop for fancy shoes and clothes; when the Catholic Church in America is weak, tourists come to America for annulments. Though it may not amount to a significant statistical bump, annulment tourism (Vasoli calls it "intercontinental forum-shopping") has been going on for decades.[380]

Even those within America have become aware that some tribunals are more likely to advance cases and grant annulments than others. The website for the Archdiocese of Newark states that tribunals "must have jurisdiction" in order to hear a case because it "prevents 'shopping around' among tribunals."[381] But this prompts the question: If the system is not broken, what possible advantage would one gain from tribunal shopping? Perhaps tribunal shoppers read about the curious case of Rev. Jack Anderson, who had served on a marriage tribunal in the diocese of Wilmington, Delaware. Though Anderson had left the Catholic Church, become an Episcopalian, and undergone a gay marriage, he nevertheless remained

---

[378] "Frequently Requested Church Statistics."
[379] Vasoli, *What God Has Joined Together,* 200.
[380] Vasoli, *What God Has Joined Together,* 174.
[381] "The Process."

on the marriage tribunal for several years. That would have been scandalous enough, but the priest had a unique position on that tribunal: the Defender of the Bond.[382]

At what point are we allowed to admit problems in the system?

Annulments in America seem to have affected almost every Catholic in some way—peripherally if not directly. But if a person even broaches the subject of annulments, he can expect a vitriolic argument. If you post something on Facebook even *questioning* the annulment process, you can fully expect angry criticism. Some of that criticism may even come from priests. It's easy to forget, but many priests are children of divorced and annulled couples, and it would be unreasonable to think that this does not—at least in some measure—create a bias in favor of annulment. After all, who wants to vicariously indict the decisions of his mom or dad? At a minimum, many of these priests have a negative impression of marriage. Consider further that some of these same men serve on tribunals. So we laity are conditioned not to question the procedure. If you question it, you can expect some form of ad hominem like, *Who are you mere laity to dare question the tribunal process?* Perhaps thinking that a tribunal judge somehow possesses infallibility, others ask: *Who are <u>you</u> to question the Church?*

But in this discussion, it's worth noting that the most substantial criticism of progressive American tribunals has not been offered by the laity. Rather, it has been offered by men at the loftiest levels of the Church hierarchy: men such

---

[382] https://spectator.org/bishop-bambera-and-the-jack-anderson-scandal/

as Cardinal Staffa, Cardinal Burke, and Pope Saint John Paul II. If it is unacceptable to question American tribunals, that news would come as a great shock to the Roman Rota, which—as we have seen—has overturned a huge percentage of annulments on appeal.

From the moment canon law was put into print in 1983, some rogue canonists and tribunalists bastardized it. Their concept of a canon law that does not preciously guard marriage violates the very *purpose* of law itself, which, as Aquinas assures us, is simply this: to make men good. If canon law is not viewed through the lens of the Faith, it is blindness. As Pope Emeritus Benedict wrote, "A balanced canon law . . . must also protect the Faith, which is also an important legal asset. . . . In the general awareness of the law, the Faith no longer appears to have the rank of a good requiring protection. This is an alarming situation which must be considered and taken seriously by the pastors of the Church."[383]

In the aggregate, five decades worth of American tribunals have widely failed to uphold marriage. While they speak of marriage being indissoluble in principle, they repeatedly find it null in practice, using methods criticized or condemned by the Roman Rota, the Signatura, and the papacy.[384] The 1970s threw open wide doors to annulments, and now we must deal with the consequences. In its entry on the "History of Marriage," the *Catholic Encyclopedia* argues that "when there is no hope of another marriage, the offenses that justify separation are less likely to be provoked or committed

---

[383] "Full text of Benedict XVI essay: 'The Church and the scandal of sexual abuse.'"

[384] Vasoli, *What God Has Joined Together,* 203.

by either party, and separation is less likely to be sought on insufficient grounds or obtained through fraudulent methods."[385] Conceding that some couples should not and cannot live together for serious reasons, it is difficult to argue against the encyclopedia's basic logic. In the annulment culture created during the past half-century, there has almost always been the hope of another marriage. But now, it is even worse: people are not even bothering with an annulment. They simply divorce.

There is an even more fundamental problem: couples are avoiding marriage. Some have observed that annulment numbers are down in recent years, as though that indicates a reform of the process. Nominally, it is true: the numbers of annulments are down. But before we celebrate that fact, we might consider another: marriage in America is suffering the most profound decline in the history of the sacrament. In the United States, the year 1969 witnessed 426,309 Catholic marriages.[386] By 2004, the number had decreased by more than half, falling to 207,112. In 2020, that number had reduced by half again, falling to 97,200.[387] Simply, there are fewer marriages to potentially annul—that would be an odd reality to celebrate. Are annulment numbers falling on a comparative basis? In 1989, for every annulment, there were fewer than five marriages confected. In 2014, for every

---

[385] *The Catholic Encyclopedia*, s.v. "History of Marriage."

[386] "Frequently Requested Church Statistics."

[387] It should be observed that the 2020 numbers were artificially low due to the outbreak of COVID-19. During 2020, in which churches were voluntarily closed, many couples could not get married even if they desired to. Following the numerical trajectory, however, it is unlikely that the number would have been much over 100,000.

annulment, there were closer to six-and-a-half marriages. That's hardly a reason to celebrate. By any rational metric, the numbers are lie-awake-at-night frightening.

It's imperative we started asking questions about annulment procedures.

Considering the prevalence of annulments in America, it is astounding how little literature is dedicated to the subject. Why is this the case? Why are marriage tribunals the one system of law we dare not question? To question the system here does not presume a lack of faith in the Mystical Body of Christ; rather, it is to help prevent the loss of Faith. And if we cannot speak out in defense of marriage, what should we speak about? If not marriage, what will we defend? For all their training, many tribunalists seem to have ignored a fundamental truth about marriage: marriage is *about* God. Adam and Eve's marriage was about God and was *ordered* to God—and so is every Christian marriage. So is every sacrament. But as it turns out, the damage to marriage is now affecting other sacraments. As we are about to see, the fallout of marriage is affecting the Holy Eucharist.

7

Come One, Come All: Eucharist for the Divorced and Remarried

"'Whoever causes one of these little ones who believe in me to sin, it would be better for him if a great millstone were hung round his neck and he were thrown into the sea' (Mark 9:42). The phrase 'the little ones' in the language of Jesus means the common believers who can be confounded in their faith by the intellectual arrogance of those who think they are clever. So here Jesus protects the deposit of the faith with an emphatic threat of punishment to those who do it harm."

—Pope Emeritus Benedict XVI[388]

THE PAST FEW decades have witnessed a vociferous push for admitting un-annulled divorced and remarried persons to the Eucharist. Many people view it as a travesty that anyone, regardless of lifestyle or public sin, would be denied. But the real travesty is that they either do not understand or simply reject the irreformable doctrine that the Eucharist cannot be

[388] "Full text of Benedict XVI essay: 'The Church and the scandal of sexual abuse.'"

received by a soul outside the state of sanctifying grace. And the idea that the divorced and remarried should be admitted to the Eucharist is particularly harmful and scandalous. If we lived in an age of belief, the mere discussion of admitting such persons to the Eucharist would be shocking. The come-one, come-all approach devastates reverence for both the Eucharist and Matrimony. But this also powerfully illustrates that respect for the sacraments tends to rise and fall together. If the bishops, priests, and laity undermine marriage, this leads to disrespect, disregard, and disbelief in the Eucharist. This is not a predictive statement; rather, it refers to a scenario that has already occurred.

To correct this Eucharistic scandal, we must first understand how we arrived here. We will begin this discussion by examining the Scriptural, Magisterial, and Traditional link between Matrimony and the Eucharist to explain the Church's consistent stance throughout ecclesiastical history.

The Necessity of Grace

The prohibition against receiving Holy Communion in the state of mortal sin dates to the Church's infancy. The foundational Scriptural text is Saint Paul's First Letter to the Corinthians: "Whoever, therefore, eats the bread or drinks the cup of the Lord in an unworthy manner will be guilty of profaning the body and blood of the Lord" (1 Cor 11:27). With the verbiage "Profaning the body and blood of the Lord," the text could hardly be more explicit regarding its level of grave evil. Even among mortal sins, this sacrilege is uniquely heinous. Aquinas explains that the objective gravity of a sin is determined, in part, by against whom the sin is directed. In this respect, sins against God are more evil than those against neighbor. As Aquinas explains in his *Commentary on First Corinthians*, "For his guilt is increased to the extent that a greater person is offended against."[389] Those who insistently receive Communion in the state of mortal sin exhibit, in Aquinas's words, "contempt of this sacrament."[390] But Saint Paul goes even further: "For any one who eats and drinks without discerning the body eats and drinks judgment upon himself" (1 Cor 11:29). The man or woman who receives the Eucharist in the conscious state of mortal sin calls down God's judgment.

This might prompt a question: Why is mortal sin so much worse than venial sin? How can mortal sin strictly prohibit someone from Communion, yet those who commit venial sin be not only allowed but *encouraged* to receive Communion? The answer is simple: those who commit mortal sin have willingly surrendered sanctifying grace by freely choosing a grave evil. Sanctifying grace, sometimes called *habitual grace*, is a state of the soul that remains even with the commission of venial sin. But mortal sin takes a man or woman out of that state of grace. In mortal sin, a man has cast aside friendship with God; he has cast aside charity.[391] And the willful reception of the Eucharist in such a state contemptuously deepens that separation.

It cannot be overemphasized that the Church provides a remedy for mortal sin: sacramental confession. Sacramental confession with true sorrow and a firm purpose

---

[389] "Patristic Bible Commentary," 1 Corinthians, Chapter 11.
[390] "Patristic Bible Commentary," 1 Corinthians, Chapter 11.
[391] "Patristic Bible Commentary," 1 Corinthians, Chapter 11.

of amendment can forgive any sins, including sacrilege—including any great number of instances above of sacrilege. Thousands of sins of fornication and unworthy receptions of the Eucharist can be absolved by one good sacramental confession. The passion and death of Jesus provide superabundant graces to forgive sins—however grave, however numerous. Therefore, there is no room for despair in the heart and soul of a Catholic—the Father of Mercies is eager to forgive His sons, however prodigal they may be.

But it is vitally important to remember that sins may not be absolved without a purpose of amendment. A man who has fornicated with his girlfriend may indeed confess this sin, but he must have a firm purpose of amendment to abstain from this sin. He may fall into that sin again, but he must confess again and have a firm purpose of amendment again. But one could not reasonably claim to have a firm purpose of amendment regarding a sin he is *planning* to commit again.

Let's apply this principle to our discussion at hand. If a man confesses sleeping with his girlfriend yet has two tickets in his pocket for a weekend rendezvous with her in Aruba, he is not making a good confession. It is not fair to expect absolution for such a sin. Just as Jesus conferred the power to forgive sins, He also conferred the power to retain them. If a man lives with his girlfriend in a sexual relationship, this indicates no firm purpose of amendment. If a sacramentally married man is divorced (absent a finding of nullity) and insists on carrying on a sexual union with his girlfriend, he clearly has no purpose of amendment. If he continues that relationship through civil marriage, that provides no moral weight to the situation. In the eyes of the Church, he is still living with his girlfriend in direct contravention of the sixth commandment.

The *Catechism* explains this with great clarity:

> Today there are numerous Catholics in many countries who have recourse to civil divorce and contract new civil unions. In fidelity to the words of Jesus Christ—'Whoever divorces his wife and marries another, commits adultery against her; and if she divorces her husband and marries another, she commits adultery.'—The Church maintains that a new union cannot be recognized as valid, if the first marriage was. If the divorced are remarried civilly, they find themselves in a situation that objectively contravenes God's law. Consequently, they cannot receive Eucharistic communion as long as this situation persists. Reconciliation through the sacrament of Penance can be granted only to those who have repented for having violated the sign of the covenant and of fidelity to Christ, and who are committed to living in complete continence.[392]

Given Saint Paul's admonitions and the *Catechism*'s teaching, this man is not in any position to present himself for Holy Communion. The priest should not admit him to Communion. Though the priest need not provide any further reference than the Letter to the Corinthians and the *Catechism* to justify withholding the Eucharist from the man, he can cite the Code of Canon Law. Canon 915 states

[392] *CCC* 1650.

that those "obstinately persevering in manifest grave sin are not to be admitted to holy communion."[393]

There are several reasons for denying him Communion, beginning with the good of the man's soul. It might appear unfair, unfeeling, or even mean to deny him Holy Communion. Yet, that denial amounts to great mercy. By denying him Communion, the priest informs the man that he must change his ways. Admonishing the sinner is a work of mercy, and it is difficult to imagine a more excellent exercise of this mercy. Withholding Communion may appear to be a denial, but it is an invitation to the mercy of God. The argument could be made that the man in question—while undoubtedly *objectively* guilty of gravely wrong acts—is not *subjectively* guilty of mortal sin. But if that is the case, then the denial of the Eucharist is also mercy, albeit a different one: instructing the ignorant. Beyond that, withholding the Eucharist is an invitation to the sacrament of Penance—to experience the reconciliation of God. But there is another reason to deny the man Communion, not because it only affects him, but because it affects everyone around him.

A Receptive Community

The *Catechism of the Catholic Church* explains that the fifth commandment demands respect not only for the bodies of others but "for the souls of others." The *Catechism*'s first sin mentioned in this regard is the sin of scandal. The *Catechism* defines scandal as "an attitude or behavior which leads another to do evil."[394] In his treatise on virtues, Aquinas

[393] Canon 915.
[394] *CCC* 2284.

lists scandal as the vice opposed to the virtue of *beneficence*, which he defines simply as "doing good to someone." Scandal harms others in the worst way possible: spiritual evil. The *Catechism* explains, "The person who gives scandal becomes his neighbor's tempter. He damages virtue and integrity; he may even draw his brother into spiritual death. Scandal is a grave offense if by deed or omission another is deliberately led into a grave offense."[395] Chilling as those words may be, they cannot equal Our Lord's warning to avoid scandal: "Whoever causes one of these little ones who believe in me to sin, it would be better for him to have a great millstone fastened round his neck and to be drowned in the depth of the sea" (Mt 18:6).

Let's look at a few examples. If I rent a pornographic movie and invite friends over to watch it with me, that would be a clear case of grave scandal. But scandal is often not so direct. If I tell my friends how much I enjoy binge-watching hardcore pornography movies, that would be a scandal to them because I am endorsing grave evil. If I brag about theft or getting drunk, that would also be scandalous. But the sin of scandal does not require that I inform anyone of my sins. Instead, my friends can see me commit these acts, which is worse in some measure. If my friends see me walk into an "adult" club, that would constitute the sin of scandal. Likewise, if they witnessed me shoplifting at a jewelry store or getting heavily intoxicated on rum-and-cokes at the neighborhood bar. The *Catechism* addresses *deliberate* scandal, but scandal can happen indeliberately; I may hope that no one sees me enter the "adult" club, but friends may still

---

[395] *CCC* 2284.

randomly drive past the club and see me enter. Aquinas calls this "accidental" scandal, but it still constitutes sin.[396]

Scandals can also occur in the reception of the Eucharist. If I operate a notorious "adult" club in town, it would be scandalous for me to receive Communion at my local church (to say nothing of sacrilege). In fact, not only would I be committing a sin of scandal, but potentially, the priest who gives me Communion would be committing the sin of scandal also. Why is that? Part of the danger of scandal is that it endorses sin—even mortal sin. I may be tempted to think along these lines: *This guy is going to Communion! I've never committed any sins like this guy commits every night!* While I may not be tempted to frequent the adult club, I may be tempted to think that my sins are not so bad in comparison. Specific to Eucharistic reception, it leaves me with less reason to examine my conscience before I receive Communion.

Someone might criticize this response as pharisaical, in reference to the incident of the Publican and the Pharisee. But does that analogy work? Let's take a look at that parable: "Two men went up into the temple to pray, one a Pharisee and the other a tax collector. The Pharisee stood and prayed thus with himself, 'God, I thank you that I am not like other men, extortioners, unjust, adulterers, or even like this tax collector. I fast twice a week, I give tithes of all that I get.' But the tax collector, standing far off, would not even lift up his eyes to heaven, but beat his breast, saying, 'God, be merciful to me a sinner!'" (Lk 18:10–13). The tax collector remains in the back of the Church, not even daring to approach the

---

[396] Aquinas, *Summa Theologiae*, II-II, Q. 43, Art. 4.

altar, not daring even to lift his head to God until he confesses his sins. While we cannot judge the heart of either man, we can observe that—in their objective actions—there is no equivalence between the two.

Nevertheless, I should not attempt to negatively judge the heart of the tax collector or the club owner. If I relationally discount the evil of my sins, that *does* amount to the sin of pride. But therein lies the problem of scandal. The club owner's actions tempt me to the sin of pride. And though I am not *permitted* to judge the man's heart, I may be *required* to judge his actions. The parish priest ought to judge actions and act accordingly. This is an important distinction: withholding the Eucharist from the club owner is not to judge his heart; rather, it is to judge his actions. Augustine says that the Eucharist "is the sacrament of unity and love."[397] But a public sinner's reception of the Eucharist lacks both charity and unity. If the man's actions publicly scandalize the faithful, the priest must act accordingly and follow Scripture, the *Catechism*, and the Code of Canon Law.

The same principles outlined above apply to the unnullified, divorced, and civilly remarried. In his 1981 Apostolic Exhortation *Familiaris Consortio*, John Paul II brings these concepts together, explaining, "However, the Church reaffirms her practice, which is based upon Sacred Scripture, of not admitting to Eucharistic Communion divorced persons who have remarried. They are unable to be admitted thereto from the fact that their state and condition of life objectively contradict that union of love between Christ and the Church which is signified and effected by the Eucharist.

[397] "Patristic Bible Commentary," 1 Corinthians, Chapter 11.

Besides this, there is another special pastoral reason: if these people were admitted to the Eucharist, the faithful would be led into error and confusion regarding the Church's teaching about the indissolubility of marriage."[398]

Thus, the prohibition on the reception of the Eucharist to the divorced and remarried is for the sake of the person and the community. John Paul II's statement was not a watershed document with a breakthrough in sacramental theology. Like *Humanae Vitae*'s contraception analysis, it was not a new statement but rather a restatement of two thousand years of teaching.

In 2006, Cardinal Estévez, the prefect emeritus of the Congregation for Divine Worship and the Discipline of the Sacraments, provided more explanation. He states the basic principle: "Any person who has divorced his or her spouse from a valid marriage and cohabits with another person is in a state of grave sin—to be precise, the sin of adultery."[399] Nevertheless, Estevez noted that the Eucharistic prohibition for the divorced and remarried was increasingly becoming considered "merely a pragmatic decision on the Church's part, which can be revised and even revoked or at least mitigated in certain cases or circumstances."[400] He explains, however, that this prohibition "is of a doctrinal nature, as is crystal clear from both the *Catechism of the Catholic Church* (cf. nn. 1649, 1650, and 1651) and the *Compendium of the Catechism* (cf. n. 349), which faithfully present the Gospel

[398] John Paul II, *Familiaris Consortio*.
[399] Estevez, "Holy Communion for Divorced and Re-married?"
[400] Estevez, "Holy Communion for Divorced and Re-married?"

teaching of Jesus Christ (cf. Mk 10:11ff.)."[401] Further, while sacramental confession is accessible to every Catholic, Penance requires a firm purpose of amendment. Estevez writes, "To receive sacramental absolution, he or she must repent and have true contrition for this sin, which means, according to the Council of Trent, *'sorrow or repudiation of the soul for sins committed, together with a purpose to turn away from sin' (DS* 1676). In the absence of such sorrows for one's grave sins, it is not possible to receive valid sacramental absolution and, consequently, one is not properly disposed to receive Holy Communion worthily."[402]

Pope Saint John Paul II does state that while the divorced and remarried cannot receive Communion, they still deserve care and attention from the parish priests. These priests must also desire to bring the divorced and remarried to confession and Communion, which requires a firm purpose of amendment. John Paul II writes:

> Reconciliation in the sacrament of Penance which would open the way to the Eucharist, can only be granted to those who, repenting of having broken the sign of the Covenant and of fidelity to Christ, are sincerely ready to undertake a way of life that is no longer in contradiction to the indissolubility of marriage. This means, in practice, that when, for serious reasons, such as for example the children's upbringing, a man and a woman cannot satisfy the obligation to separate, they "take on themselves the duty to live in complete

[401] Estevez, "Holy Communion for Divorced and Re-married?"
[402] Estevez, "Holy Communion for Divorced and Re-married?"

> continence, that is, by abstinence from the acts proper to married couples."[403]

Of course, to "undertake a way of life that is no longer in contradiction to the indissolubility of marriage" might very well include leaving one's civil partner and returning to one's actual sacramental spouse.

Pope Saint John Paul II also stresses the need for pastoral care for the larger community. He writes, "Besides this, there is another special pastoral reason: if these people were admitted to the Eucharist, the faithful would be led into error and confusion regarding the Church's teaching about the indissolubility of marriage."[404] In short, pastoral care must avoid incidents of scandal, but pastoral care also requires the affirmation of indissolubility. John Paul II warns priests against those actions that can scandalize others. Thus, he includes another prohibition beyond that of a Eucharistic prohibition, writing, "Similarly, the respect due to the sacrament of Matrimony, to the couples themselves and their families, and also to the community of the faithful, forbids any pastor, for whatever reason or pretext even of a pastoral nature, to perform ceremonies of any kind for divorced people who remarry. Such ceremonies would give the impression of the celebration of a new sacramentally valid marriage, and would thus lead people into error concerning the indissolubility of a validly contracted marriage."[405]

The Church's doctrine on this matter is clear and precise, dating back to the beginning of the Church. Her practice of

---

[403] John Paul II, *Familiaris Consortio.*
[404] John Paul II, *Familiaris Consortio.*
[405] John Paul II, *Familiaris Consortio*

Eucharistic prohibition exhibits truth and charity. Nevertheless, John Paul II's statements would be ignored in coming years and countered by some loud voices in the Church.

Amoris Laetitia

Cardinal Walter Kasper is often seen as the leading advocate for allowing Communion for the divorced and remarried, a position he has advocated for five decades.[406] But the credit (or more accurately, discredit) for such a position goes back much further in time. Archbishop Samuel Aquila pointed out in a *National Catholic Register* article in 2015: "The idea that Catholics should be allowed to remarry and receive communion did not begin with the letter signed by Cardinal Kasper and other members of the German episcopate in 1993. Another country's episcopate—England's—pioneered this experiment in Christian doctrine nearly 500 years ago."[407] If one wants to award credit, he should cite King Henry VIII, who did not want his divorce to interfere with the reception of the Eucharist. As Archbishop Aquila puts it, "The King could hardly be bothered to skip communion as the result of an irregular marriage."[408] As seen earlier, Henry's insistence on sacrilege led to countless others, including the beheadings of numerous priests and a bishop. The idea of Communion for the divorced and remarried is not new. These past several decades have simply seen the argument repackaged and reargued.

---

[406] Levering, *The Indissolubility of Marriage*, loc. 958 of 4735, Kindle.
[407] Aquila, "Did Thomas More and John Fisher Die For Nothing?"
[408] Aquila, "Did Thomas More and John Fisher Die For Nothing?"

In 2016, Pope Francis issued an apostolic exhortation titled *Amoris Laetitia*. Its English title is "On Love in the Family."[409] At over 250 pages in length, it is a sweeping consideration of family life and marriage—easily one of the longest papal exhortations in history. There are certainly many beautiful passages in the text, but those are rarely noted when the discussion of *Amoris Laetitia* arises. Instead, much of the attention has focused on a footnote. It is footnote number 351. Footnote 351 appears in chapter 8, which discusses the pastoral approach toward the divorced (and not annulled) and remarried. Here is the sentence that is footnoted: "Because of forms of conditioning and mitigating factors, it is possible that in an *objective* situation of sin—which may not be *subjectively* culpable, or fully such—a person can be living in God's grace, can love and can also grow in the life of grace and charity, while receiving the Church's help to this end."[410] Before getting to the footnote, let's unpack this sentence.

It is undoubtedly true that Catholic moral theology has long recognized a distinction between objective evil and subjective guilt. For instance, someone may have either vincible or invincible ignorance that a particular act is wrong. It could also be the case that internal or external pressures alleviate one's level of culpability. An objective mortal sin might amount to a subjective venial sin for its doer. But nothing can change the nature of the act: grave evil is always grave evil. If I am forced under gunpoint to get drunk, my culpability is certainly lessened, but that drunkenness does not

---

[409] Francis, *Amoris Laetitia*.
[410] Francis, *Amoris Laetitia*, 236–37, emphasis added.

somehow become *good* in that instance—or any instance, ever. Irrespective of my state of mind and external pressures, I cannot make an evil act good. God cannot be pleased with my evil act by His very nature.[411]

When this distinction between objective nature and subjective culpability is discussed in catechetics, an important point is often made: though personal culpability can be lessened, it is rarely removed. Saint Thomas Aquinas teaches that passion can lessen guilt but does not entirely excuse responsibility. If passion eased guilt to venial sin, most sexual sins would not be mortal, which is clearly not Church teaching. If a man, driven by passion, commits an objectively grave act, he may indeed still be committing a mortal sin—for mortal sin has its levels of culpability. In other words, if we say that one's culpability for an objective mortal sin is lessened, that does not automatically mean that he is, therefore, only guilty of venial sin; he is very likely still guilty of mortal sin. Catechists should be careful to make this point, largely because we fallen humans can be overly forgiving of our sins, looking for reasons why our guilt might be lessened or removed altogether.

As to the idea that the Church should "help" those in adulterous unions, how could one argue otherwise? The Church should seek to help everyone, which varies by person and requires charity, prudence, and justice. Any action devoid of those virtues is not helping. Imprudent and unjust acts that lack charity are not "help" either to a person or to the common good. Regarding adulterous unions, the Church welcomes them to come to Church, participate in

[411] Murray, "World Over - 2018-01-11."

the Mass, pray the Rosary, and so forth. God desires the salvation of all men, and no one on earth is disinvited to these things. (Even the formally excommunicated are welcome to pray the Rosary in church.) That said, not all are invited to participate in the sacraments for the many reasons outlined above by Scripture, Saint Thomas Aquinas, and Pope Saint John Paul II.

Let's now return to Pope Francis's statement: "Because of forms of conditioning and mitigating factors, it is possible that in an objective situation of sin—which may not be subjectively culpable, or fully such—a person can be living in God's grace, can love and can also grow in the life of grace and charity, while receiving the Church's help to this end." This statement, while vague, is supported by the basic norms of Catholic moral theology. But then comes the footnote: "In certain cases, this can include the help of the sacraments. Hence, 'I want to remind priests that the confessional must not be a torture chamber, but rather an encounter with the Lord's mercy' (Apostolic Exhortation *Evangelii Gaudium* [24 November 2013], 44: AAS 105 [2013], 1038). I would also point out that the Eucharist 'is not a prize for the perfect, but a powerful medicine and nourishment for the weak' (*ibid.*, 47: 1039)."[412]

From poor sinners to cardinals, many Catholics found this statement confusing and troubling. What "forms of conditioning?" What "mitigating factors?" Since the footnote mentions the Eucharist, the footnote insinuates that the "help" of the Church toward those in adulterous unions "can include" the Eucharist. (If it referred to those living

---

[412] Francis, *Amoris Laetitia*, 237.

in non-sexual unions, it should have stated that explicitly.) It gets more unclear with its statement about the confessional being a "torture chamber." In context, what does that mean? Does it refer to the requirement for the penitent's firm purpose of amendment—in this case, the firm purpose to explicate oneself from the adulterous relationship? Further, the "prize for the perfect" comment is also confusing. The Church has never claimed that reception for the Eucharist requires perfection; what she *has* claimed—and claimed repeatedly and insistently since apostolic times—is that the Eucharist requires the state of sanctifying grace. To be in the state of grace means that one has an indwelling of the Trinity, and one cannot receive the Body, Blood, Soul, and Divinity of Christ without a prior indwelling of the Trinity. And while there is no requirement for perfection in reception, Christ Himself commanded us to pursue perfection, and that includes turning away from sin. In its overall reception, *Amoris Laetitia* produced more questions than answers.

The *Dubia*

Some of those questions were made public; the most noteworthy were those formally drawn up by Cardinals Burke, Brandmüller, Caffarra, and Meisner in 2016. Though the document was private initially, it was later made public, titled "Seeking Clarity: A Plea to Untie the Knots in *Amoris Laetitia.*" This document came to be known as "the *dubia*," in reference to the Latin word for "doubt" mentioned in the letter. Noting that *Amoris* had caused significant confusion—even to the point where bishops fundamentally disagreed about its specific meaning—the cardinals explained that they were motivated by a "deep pastoral concern."[413] They make the unassailable point that "doubt and uncertainty are always highly detrimental to pastoral care."[414] Along with explanatory notes and observations, the document posed five lengthy questions. The questions involved the nature of "absolute moral norms," "conscience," and what specific "circumstances" mitigated the objectively evil actions.[415]

> The first question gets to the heart of the matter: "It is asked whether, following the affirmations of *Amoris Laetitia* (nn. 300–305), it has now become possible to grant absolution in the sacrament of penance and thus to admit to Holy Communion a person who, while bound by a valid marital bond, lives together with a different person *more uxorio* without fulfilling the conditions provided for by *Familiaris Consortio* 84 and subsequently reaffirmed by *Reconciliatio et Paenitentia* n. 34 and *Sacramentum Caritatis* n. 29. Can the expression "in certain cases" found in note 351 (n. 305) of the exhortation *Amoris Laetitia* be applied to **divorced persons who are in a new union and who continue to live *more uxorio*?"**

It was not that the cardinals were unaware of the answer; instead, they were seeking a widespread clarification for the good of souls.[416] The cardinals were criticized in some circles

[413] Montagna, "Seeking Clarity."
[414] Montagna, "Seeking Clarity."
[415] Montagna, "Seeking Clarity."
[416] Murray, "World Over - 2018-01-11, 19:00–19:10.

for making their document public, but there were excellent reasons for their urgency. The issues involved here regard matters that are both serious and immediate. The cardinals' question here does not involve an esoteric matter of speculative theology; the answer to this question directly or indirectly affects nearly every Catholic worldwide. Whose life has been unaffected—at least peripherally—by divorce and remarriage? Which of us is unacquainted with a divorced and remarried friend or a child of a divorced friend? In 2014, the USCCB reported that "20.7% of Catholic adults have experienced divorce at some point in their life."[417] This is troubling but more alarming considering that the same report noted that only "53.9% of adult Catholics are currently married."[418] Since divorce only occurs after marriage, and marriage numbers are dwindling, the 20.7% number is deceptively low. Thus, the *dubia* was asking for fundamental clarification on a prevalent issue that immediately pertains to the salvation of souls.

The *dubia* illustrates the practical problem of admitting the Eucharist to those divorced and remarried persons. If a man and woman live together, it is generally assumed that they are engaging in sexual intimacy. As the administrator of the sacraments, the Church must be acutely aware and sensitive to the scandal of allowing such persons to the Eucharist. The *dubia* points out that if such persons are admitted to the Eucharist, it would appear that the Church was to "teach by her practice" one of three possible things. First, while "divorce does not dissolve the marriage bond," nevertheless,

---

[417] "Catholic Marriage and Family in the United States."
[418] "Catholic Marriage and Family in the United States."

"*people who are not married can under certain circumstances legitimately engage in acts of sexual intimacy.*"[419] *Second, that "divorce dissolves the marriage bond," which would mean that* "the divorced and remarried are legitimate spouses and their sexual acts are lawful marital acts."[420] Third, even though the Church disallows divorce and sexual acts for unmarried persons, the Church still allows reception of the Eucharist because such persons have confessed their sins—albeit with no purpose of amendment.[421] There is no good scenario.

Pope Saint John Paul II allowed reception of the Eucharist to divorced and remarried under three specific and simultaneous conditions. The *dubia* rephrases John Paul II's conditions: "The persons concerned cannot separate without committing new injustices (for instance, they may be responsible for the upbringing of their children); They take upon themselves the commitment to live according to the truth of their situation, that is, to cease living together as if they were husband and wife (*more uxorio*), abstaining from those acts that are proper to spouses; They avoid giving scandal (that is, they avoid giving the appearance of sin so as to avoid the danger of leading others into sin)."[422] Even given these conditions, it must be stressed that a husband or wife can only separate from bed and board in the first place for either *serious reason(s)* or *mutual agreement*. For instance, a wife is not compelled to remain with an abusive husband—that would be a serious reason to separate from bed and

[419] Montagna, "Seeking Clarity."
[420] Montagna, "Seeking Clarity."
[421] Montagna, "Seeking Clarity."
[422] Montagna, "Seeking Clarity."

board. A husband and wife could separate by mutual agreement after raising their children. But a husband cannot unilaterally decide to leave his wife—or vice versa. John Paul II's three conditions require that a prior condition of *serious reason* or *mutual agreement* has already been met. According to Pope Saint John Paul II, if one (or more) of the above three conditions fails to be met, the party cannot receive the Eucharist.

Regarding the first condition, a man may have undertaken a financial responsibility to a new family, and that obligation must be taken seriously. It must be noted, however—as the *dubia* references by speaking about "new injustices"—that the man (or woman) may very well have a *prior* obligation to support the family that is the product of his or her sacramental marriage. That is, it could be that the father or mother must atone for his or her prior injustices. If a man abandons his wife and three children from his valid marriage, he still owes *them* financial support in justice; even civil law recognizes that principle.

Regarding the second condition, it is blunt: a man must cease having sexual relations with his civil—rather than sacramental—"wife" because his first marriage remains intact until one of the parties dies. This requirement is fundamental to the entire notion of Matrimony. Extramarital sex violates the sacrament, squashes fidelity, and mocks indissolubility. Sexual relations outside marriage are intrinsically grave matters, regardless of party or circumstance.

Regarding the third condition, the couple *and the Church* must avoid scandal. The avoidance of scandal is also a fundamental principle for reasons outlined by the *dubia*, but we might also narrow that focus on another: the direct scandal to the families involved. Consider the following example. Forty-five-year-old Charlie leaves his fifty-year-old wife, Nicole, and his nineteen-year-old daughter, Veronica, to live with Stephanie. Charlie files for a no-fault divorce, which is granted a few months later. The day after his divorce decree, he civilly marries Stephanie. A few days later, Charlie receives Communion from his parish priest. Does Charlie's reception scandalize the Catholics in the pews? The parish lacks some elemental Catholic sensitivities if it does not. But another group of Catholics in the pew might be confused and even angered by Charlie's reception of the Eucharist: his family. Given her father's actions and the priest's apparent laissez-faire stance regarding those actions, Charlie's nineteen-year-old daughter might naturally wonder why she is not permitted to engage in sexual acts with her boyfriend. This is a clear scandal. Charlie has committed a "behavior which leads another to do evil."[423] It is also likely that if Veronica sees her father in a confession line one Saturday but is still living with Stephanie a month later, that is *also* a scandal to Veronica. His purpose of amendment did not seem to include returning to his family or even leaving his adulterous union with Stephanie. Charlie goes back to Communion; he goes back to confession, and he goes back to a woman who is not his wife. Scandal is the common denominator.

The topic of scandal demands to be addressed for reasons of both severity and ubiquity, but in the entire 260 pages of *Amoris Laetitia*, including all the 391 footnotes, the word

---

[423] *CCC* 2284.

"scandal" appears twice—and neither usage references the scandal of the divorced and remarried.

With a few variances, the family discussed above involving Charlie and his family is widespread. The discussion above will remind many readers of at least one real-life family going through something similar. Very little is being done to protect the innocent victims of scandal. At present, the Church seems more focused on "walking with the divorced and remarried" rather than walking with the victims—that is, the Veronicas and Nicoles of the world. In this discussion, it becomes straightforward to see how the sacraments are intertwined: the failure to protect one sacrament eventually results in the failure to protect all the sacraments.

It is estimated that 60 percent of Catholics believe that divorced and civilly remarried persons should be admitted to the Eucharist. That, in itself, is scandalous. But sadly, it is easy to see *why*. Though the topic of reception of the Eucharist for the divorced and remarried is discussed academically, the *practice* of such reception is widespread. Reliable statistics may not be available on the number of divorced and remarried Catholics who regularly receive Communion; however, just about any Catholic can anecdotally tell you that—on a given Sunday—nearly everyone in the church receives Communion. Considering the prevalence of divorce and remarriage, one might think it reasonable to expect priests to—at least occasionally—discuss the proper disposition of reception in relation to divorce. But after a half-century of faithful Mass attendance, including numerous Latin Masses and Byzantine Divine Liturgies, this author has heard such discussion a total of *once*. If 60 percent of Catholics believe that divorced and civilly remarried persons should not be barred from the Eucharist, there might be a simple explanation: they have never heard otherwise. Respectfully, if Pope Francis would simply provide an official answer to the *dubia*, that may help matters in this regard. But as of this writing in 2023, he has not answered the cardinals.

Conclusion

Freely allowing the un-annulled divorced and remarried to receive Communion directly harms Matrimony. At least in appearance, it puts divorce on par with marriage, which is scandalous. Just as a husband and wife must work to strengthen their marriage, so must the Church work to support Matrimony. To protect and nourish one sacrament is to protect and nurture them all. If marriage is not strengthened, the diminution of other sacraments will follow. As we have seen, a diminution of marriage can easily lead to a lack of reverence and even sacrilege toward the Eucharist. And this leads to a lack of respect for the sacrament of Penance, as though penitents do not need a firm purpose of amendment. By divine design, there is an inescapable link between and among the sacraments. We are meant to live sacramental lives, which demand respect and awe for all seven sacraments. If a Catholic loses respect for the mystery of Matrimony, the Eucharist, and confession, he runs the risk of becoming lukewarm, causing scandal himself, or even leaving the Church. Sadly, this is true not only for individual Catholics but also for parishes and nations. During the first months of the coronavirus outbreak, some priests were forbidden by their superiors to go into hospitals to administer Anointing of the Sick. Confirmations were delayed, and parents were not permitted to have their newborn babies baptized. We were told these were exceptions. Of late, we have become a Church of exceptions.

The one sacrament not mentioned above is Holy Orders. But we might note that there are but two vocational sacraments. If the vocational sacrament of Matrimony continues to be weakened, what will become of Holy Orders? It is a tragic scandal that many priests seem to champion annulments and give Communion to those living in sin. In the exercise of their vocation, they have failed to protect Matrimony. Ironically, the best way to protect Holy Orders is to protect Matrimony. Priests must recognize that. Matrimony and Holy Orders are the symbiotic heart and lungs of the Church. The Mystical Body of Christ requires both.

8

Before Marriage: Taking Pre-Cana Seriously

"We've only just begun to live.
White lace and promises,
A kiss for luck, and on we're on our way."

—The Carpenters,
"We've Only Just Begun"

NAMED IN REFERENCE to the little village where Jesus performed His first public miracle, "pre-Cana" Catholic marriage preparation programs differ greatly in quantity and quality. Some programs take place in person; others take place online. Some programs take a few hours to complete; others take weeks.[424] Some parishes offer "encounter" weekends. This is all to say that pre-Cana, largely depending on the particular diocese, is pretty random. That is, it could be an exceptional experience that you remember always; it could also be a miserable experience that you can't seem to forget. Preparing for marriage is reasonable and necessary. It is even recognized in Canon Law: "The

[424] "Pre-Cana: Living Our Faith in Love."

couple should receive appropriate education and pastoral preparation through participation in a marriage preparation program approved by the diocesan bishop."[425] Some excellent pre-Cana programs faithfully communicate doctrinal teaching of the Church, but in the aggregate, there is a problem. If the pre-Cana process is designed to curtail divorce and annulment, no one can be happy with the overall results. And that puts it mildly. Can it be done better, and if so, how? How would a solid pre-Cana program be structured?

Pre Pre-Cana

As Pope Saint John Paul II reminds us in *Familiaris Consortio*, "remote preparation" for marriage "begins in early childhood."[426] As her father gently sings to her while her mother nurses her, the baby may certainly sense that she is, indeed, the primary purpose. In her highchair, she notes how the husband and wife—Daddy and Mommy—assist and love each other. This is the baby's universe—as orderly as the mother and father care to make it. Dr. Meg Meeker has noted the direct relationship between a father's involvement in his child's life and the mental development of that child—and that is evidenced even in infancy.[427] It follows that a father and mother's relationship influences a child's cognitive development even in the first weeks of life. It may not even take that long. Dr. Thomas Verny and John Kelly

---

[425] Canon 1067.

[426] John Paul II, *Familiaris Consortio.*

[427] Pedersen, et al., "Parent-Infant and Husband-Wife Interactions," 65–91. From Meeker, *Strong Fathers, Strong Daughters*, n. 252.

also declare that "during these months, a woman is her baby's conduit to the world. Everything that affects her, affects him. . . . Virtually everyone who has studied the expectant father's role—and, sadly, so far, only a handful of researchers have—has found that his support is absolutely essential to her and, thus, to their child's well-being."[428] They further explain that a "vital factor in the child's emotional well-being is his father's commitment to the marriage."[429] In large measure, a child's fundamental impression of marriage has been formed well before the age of reason. Pope Pius XI observed, "For it cannot be denied that the basis of a happy wedlock, and the ruin of an unhappy one, is prepared and set in the souls of boys and girls during the period of childhood and adolescence."[430] The domestic church teaches domestic pre-Cana.

The father and mother's participation in Church also forms a powerful and lifelong impression. The child sees her parents kneel in adoration together at Mass. In mysterious ways, dad and mom are united together with God. And her parents are bringing her to God. At a young age, the little girl may not even be able to pronounce the word *catechism*, but she has a happy and powerful impression of marriage that is mapped out in her brain. The family is not the only pre-Cana influence: the Church is designed to be a constant witness to marriage for children. For her parish priest, that witness is beautifully expressed in the sacraments: baptizing children, hearing confessions, saying Mass, and performing

---

[428] Verny, *The Secret Life of the Unborn Child,* 30.
[429] Verny, 30.
[430] Pius XI, *Casti Connubii.*

weddings. Marriage revolves around the sacramental life only priests can provide; that fact is illustrated at every Mass.

Pope Saint John Paul II explains that following the stage of remote preparation comes "proximate preparation" for older children and young adults.[431] He explains that Christian marriage as an essential element in their catechetical programs of this audience. He writes, "This renewed catechesis of young people and others preparing for Christian marriage is absolutely necessary in order that the sacrament may be celebrated and lived with the right moral and spiritual dispositions."[432] He also writes that young people must understand the practicalities of married life, like "stable work, sufficient financial resources, sensible administration, notions of housekeeping."[433] This remote stage of preparation should also examine what makes a good husband and father or wife and mother. As Pope Pius XI wrote in *Casti Connubii*, "To the proximate preparation of a good married life belongs very specially the care in choosing a partner; on that depends a great deal whether the forthcoming marriage will be happy or not, since one may be to the other either a great help in leading a Christian life, or, a great danger and hindrance."[434] Even before he begins dating, if a young adult is taught to view marriage through the lens of its sacramentality, fidelity, and indissolubility, he should be in a position to identify what makes a suitable marriage partner.

---

[431] John Paul II, *Familiaris Consortio*.
[432] John Paul II, *Familiaris Consortio*.
[433] John Paul II, *Familiaris Consortio*.
[434] Pius XI, *Casti Connubii*.

Before marriage preparation, there should be preparation for dating.

Of course, the above examples present an ideal: that children be brought up in strong and loving marriages. But that ideal—even though even the holiest among us are fallen sinners and far from perfect—is achievable. It is imperative that Catholic parents realize that they are the first marriage educators. The continuous influx of grace admits the possibility of a healthy and holy marriage to raise children. And if we are going to have a serious discussion about marriage, we must look to an achievable ideal. Thus, before discussing formal marriage preparation programs for our children, we must understand that marriage *is* a pre-Cana program.

Formal Pre-Cana

This brings us to formal pre-Cana. Though some excellent pre-Cana programs exist in America, others are badly subpar. In many dioceses in America, pre-Cana programs are taught by an older couple or several couples. While many couples might be in solid command of doctrine, others are unqualified to stand in front of a room to explain the Catholic faith. Although a priest will eventually witness these couples' exchange of consent or vows, many pre-Cana programs do not require ever meeting with a priest. The programs often attempt to address a wide range of topics like sexuality, finances, jobs, and skills for communicating with each another. Some programs perform skits ostensibly to illustrate resolution and forgiveness. Many have breakout sessions at which couples are instructed to speak among each other for reasons that are not always clear. The online world abounds with criticism and mockery of many such programs. ("Pre-Cana is the opposite of a concert. The back rows fill up first. . . . Imagine if you will, bad actors reading a bad play in a mediocre theatre with shoddy equipment in front of a captive audience of miserable critics. If you're able to do that well, you'll be able to recreate the experience any time.[435]) Nevertheless, after a mere six hours or so, couples are given a certificate of completion that they can present to the diocese.

It is simple enough to attain a basic understanding of marriage—of its requirement to be open to children, to commit for life, and to be faithful—in less than six hours, but if pre-Cana is to serve a definite purpose, it must offer more than this. Expressed in *Familiaris Consortio*, Pope Saint John Paul II envisioned something much more. He writes, "The immediate preparation for the celebration of the sacrament of Matrimony should take place in the months and weeks immediately preceding the wedding, so as to give a new meaning, content and form to the so-called premarital enquiry required by Canon Law. This preparation is not only necessary in every case, but is also more urgently needed for engaged couples that still manifest shortcomings or difficulties in Christian doctrine and practice."[436] Thus, marriage preparation for engaged couples can serve as a catechetical program of its own. In some measure—perhaps in considerable measure—such a marriage preparation program can

[435] Sack, "Those Who Pre-Cana Don't Really Wanna."
[436] John Paul II, *Familiaris Consortio*.

perform what RCIA (Rite of Christian Initiation of Adults) seeks to accomplish. The benefit of such a program extends well beyond the couple. After all, the primary purpose of marriage is the procreation and education of children, and the education component primarily concerns an education in the Faith. Parents need to learn the Faith in order to pass on the Faith. But it is unreasonable to believe such a program can be accomplished in six hours. Instead, the pontiff envisions such programs as taking weeks or even months.

In 2022, the Dicastery for the Laity, the Family, and Life issued a document that recommended a marriage preparation program of over one full year. Referred to as a "marriage catechumenate," the program would consist of three phases: the first lasting one year, the second lasting a matter of months, and the third phase involving the first years of marriage.[437] The document, *Catechumenal Itineraries for Married Life*, noted the inadequacy of brief marriage preparation programs. An article in *Northwest Catholic* paraphrased the document's argument, "Just as preparations for living the vocations to priesthood or religious life extend over time—years, not a few weeks—so should preparations for the vocation of marriage."[438]

Though many of this program's goals are admirable, its lengthy approach seems unwise. Bluntly, it's hard to imagine how a fifteen-month preparation program does not occasion the sin of fornication for young couples in love. Oddly

---

[437] Wooden, "Vatican releases suggestions for lengthier, revamped marriage preparation."
[438] Wooden, "Vatican releases suggestions for lengthier, revamped marriage preparation."

enough, the program seems to acknowledge this, noting—while not endorsing—that such programs would include those already cohabitating. Such a program penalizes those couples who are practicing chastity. Moreover, though the priesthood and married life are both vocations, the dicastery's comparison regarding preparation is flawed. Unlike the priesthood, men and women have a natural right to marriage, which cannot be denied or obstructed without clear and serious reason. Further, the nature of the priesthood is such that comprehensive and precise theological training is demanded. On the other hand, the majority of married people in history—even the canonized ones—were not doctrinal experts. Nor did their perfectly valid vows require them to be.

Fifteen months is far too long a duration. Love desires union, and young couples in love are already battling to maintain chastity. Pre-Cana programs must be cognizant of that fact. As John Paul II viewed it, "Although one must not underestimate the necessity and obligation of the immediate preparation for marriage—which would happen if dispensations from it were easily given—nevertheless such preparation must always be set forth and put into practice in such a way that omitting it is not an impediment to the celebration of marriage."[439] Years ago, Aristotle wrote about a "golden mean" between two extremes. Certainly, that golden mean lies between the extreme of six hours and the extreme of fifteen months—and not necessarily in the middle. Anything over six months in duration seems both unwise, unfair,

---

[439] John Paul II, *Familiaris Consortio*.

and in violation of the natural right to marriage. Nevertheless, the argument that pre-Cana programs need an overall upgrade is correct and necessary.

Priestly Involvement

A snarky online critic once complained of the Church's marriage preparation process: "Pre-Cana is a series of lectures on how to have a functional marriage, organized by people not allowed to have one."[440] His own statement was ironic: in many marriage preparation programs, the priest is not involved at all. In fact, in his description of his pre-Cana course, he never saw a priest. This is common in America. How did it originally come to this? Why the lack of priestly involvement? Perhaps the reason was a time constraint. To be sure, the shortage of priests has undoubtedly left many parish priests overextended. Yet, as far as marriage is concerned, the numbers are less than daunting. In 2020, there were just over twenty-four thousand priests in America and fewer than one-hundred thousand weddings. That would mean that each priest would oversee four couples per year on average. If there is to be reform of the marriage process, that process must include more parish priest involvement.

There are certainly some very dedicated and generous couples who regularly devote their time to pre-Cana instruction; that fact is not under dispute. But if a pre-Cana program does not involve meeting with a priest—even if the material itself is excellent—the program is flawed. If the pre-Cana instruction does not include a priest, it gives the impression

[440] Sack, "Those Who Pre-Cana Don't Really Wanna."

to the engaged couple that the priest has better things to do than oversee marriages. That's a terrible impression to give the future husband and wife. By contrast, meeting with a priest illustrates his belief in the marriage and signifies his continued commitment. If there's any doubt, he should emphasize his continued commitment.

The role of the priest should begin much earlier than pre-Cana. We spoke previously about the early influences of marriage on children and how part of that involves viewing the actions of the priests. As the child grows up, she will listen more intently to the homilies, perhaps expecting to hear more about Matrimony. But it is here that many priests have struggled—and can improve. While no scientific data is available that details and indexes the content of Sunday sermons, it can be anecdotally observed that comparatively little is spoken about marriage from the altar. Outside of nuptial Masses, which are becoming increasingly uncommon, congregations are very unlikely to hear the word "matrimony." They are unlikely to hear about the vocation of marriage, the joys of marriage, overcoming the challenges of marriage, the holiness of marriage, or how to act gracefully within marriage. They are even more unlikely to hear about a future spouse's recommended qualities. But faithful men, women, and children need these sermons. The laity need to turn their hearts and minds toward Matrimony and the transformative graces of that sacrament.

The laity needs to hear about the vocation of marriage. If a priest discusses "vocations" from the pulpit, it almost always refers to Holy Orders rather than marriage. This creates an impression for the faithful that there is but one vocational sacrament rather than two. The laity has grown to employ similar verbiage. If a mother excitedly informs someone that her son "may have a vocation," it is assumed that she is saying her son is investigating the priesthood. If a mother said that her son "may have a vocation," then she explained it was a "vocation to marriage," her listener would be confused or laugh. Priests must endeavor to explain that marriage is a vocation. Marriage is a vocation that is reflective of the love of Christ for His Church. The laity also need to hear about the holiness of marriage. They need to hear that, as Matthew Levering writes, "Christian marriage and family are—without being superior to consecrated singleness—at the very center of human flourishing."[441] Matrimony is a wellspring of holiness. The term "Holy Matrimony" should be spoken often because it affirms the universal call of every couple to holiness.

Regarding the immediate preparation, this would be a good time for the priest to catechize the couple. The priest can quickly ascertain which couples need additional catechetics. Pre-Cana preparation by the priest also allows the pastor the chance to befriend the couple. He should let the couple know that he is available for advice and counsel—that this pre-Cana instruction is the beginning of a process rather than the completion. He should offer each engaged man and woman the opportunity for a general confession before Matrimony. Unless a person has problems of scrupulosity, a general confession—in which one confesses all the sins of his life—is entirely appropriate before entering

[441] Levering, *Engaging the Doctrine of Marriage*, 12.

married life. It is also a great reminder of God's mercy. He should let the couple know he is looking forward to baptizing their children. He should offer to bless their homes after marriage; sadly, this practice is less and less common. But a house blessing can be the occasion for tremendous grace and a reminder that a Catholic home is a domestic Church. The priest should pray with them together, asking God for His graces for their engagement, that it may be holy and happy. As the classic Morning Offering informs, he should explain that their marriage will experience "prayers, works, joys, and sufferings." But Matrimony confers grace that will get the couple through any and every suffering and setback. He should speak to them of the joy of marriage even in old age. Even if the marriage seems to have run out of wine, Jesus is ready to perform abundant miracles to assist the couple. If wine is a metaphor for grace, it can surely be that Christ saves the best for last.

Other than the place of their wedding, we know little about the couple married in Cana. But we do know this: they invited Jesus. Christ was at the center of their marriage from the beginning. So must it be for ours. Thus, engaged couples need priests, who act *in persona Christi*, in their lives from the very beginning. As Cormac Burke puts it, "When she joins her children together in matrimony, the Church is the first to rejoice at their love and happiness. The divine Master is always a willing guest if he is invited to the marriage feast; with his presence he wishes to confirm the joy of Cana. But it is to him that a young couple must look if they want the wine of their present happiness to grow richer."[442] The role of the priest cannot be overstated here; his involvement may easily prove the difference between a happy marriage and a troubled one.

Moreover, the benefit of priestly involvement in pre-Cana is not just for the couple; it will undoubtedly benefit the priest. Though sad, priests often only meet couples after their marriages have become adversarial. This can have a jading effect on his view of marriage; if the priests serve on marriage tribunals, it can be doubly worse. But if priests meet regularly with couples who are head over heels in love, this will help produce a balanced and healthy view of marriage.

Conclusion

In this discussion, parish priests should follow the example of Saint John Vianney, the patron saint of parish priests, who witnessed marriage's happiness, suffering, and challenges. In one of his sermons, Vianney counseled, "Husbands and wives should live peacefully in their union of marriage; they should be mutually edifying to each other, pray for one another, bear patiently with one another's faults, encourage virtue in one another by a good example, and follow the holy and sacred rules of their state, remembering that they are the children of the saints and that, consequently, they ought not to behave like pagans, who have not the happiness of knowing the one true God."[443] Vianney well-understood

[442] Burke, *Covenanted Happiness*, 16.
[443] Morrissey, *The Sermons of the Cure of Ars*, 45–46.

that marriage is designed to be a path to heaven—a path well worn by saints throughout history.

But Vianney also understood the joys of marriage and was not afraid to communicate this to other people who were considering Matrimony. As so many of his penitents quickly discovered, Father Vianney was graced with the gift of reading hearts, which assisted penitents in making good confessions. So powerful was this gift, and so powerful was the impression of mercy by Father Vianney's absolution, that people traveled from America—by boat—to confess their sins to him. Father Vianney was also able to predict some future events. Much of this would be difficult to believe, even for many Catholics, except that it is well documented. It is important to understand these facts about Father Vianney so that the following story makes more sense.

A Catholic noblewoman in France had learned that her teenage son was planning to ask his girlfriend to marry him. The noblewoman considered this marriage a terrible idea. Perhaps she thought her son was too young for marriage or that her son was too good for his intended bride. Whatever the reason, she was terribly worried about the proposed marriage, so she came up with the idea to travel to Ars for Father Vianney's advice. Surely, Father Vianney would know what to do. The journey took three days, and the noblewoman's schedule only allowed her a few hours window to meet with Father Vianney. When she arrived at the church, she saw it was filled, and the line for confession stretched to the outside. It seemed her whole trip had been in vain: there was simply no reason to think she would have a chance to speak with Vianney about her son and his plans to marry.

But she could find a place to stand by the holy water font, so she decided to pray. As she blessed herself and prayed, she saw the door open to the confessional. Father Vianney came out of his confessional and walked right toward her. She was shocked when she began to understand that Father was coming to see her. When he reached her, Father Vianney smiled and quietly whispered to her, "Let them marry; they will be very happy!" With that, Father John Vianney went back to hearing confessions.[444]

We need to hear those very words from the pulpit. We need to hear those words from a priest in pre-Cana. For all you priests reading this, please help us. We laity need your involvement. Our children need your assistance and guidance in preparing for marriage. Your presence is irreplaceable. Please help us, and please know that you are in our prayers. And in the prayers of our children.

---

[444] Rutler, *The Cure d'Ars Today*, loc. 175–76, Kindle.

9

Endless Honeymoon: How the Church Can Help Married Couples and Families

"You've got to laugh a little, cry a little,
Until the clouds roll by a little,
That's the story of,
That's the glory of love."

—Billy Hill, "The Glory of Love"

MARRIAGE IS IN trouble. But there is hope. There are many things the Church can do to safeguard, promote, and nourish marriage. Some things can occur in Rome, others at the diocesan level, and others at the individual parish level. The ideas below will assist healthy marriages, those in crisis, and those marriages yet to come. Each of these ideas is offered in light and in response to a message by Pope Saint John Paul II to the Roman Rota in 2004: "It is necessary instead to rediscover the truth, goodness and beauty of the marriage institution. Since it is the work of God himself, through human nature and the freedom of consent of the engaged couple, marriage remains an indissoluble personal reality, a bond of justice and love, linked from eternity to the plan of salvation and raised in the fullness of time to the dignity of a Christian sacrament. It is this reality that the Church and the world must encourage! This is the true *favor matrimonii!*"[445]

Eliminate the Divorce Mandate

As discussed in chapter 6, dioceses in America require a couple to obtain a civil divorce before even hearing their case for annulment at a tribunal. This requirement is problematic, imprudent, and gives rise to scandal.

To understand why, let's begin this discussion by distinguishing between *separation* and *divorce*. The Church has long allowed a husband to separate from his wife (or vice versa) for particular and grave reasons, including adultery, apostasy, or abuse.[446] Nevertheless, the Church has simultaneously affirmed the permanence of marriage. As Session XXIV of the Council of Trent declared, "If anyone shall say that the bond of matrimony can be dissolved for the cause of heresy, or of injury due to cohabitation, or of wilful desertion; let him be anathema."[447] Thus, in no sense does separation imply invalidity; in fact, deeming it "separation" presumes its validity. Separation also leaves the possibility, but certainly not the requirement, for reconciliation. Even in those cases where prudence demands that the separation be permanent, the marriage is presumed valid.

---

[445] John Paul II, "Address of John Paul II to the Members of the Tribunal of the Roman Rota for the Inauguration of the Judicial Year."
[446] *The Catholic Encyclopedia*, s.v. "Divorce (in Moral Theology)."
[447] *The Catholic Encyclopedia*, s.v. "Divorce (in Moral Theology)."

One of the problems in this discussion is that the word "divorce" often suffers from ambiguity and equivocation.[448*] "Divorce" can refer to a civil action that admits an intact and permanent sacrament of Matrimony, but "divorce" can also refer to the attempt to abolish a valid sacramental union. While the former is allowed under some circumstances, the latter is never allowed—or even ontologically achievable, for that matter. One cannot abolish his sacramental marriage any more than he can abolish his baptism.

The *Catechism of the Catholic Church* states, "Divorce is a grave offense against the natural law. . . . Divorce does injury to the covenant of salvation, of which sacramental marriage is the sign. . . . Divorce is immoral also because it introduces disorder into the family and into society."[449] While the *Catechism* recognizes the indissolubility of sacramental marriage, the *Catechism* does permit for "civil divorce." It states, "If civil divorce remains the only possible way of ensuring certain legal rights, the care of the children, or the protection of inheritance, it can be tolerated and does not constitute moral offense." And for purposes of our discussion of the divorce mandate, the *Catechism*'s statement here is key. In fact, the *Catechism*'s verbiage here regarding civil divorce is reminiscent of its just war doctrine: war is begrudgingly "tolerated" but must be a last and "only possible" resort. Like war, for civil divorce to even be tolerated, all other possibilities must have been exhausted.

---

[448] For a further discussion of this point, see Miller, "When Does the Church Tolerate Divorce."

[449] *CCC* 2384–85.

Considering all this, why is divorce mandated before an annulment case is even heard? Requiring divorce before an annulment hearing is tantamount to declaring war as an opening act of diplomacy. Moreover, the divorce requirement is opposed to Canon Law. The Code of Canon Law reads, "Marriage possesses the favor of law; therefore, in a case of doubt, the validity of a marriage must be upheld until the contrary is proven."[450] But in what sense does requiring divorce enjoy canon law's favor? In what sense does it uphold validity on any level? Consider the following. Instead of upholding marriage's validity, imagine for a moment that canon law stated: "In a case of doubt, the *invalidity* of a marriage must be upheld until the contrary is proven." If invalidity were presumed, how would the dioceses act any differently?

But it gets much more insidious. Tribunal judges are charged with attempting persuasive reconciliation between the parties, and this is stated explicitly in canon law: "Before accepting the case and whenever there is hope of a favorable outcome, the judge is to use pastoral means to reconcile the spouses and persuade them to restore conjugal living."[451] Canon law's requirement here is eminently reasonable and eminently pastoral; however, there's an enormous problem with the tribunal as we have seen. By diocesan mandates, un-divorced couples cannot appear before judges. The judge won't hear a word until the divorce decree is in his files. In the eyes of judges, this divorce decree can constitute the very

[450] Canon 1060.
[451] Canon 1695.

proof that reconciliation is impossible—a decree required before the case.[452]

Dear reader, even if you disagree with every premise and conclusion in this book, can we at least agree that reconciliation is more likely *prior* to divorce? God loves reconciliation; God hates divorce. Every procedure and structure of the parish, the chancery, and the tribunal must reflect that twofold divine reality.

Enforce the Separation of Sacrament and State

If a Catholic couple presents themselves for sacramental Matrimony, they normally must have a state-issued marriage certificate in hand. If one or both of those parties wish to begin an annulment proceeding, they must have a state-issued divorce decree in hand. Martin Luther would have loved this system. It is literally true that the priests of the Catholic Church will not perform a marriage (or annul one) without prior state permission. This system has been in place for so long that few people question it. It's time we did.

Imagine if this same system were in place not in the sacrament of Matrimony but in any other sacrament. A child could not be baptized without a decree from the state authority; a bishop could not confer Confirmation without proper civil paperwork; the Eucharist could not be administered without government approval; Holy Orders would require a signed document from the county; penitents would be required to produce documentation before absolution; Anointing of the

---

[452] Vasoli, *What God Has Joined Together*, 211.

Sick could only be administered to the dying with the consent of the regime.

Why mention this here? After all, what sort of government would require sacramental permission?

It's worth noting that this is not the stuff of dystopian fantasy. Instead, it is a common tactic of totalitarian governments to intercede in the sacraments—a fact witnessed from Henry VIII to today's communist Church in China. Of course, intercessions tend to be followed by hostile takeovers and redefinitions of the sacraments. In his book *Earthly Powers*, Michael Burleigh outlines the French Revolution's appropriation of the sacraments. Burleigh writes, "The discourse of the Revolution was saturated with religious terminology. Words like catechism, credo, fanatical, gospel, martyr, missionary, propaganda, sacrament, sermon, zealot, were transferred from a religious to a political context."[453] Catechisms were rewritten by the French government to reeducate the once-faithful:

> Question: What is Baptism?
>
> Answer: It is the regeneration of the French begun on 14 July 1789, and soon supported by the entire French nation. . . .
>
> Question: What is Communion?
>
> Answer: It is the association proposed to all peoples by the French Republic henceforth to form on earth

[453] Burleigh, *Earthly Powers*. loc. 1588 of 11683.

> only one family of brothers who no longer recognise or worship any idol or tyrant.
>
> Question: What is Penitence?
>
> Answer: Today it is the wandering existence of traitors to their Fatherland. It is the banishment of all those monsters who, unworthy to inhabit the land of Liberty and to share the benefits which their villainy has only delayed, will soon be driven out of every corner of the globe.[454]

It turns out, totalitarian governments have often exhibited a strong interest in redefining the sacraments.

It is an essential function and duty of the Catholic Church to administer the sacraments; that function directly pertains to the salvation of souls. Someone might attempt to argue that the Church, in requiring government documents before sacramental Matrimony, must be obedient to duly appointed civil authorities. But there is a rather glaring problem with the argument: it has been formally condemned. Pope Pius IX condemned the following proposition in *The Syllabus of Errors*: "The ecclesiastical power ought not to exercise its authority without the permission and assent of the civil government."[455] Thus, a Catholic is not permitted to hold that position. Ideally, the sanctioned and holy ecclesiastical functions of the Church do not violate local civil ordinances, but the Church cannot walk away from its divine mission if they do. The Church must conduct the business of saving souls,

---

[454] Burleigh, loc. 1611.
[455] Pius IX, *The Syllabus of Errors*.

and—lest we forget—the Church has an eternal goal rather than the state's merely temporal one.

If a couple wants a civil marriage certificate, so be it. But that is far different than *requiring* it to proceed with a sacrament. And what if civil marriage is, for whatever reason, not granted? Under the current ecclesiastical practice, the state can prevent a couple from sacramentally marrying. As same-sex marriage becomes increasingly prevalent, the Catholic Church must remove this forced-documenting process.

Break the Canon Law Monopoly

We've previously discussed the monopolistic aspects of canon law and that the monopoly is part of the problem with widespread annulment. The word "monopoly" comes to English from the Greek word meaning "one seller," and the story behind the word illustrates our present ecclesiastical problem. Twenty-five centuries ago in Greece, there lived a man named Thales, who was an elemental philosopher. Thales was criticized because it seemed like all he did all day was sit around and think about things like causation and being rather than make money. His detractors thought it was easy to sit around and think; in their eyes, what was hard was running a business. Surely, as brilliant as Thales thought he was, he was nowhere near smart enough to run a successful business. At some point, Thales had heard enough, so he took a break from philosophy and quickly cornered the local olive market. If you wanted an olive, you had to buy it from Thales and pay his inflated prices. The men who criticized him had to come to him for olives. For without competition, Thales could set his price.[456]

It's easy to see how such commodity monopolies are dangerous to the common good, but they are not the only sort of monopoly nor the least dangerous. Far more harmful are monopolies of thought. It is not "one seller" that is to be so much feared as "one teacher." Does anyone honestly think America would be better off if it had but a single university? How about one law school? This would create a dangerous groupthink and could easily disallow any who disagreed. The academic monopoly of Catholic University, coupled with the CLSA monopoly, has created groupthink regarding annulment.

It's time to break up that monopoly, and it must begin with academics. To confer a degree in canon law, an academic institution must have a pontifical status for doing so. In the United States, only the Catholic University of America currently has that status. The only school allowed to confer a canon law degree is the same school with a notorious heretic on its payroll for over two decades. What part of *scandal* is this lacking? A Catholic graduate school like Ave Maria University's or Christendom College's Notre Dame Institute could certainly teach canon law but cannot confer a degree. Pontifical status should be quickly granted to such schools.

Beyond that, bishops should seek to add people to tribunals who have received their canon law degrees from countries *outside* America. The Church should also incentivize lay men and women to receive canon law degrees. The process

---

[456] McKeon, *The Basic Works of Aristotle*, loc. 28454 of 37581, Kindle.

should not be overly dominated by priests, yet it often has been. It was not until 1969 that a degree in canon law was even conferred upon a woman in America. Marriage, a contract between a man and a woman, should have representation by both on tribunals. This would also help with the interview process, as women would more readily speak with other women on intimate matters.

Lastly, tribunalists whose cases are commonly overturned by the Roman Rota should be removed from office. If a higher court overturns 90 percent of a judge's findings of annulment, what are we to make of that judge? How can we conclude anything other than incompetence or bias? In civil courts, incompetence or bias is cause for removal. Why should canon law proceedings be any different? Remember, we are not discussing a matter of simply *losing* a case; many lawyers lose defense cases, for instance. Here, we are talking about a higher court overruling a judge—that is, they declare that the lower court was acting incorrectly. And in the case of the Roman Rota, the overturns came with admonitions to American tribunals—flatly telling them they were misbehaving. Of course, one might object that such a system of removal would demand an initial assumption of validity on the part of a judge. It sure would. Of course, so does canon law—the very law they promised to protect.

Recognize Sacramental Connection

History illustrates that the two vocational sacraments rise and fall together. One might assume that a significant ordination boom would result in a dearth of marriages—except that has never happened. No age saw a great devotion to Matrimony and a diminution of Holy Orders. By contrast, our present age is witnessing a fall in Matrimony and Holy Orders. These two sacraments are mystically bound by another sacrament: the Eucharist. As we have seen, the saints recognized this in practice. Saint John the Baptist died not for baptism but to uphold marriage. Saint Valentine risked his life to undertake Holy Orders, but it was for Matrimony that he was martyred. Saint Tarcisius was entrusted with the Eucharist by a priest and died clutching the Eucharist to his chest, but he likely died on his way to deliver that sustenance to married couples. Two millennia have witnessed that Holy Orders, Matrimony, and the Eucharist are symbiotic by design and practice. The leaders of the Church need to illustrate that link, but establishing that connection has been lacking.

On the feast of Corpus Christi 2022, the USCCB announced a three-year Eucharistic revival. It was launched with numerous Eucharistic processions, plans for increased preaching on the Eucharist, and designs for increasing Eucharistic adoration in parishes. It is a beautiful program in many ways, and the connection between the Eucharist and the priesthood runs throughout, but Matrimony is largely absent from the discussion. As part of the revival, the USCCB had drawn up a document in 2021 called *The Mystery of the Eucharist in the Life of the Church*. It's difficult to imagine any "life of the Church" without marriage, and yet, neither marriage nor Matrimony is once mentioned. Referencing the announced revival in an article for the *National Catholic Register*, Father Roger Landry observed that any profound Eucharistic revival must focus on "the indispensable importance of the priest in the Eucharistic life of the Church."[457] There can be no doubt about that fact. Father Landry continues, "Without the priest, there is no Eucharist, and without the Eucharist, there is no Church." Again, that is certain. But we might add a prior reality: without Matrimony, there are no priests.

Some years ago, a man named Giuseppe Sarto—the future Pope Pius X—received his bishop's ring. Shortly after that, he visited his mother to show her the ring. That seemed appropriate; after all, his mother had raised him in the Faith. Affectionately known as "Bepi" by his mother, Giuseppe held out his hand to show his mother his elegant ring. Upon seeing the ring, his mother held out her hand, adorned with her humble wedding band. His mother responded, "Bepi, your ring is beautiful. But if I were not wearing this ring, you would not be wearing yours."[458]

Mrs. Sarto's observation was unshakably accurate, yet somehow we seem to have forgotten. Asking *Where do priests come from?* is a bit like asking *Where do babies come from?* Is it that we don't know or that we don't want to talk about it? When we hear about the "vocations crisis" in the Church, we reflexively think of the vocation to Holy Orders. Of the two vocational sacraments, however, it is Matrimony that is undergoing the more severe crisis. But the numbers indicate that the priesthood is about to have another dearth in vocations like nothing we have ever seen before. In economic

[457] Landry, "Without Vocations, There Will Be No Eucharistic Revival."
[458] Diethelm, *Saint Pius X*, 63.

terms, a radical drop in marriage numbers is a leading indicator for a decline in priestly vocations. A generation without marriages will be naturally followed by an age without priests. If we are going to have a Eucharistic revival and a revival of priestly callings, we first need a revival of marriage.

Police Heresy and Heretics

There is a quote attributed to Saint John Vianney: "A priest goes to heaven or a priest goes to hell with a thousand people behind." Vianney's contention about the wide influence of priests is simultaneously inspirational and chilling. But it is essential to note that Vianney made that observation many decades prior to the internet, mass media, and social networking. Today's priests are able to influence not a *thousand* souls, but a *billion*. Whereas Vianney hungered for anonymity, some of today's prelates seem to thirst for celebrity. That's not good. Had Saint Thomas Aquinas written his *Summa Theologica* today, he may have included an entry on "celebrity" as a vice opposed to humility, or justice, or charity—for celebrity often violates all three. But while celebrity is potentially harmful for each of us, it can be exponentially more harmful for the clergy—a danger manifested in multitudes of souls.

Of course, it must be said that fame itself is not evil. Fame is similar to money, as it tends to make its owner—and those who desire to be its owner—more virtuous or vicious. Vianney was certainly famous by the standards of his time, but the more famous he became, the holier he became. The same could be said of Bishop Fulton Sheen and Father Patrick

Peyton. Many non-Catholics tuned into Sheen's show every week until they became Catholic. Peyton's love and devotion to Mary in the Rosary made grown men publicly weep and pray in public. But for every Father Patrick Peyton, one could rattle off names of priests whose celebrity has corrupted them. Sadly, dissent often proves a quicker path to fame than fidelity.

It is not the objective of this book to name names and identify villains; suffice it to note that rogue prelates travel the country dissenting on contraception, indissolubility, and fidelity, dissenting on homosexual actions, and putting same-sex marriage on par—or above—sacramental marriage. This constitutes textbook scandal. The damage of these speeches, tours, and books is devastating to marriage, and their fame often becomes widespread. If a priest gives a sermon affirming fidelity, that is not news, nor does it give rise to celebrity. But if a priest gives a contrary speech, the world's ears perk up.

The Church recognizes the influential power of her priests and her role in tempering that influence when prudence demands. Just as the Church has the mission to teach and sanctify, she also has the duty to govern. Without performing that duty, her ability to teach and sanctify is jeopardized. Just as the responsibility to govern involves executive, legislative, and judicial powers, so does the Church have police powers of a sort. We have already seen the extensive damage that a Charles Curran-type prelate can cause the faithful, but his influence occurred before the advent of the internet. Thus, the Church's duty to reprimand, censure, and excommunicate prelates is much more immediate in the world of instant and global communication.

In the Middle Ages, excommunication was far more prevalent than today. Arguably, it was used too often, and the Council of Trent cautioned against this. Trent proclaims that excommunication "is, however, to be used with moderation and great discretion, since experience teaches that if wielded rashly or for trifling reasons, it is more despised than feared and is productive of destruction rather than of salvation."[459] But the pendulum has swung back the other way in the past few decades. The leadership of the Church has expressed an extreme reticence to reprimand dissenting prelates even in comparatively minor ways, to say nothing of excommunication. And it should not go without mentioning that many dissenters are also the same men directly involved in the Luciferian sexual abuse of children and seminarians. As a matter of prudence, justice, and charity, the Church must police and prosecute those who deny the integrity of Matrimony.

Promote and Encourage Catholic Education

In addition to the procreation of children, the Church must also stress the other primary purpose of marriage: the education of children. In 1929, exactly one year before the release of *Casti Connubii*, Pope Pius XI issued *Divini Illius Magistri*, known in English as *On Christian Education*. Pope Pius XI wrote that the parents hold "directly from the Creator the mission and hence the right to educate the offspring," a right

[459] Schroeder, *Canons and Decrees of the Council of Trent*, loc. 5146.

that is "inviolable on the part of any power on earth."[460] Pius XI also clarified the end of education, declaring that "there can be no true education which is not wholly directed to man's last end," thus, "there can be no ideally perfect education which is not Christian education."[461] He further illustrated the sweeping scope of this pedagogical process by quoting Pope Leo XIII: "It is necessary not only that religious instruction be given to the young at certain fixed times, but also that every other subject taught, be permeated with Christian piety. If this is wanting, if this sacred atmosphere does not pervade and warm the hearts of masters and scholars alike, little good can be expected from any kind of learning, and considerable harm will often be the consequence."[462]

Less than a half-century after *On Christian Education*, during his brief pontificate, Pope Blessed John Paul I delivered a powerful reminder to the assembled American bishops: "We must encourage parents in their role as educators of their children—the first catechists and the best ones."[463] Pope Saint John Paul II echoed his predecessors: "The right and duty of parents to give education is essential, since it is connected with the transmission of human life; it is original and primary with regard to the educational role of others, on account of the uniqueness of the loving relationship between parents and children; and it is irreplaceable and inalienable,

---

[460] Pius XI, *On Christian Education.*

[461] Pius XI, *On Christian Education.*

[462] Pius XI, *On Christian Education.*

[463] John Paul I, "Address of John Paul I to a group of American Bishops on their Ad Limina Visit."

and therefore incapable of being entirely delegated to others or usurped by others."[464] In 2015, Pope Francis lamented that "so-called 'experts' have assumed the role of parents in even the most intimate aspects of education."[465] He urged, "It is time for fathers and mothers to return from their exile—for they have exiled themselves from their children's upbringing—and to fully resume their educational role."[466]

Regarding education, the deficiency has not been in Rome's defense of parents' duties, rights, and abilities to educate their children; rather, the issue has been in the practical translation of that message. Bluntly, these words and teachings of the popes are rarely expressed from the pulpit. Anecdotally, when was the last time you heard a sermon about parents' duties or rights to educate their children? Or of the importance of genuinely Catholic education? Or the last time you heard the term "primary educators" with regard to parents? This message would be vital to any age, but it is more important in our generation and culture, which is rejecting the importance of fathers and mothers and families.

There's another subject we fathers and mothers in the pews hear little about: homeschooling. If procreation and education of children is the primary purpose of marriage, if the end of education is a truly Christian education, if parents are the best catechists, and if education should take place in a sacred atmosphere (such as a domestic Church), what are Catholic homeschooling parents lacking in heroism? Homeschooling strengthens families.

[464] John Paul II, *Familiaris Consortio*.
[465] Francis, "General Audience," May 20, 2015.
[466] Francis, "General Audience," May 20, 2015.

It's worth noting that homeschooling also strengthens the Church, and concrete numbers can back that statement. Drawing on research from CARA, Patty Knap notes in the *National Catholic Register*, "Young men with a homeschool background are four times more likely to enter seminaries than those educated in Catholic institutions."[467] It's high time we stopped overlooking the obvious: heroic homeschooling parents are raising priests. All that said, homeschooling is not the easy way; it is often difficult and requires heroic sacrifice. Thus, priests must offer homeschooling mothers and fathers encouragement.

Parochial schools must also find ways to offer free education for Catholic students. The objection could be made that the Church cannot afford to offer free education. But what expenses and programs could be more important than educating children in their Faith? The principle of subsidiarity dictates that no money should leave the diocese before appropriate money has been spent on education. The Church has a fundamental right and duty to help educate her members. Without free education, many poorer Catholic parents will opt for public schools for financial reasons, which should never happen. No child should be deprived of parochial school education for monetary reasons.

Reaffirm the Living Wage Doctrine

According to the United States Department of Agriculture—which tracks such figures—the cost of raising a child

[467] Knap, "Homeschooling is Bringing Us More Priests."

is increasing rapidly and has been for decades. When people hear this news, they might naturally respond that this is simply the effect of inflation; meaning that, due to inflation, the price of *everything* is higher. Of course, there is some truth to that statement. But to get a more accurate picture of what is truly occurring, economists use what is known as inflation-adjusted dollars. This number provides us with a look at what is called *purchasing power*. For instance: What did a one-dollar bill buy me in 1980, and what does it buy me now? Here's a real-life example: an American worker in 1973 making $4.03 an hour had the *same purchasing power* as a worker making $23.68 an hour in 2018.[468] That worker, in inflation-adjusted dollars (sometimes called "real dollars"), makes the same amount of money.

Adjusted for inflation, the real cost of raising a child rose about 23 percent from 1980 to 2010.[469] (If you're curious about the actual number, here it is. In 2017, the United States Department of Agriculture estimated that—for a child born in 2015—it would cost $233,610 to raise him to age eighteen.[470])

The more pertinent question, however, is not whether the cost of raising children has outpaced inflation; the real question is whether the cost of raising children has outpaced *wage growth*. In other words, if the cost of raising children outpaced inflation by 23 percent, one would hope that his or her wages (salary) also outpaced inflation by at least

---

[468] DeSilver, "For most U.S. workers, real wages have barely budged in decades."

[469] McIntyre, "Skyrocketing Costs of Child Care: 1960 to Today."

[470] "2015 Expenditures on Children by Families."

23 percent. Of course, it would be ideal if wages grew by *more* than 23 percent; after all, most parents would hope to improve the material condition of their children. But as long as wage growth was at least 23 percent, the family's material condition is not regressing. Only that's not what has happened. Instead, according to Pew Research, wage growth "has barely budged" between 1979 and 2018.[471] To make matters worse, Pew reports that the largest wage growth has "gone largely to the highest earners."[472] In sum, the harsh reality is that raising children has become considerably more expensive over the past few decades. But what does the Catholic Church have to say about all this? Quite a bit.

In his 1891 encyclical *Rerum Novarum*, Pope Leo XIII explains, "The preservation of life is the bounden duty of one and all, and to be wanting therein is a crime. It necessarily follows that each one has a natural right to procure what is required in order to live, and the poor can procure that in no other way than by what they can earn through their work."[473] In 1931's *Quadragesimo Anno*, Pope Pius XI affirmed this teaching, writing that "the worker must be paid a wage sufficient to support him and his family." In 1963's *Pacem in Terris*, Pope Saint John XXIII wrote, "The amount a worker receives must be sufficient, in proportion to available funds, to allow him and his family a standard

---

[471] DeSilver, "For most U.S. workers, real wages have barely budged in decades."
[472] DeSilver, "For most U.S. workers, real wages have barely budged in decades."
[473] Leo XIII, *Rerum Novarum*.

of living consistent with human dignity."[474] In 1991, Pope Saint John Paul II wrote in *Centesimus Annus*, "A workman's wages should be sufficient to enable him to support himself, his wife and his children."[475] What might be called a *living wage doctrine* or a *family wage doctrine* has been formally and consistently taught by the Church since her first social encyclical. This is official Church teaching and, thus, binding on the faithful.

Nevertheless, the doctrine has its objectors. The most common argument is that the precise payment point cannot be determined; thus, the doctrine is not workable. (For example, is this family's living wage $72,000 or $80,000?) But that is a specious argument. The moral law is not always a precise science, but that does not nullify its validity. Procreation and upbringing of children is the primary purpose of marriage. But "upbringing" is not easy to define, much less pinpoint. Does upbringing mean violin lessons and a math tutor? Although not mathematically precise, the doctrine is still doctrine. The same principle applies to living wages.

Priests must affirm the family wage doctrine from the pulpit. The employers in the congregation need to hear the teaching, and the employees need it to be heard. Without a living wage, the family is in dire straits. Many men and women will refuse to get married without the assurance of a living wage. Marriage numbers are hemorrhaging, in considerable measure, for economic reasons. Clergy can help turn this around.

---

[474] John XXIII, *Pacem in Terris*.
[475] John Paul II, *Centesimus Annus*.

Reaffirm the Sanctity of Matrimony

Perhaps due to their upbringing, some Catholics have the persistent notion that holiness is something only for priests and religious. Of course, the idea is erroneous: the Church has taught since her origin that all Christians, regardless of their state, are called to holiness. But we laity need reminders of that calling. And while we must remind each other, we need regular reminders from the pulpit.

Sexual union within marriage is an act of holiness and innocence, but our world relentlessly presents sexual activity as anything but holy or innocent. No surprise there. But here is what may come as a surprise to clergy members: because sex is portrayed in the media and society as lustful, virtuous husbands and wives can feel a sense of guilt for sexual activity even *within* marriage. Some readers may find this notion very odd—that married people would ever feel guilty in making love to their spouse. To counter this temptation, married couples need to hear the beautiful words of Pope Pius XI: "For matrimonial faith demands that husband and wife be joined in an especially holy and pure love, not as adulterers love each other, but as Christ loved the Church."[476] Priests, please trust me when I say that this one teaching—this one quote uttered from the pulpit—can improve the lives of your parishioners. It will strengthen marriages. It is time to begin standardizing the term "Holy Matrimony."

Another practical thing that will help marriages is to celebrate them. The Eastern Catholic diocese of Passaic, New Jersey, did something extraordinary in that regard. On each

[476] Pius XI, *Casti Connubii.*

fifth anniversary of their marriages (fifth, tenth, fifteenth, etc.), every couple in the entire diocese is invited to have their marriage blessed by the bishop. The bishop says a special liturgy for the couples, presenting each with a signed scroll in front of the Church that pronounces his continued blessing. A formal dinner follows the liturgy and presentation for the couples and their children. It is a beautiful marriage celebration and should be the template for every diocese in America.

Another thing the Church can do to highlight the holiness of marriage is to canonize more married couples. In 2015, Louis and Zélie Martin were the first married couple with children to be canonized together. It was a beautiful and enduring blessing, especially for married couples. But simultaneously, it might naturally strike Catholics as odd that it took two thousand years to occur. For they raised one of the greatest saints in Saint Thérèse, the "Little Flower," and inspired her four older sisters to become nuns. But it is also true that Saint Bernadette had holy parents, as did hundreds of other canonized saints. Efforts should be made to open more cases for canonization, and some are in the works, such as Pope Saint John Paul II's parents along with Saint Don Bosco's mother. If there is a universal call to holiness, and if many husbands and wives and fathers and mothers answered that call, why should there not be a significant movement to highlight their sanctity and the holiness possible within every marriage?

Pope Saint John Paul II certainly made efforts in that regard, as has Pope Francis. This is a huge step in the right direction, and hopefully, the Church has only just begun what will prove to be a significant wave of canonizations. It must continue. Of course, there is a formal process for canonization, which should be followed. But even opening the cases for more married couples would tremendously benefit the earthly members of the Mystical Body of Christ.

One last recommendation on affirming the holiness of Matrimony, and it is a rather simple one: amend the Scriptural readings concerning marriage. Back in the first chapter of this book, we read the story of Tobias and Sarah. The story beautifully and powerfully illustrates the virtues of marriage such as perseverance, chastity, charity, faith, and hope. The story illustrates the primary purpose of marriage and the destiny of married love. It is one of the greatest tributes to the romance of marriage ever written. Most of all, it illustrates the providence and continued presence of God within marriage. Catholic children should grow up hearing this story from their infancy because it creates a wondrous respect for the sacrament of Matrimony. It is easy to see why Martin Luther, who denied Matrimony, threw out the book of Tobit from his new Protestant Bible. But while Tobit will always and everywhere be part of the defined Catholic canon, Tobit has been largely ignored in the Mass readings.

The Sacred Congregation for the Sacraments and Divine Worship determines the structure of the readings for the Roman Rite Masses. The basic design is for the entire Bible to be read over the course of three years of Sunday and weekday Masses. Under the current structure, however, the Sacred Scripture is not read entirely. In some cases, single verses are skipped; in other cases, multiple verses are skipped. One could respectfully argue against the wisdom of omitting *any* verses; after all, Scripture was inspired in totality by the Holy

Spirit. But the treatment of the book of Tobit is particularly glaring. The current design does not merely omit a verse of Tobit; instead, under the current design, not a single verse of the book of Tobit is ever read during a Sunday Mass. Not a single verse. Even during the weekday Masses, selections from the book of Tobit are read only one week in the three-year cycle.[477] And even then, Raphael's beautiful statement of faith and assurance in chapter 6—"Do not be afraid, for she was destined for you from eternity" (Tb 6:17)—is omitted, as are several full chapters. Unless they are daily communicants, the average Catholic will never hear these readings in Church. And even if they attend daily Mass, Catholics will only hear these abbreviated readings 1 week out of 156 weeks. Particularly in a time of marriage crisis, this is not enough. The lectionary should be amended to include reading Tobit at Sunday Mass.

Conclusion

This chapter intends to offer helpful critique as to how Church officials can strengthen marriage and the Catholic Church. But the prayerful motivation for this has been charity. And in all this discussion, there should be no mistake about the role of priests by the Catholic faithful: Dear priests, we pray for you, we need you, we love you, and we want you involved in our marriages.

---

[477] Bergsma, *A Catholic Introduction to the Bible*, loc. 10118 of 30084, Kindle.

10

Battling Dragons: How the Laity Can Nourish Our Marriages

"But to look beyond the glory is the hardest part
For a hero's strength is measured by his heart . . .
I will search the world, I will face its harms,
Till I find my hero's welcome, waiting in your arms."

—Michael Bolton, "Go the Distance"

WE BEGAN THIS examination of marriage by looking at the Garden of Eden, the first marriage, and the serpent's temptation. To conclude our study, we return to the garden to make another observation because therein lies a clue about how to protect our marriages.

It is often assumed that the serpent in the Garden of Eden was a snake, or at least *appeared* to be a snake. Thus, we envision a comparatively small, albeit venomous, creature. Genesis doesn't provide much description; the focus is on the serpent's actions rather than his physical attributes. But the book of Revelation provides us with more insight. Revelation 12:9 reads, "And the great dragon was thrown down, that ancient serpent, who is called the Devil and Satan, the deceiver of the whole world—he was thrown down to the earth, and his angels were thrown down with him." The passage here is clearly referencing the very same being who tempted Adam and Eve, only now the serpent is described as a "great dragon." Thus, it was a dragon that endeavored to destroy the first marriage. Adam refused to battle the dragon, thus failing to protect his marriage. Today, the weapons have changed, but the enemy remains, as does the battle. To champion marriage, we must battle a dragon. That's not an easy task. But as any young child can tell you, battling dragons is the stuff of heroes. As that same child can assure you, the battle can be won. Matrimony can be championed. And you, dear reader, are called to do just that.

The world is hostile to marriage; that much is true. It's worth remembering that this was true in the beginning and will be true until the end. Regardless of time and place, we must protect and defend our marriages even if the whole world is against us. And we must always remember this: as much as you love your marriage, God loves it more. God will give you the grace to save your marriage and help it blossom forever. Below are a few ideas for nourishing and defending your marriage.

Remember the Romance of Matrimony

Every Catholic couple must practice romance. I state this at the outset because the Catholic view of marriage is sometimes viewed as unromantic. That's nonsense. The problem is not with the Catholic view; the problem is that romance has been dumbed down so far that it now excludes permanence. In storybook lingo, "living happily ever after" has come to be viewed as passé and unromantic. Think about that: the world's concept of romance negates happiness. But the Catholic view offers something better: we believe in "living happily ever after." And we firmly believe in romance.

To support that claim, let's consider the Catholic concept of marriage. You fall in love with a woman and choose to unite with her for life in Matrimony because Jesus raised Matrimony to the level of a sacrament. In His omniscience, when Jesus raised Matrimony to a sacramental level, He thought precisely of *your* marriage. The angels in heaven love each other, but no two angels will ever be united like you and your wife. Your hope and prayer together is that your ecstatic love brings forth new life. Not a single angel in a single choir in heaven can even dream of such a thing; for all their powers, their love was not designed to bring forth new life. You not only want to be her husband but also the father of her children. Even though the world mocks fidelity—*you* will be forever faithful. And the band of gold on your finger symbolizes not merely an earthly love but a heavenly one. The world seeks fleeting pleasure, but you desire something infinitely greater for yourself and your wife: the fulfillment and happiness that comes with fidelity. You realize that Matrimony does not negate illness, poverty, or tragedy, for the married must also walk through shadows and valleys of death. But just as the Lord is with you through those valleys, you look down and see your wife's hand in yours. There will be dragons, but you will battle any dragons along her path—for you are her knight in shining armor. You wear the belt of truth, the breastplate of righteousness, the shield of faith, the helmet of salvation, and the sword of the Spirit for her protection. And no armor ever shone more brightly. You never feel worthy of her, and she never feels worthy of you; thus, you strive for perfection because your heavenly Father and earthly wife deserve no less. Matrimony does not absolve you from death, but you know that death is only a temporary separation. For at the end of the marriage's journey, you and your wife and children will stand in the all-beautiful presence of God in complete and total happiness.

That's the proper view of marriage since the time of Adam and Eve, affirmed by Tobias and Sarah, continued at Cana, cruciformly confirmed by Saints Timothy and Maura, witnessed by the beheading of Saint John the Baptist, testified on the scaffold by Saint Thomas More, declared by the Council of Trent, and guaranteed by Saint John Vianney.

In all its glorious stages, there is nothing more romantic than Catholic marriage.

Some will criticize the above description of marriage as idyllic. Is it? My dictionary defines "idyllic" as "pleasing or picturesque in natural simplicity."[478] By that definition, we can conclude that marriage is idyllic by divine design: marriage is simple. Saint Augustine assures us that God is simple.[479] We can say that sanctifying grace is simple. Thus, there is a certain simplicity in a marriage united in God's grace. It is not sacrament but sin that introduces complexity

---

[478] *Merriam-Webster.com Dictionary*, s.v. "idyllic," accessed October 24, 2022, https://www.merriam-webster.com/dictionary/idyllic#h1.

[479] Aquinas, *Summa Theologiae*, First Part, Q. 3.

in marriage. If your marriage has become complex, endeavor to make it simple again.

Live a Sacramental Life

Matrimony is designed to be assisted by the sacraments of confession and the Eucharist. Confession brings me closer to God and closer to my wife Lisa. That is not just some vague or poetic expression; instead, that is a tangible knowledge, emotion, and sensation. I immediately feel drawn to her when I walk out of the confessional. When Lisa and I receive the Eucharist together, we deepen our relationship with God and each other. Marriage is *about* God. Thus, proximity to God strengthens marriages. It is unrealistic to expect Matrimony to flourish when a married person allows the other sacraments to flounder in his or her life.

Am I saying that many marriages in trouble could be simply one sacramental confession away from significant improvement? Am I saying that praying a Holy Hour once a week with your husband could drastically improve your marriage? Am I saying that going to daily Mass together for one month as husband and wife might completely change the trajectory of a marriage for the better? Yes. That is precisely what I am arguing. We can concede that some marriages, though sacramentally valid, have reached a stage in which prudence dictates separation; canon law allows for this. But we must also be honest enough to admit that many couples give up long before that stage. Even very troubled marriages can be rescued through sacramental grace, and there is plenty of such evidence.

In the Eastern Catholic Liturgy of Saint John Chrysostom, we implore Jesus, "Cure the sick, O physician of our souls and bodies." Lest we forget that same physician of souls and bodies is the physician of marriages. Jesus healed the sick, raised the dead, cast out demons, and forgave sins; there should be no doubt that He can save our marriages. Perhaps we lack faith, and if we do, we should consider an account in the Gospel of Mark. In the ninth chapter of Mark's Gospel, we read about a father who brings his child to Jesus and tells Him: "Teacher, I brought my son to you, for he has a mute spirit; and wherever it seizes him, it dashes him down; and he foams and grinds his teeth and becomes rigid; and I asked your disciples to cast it out, and they were not able" (Mk 9:17–18).

Jesus asks him, "How long has he had this?" (Mk 9:21).

The father responds, "From childhood" (Mk 9:21). The father continues to explain the agony and suffering that his beloved son has endured for those years, "And it has often cast him into the fire and into the water, to destroy him; but if you can do anything, have pity on us and help us" (Mk 9:22).

Jesus takes exception to the father's doubt: "If you can!" (Mk 9:23). Jesus is essentially telling the father that there are no "ifs" with God. What's more, those ifs have been standing in the way of healing. Jesus continues, "All things are possible to him who believes" (Mk 9:23).

The father realizes his lack of belief and immediately repents, throwing his heart on Jesus's mercy. The father realizes that it is not only his son who needs healing but himself. Like Saint Peter on the water, his lack of faith is sinking him.

He knows he is in desperate need of healing and cries out, "I believe; help my unbelief!" (Mk 9:24). His son is cured. The apostles ask why they could not exorcise the demon who afflicted the son. Jesus tells them that some demons can only be exorcised with prayer and fasting.

Many of us pray for our marriages but begin that prayer with *if.* As in, *Dear God, if you can save my marriage.* If? "All things are possible to him who believes." For those in troubled marriages, remember that you are battling dragons. Troubled marriages require faith, prayer, fasting, and the sacraments. Even storybook marriages require those things.

Devote Yourself to Mary

Years ago, I began reading *The Mystical City of God.* The book is a series of private revelations from Our Lady to the mystic nun Venerable Mary of Agreda. The book details the events in the life of Mary from her infancy to her assumption. Among my mother's wealth of TAN Books, I remember seeing the book on the Clark family shelves growing up, but I hadn't bothered to read it until a few years after Lisa and I were married. One afternoon as I was reading the book, Lisa asked me how I liked it. I turned to Lisa and announced, "I have good news and bad news. The bad news is that I'm falling in love with another woman. The good news is that the woman is the Mother of God."

Following her Mexican tradition, Lisa has always had an intense devotion to Our Lady of Guadalupe. And my falling in love with Mary simply meant that I had arrived where Lisa already was. Our devotion to Mary, most evident in our family Rosary, has powerfully helped our marriage both in ways that I know and in ways I will never fully grasp.

Mary loves marriage; she proved that at Cana. She loves her marriage to Saint Joseph, and she loves *your* marriage. She wants to help you and has given us the Rosary to do so. Whatever ails you and your marriage, Mary can help. Mary will help. As the *Memorare* attests, "Never was it known that anyone who fled" to Mary's protection "was left unaided."

Especially in a terrible age that is rife with sins and temptations against the sixth and ninth commandments, married persons must turn to Mary for purity. In chapter 4, we referenced the temptations of the flesh, especially pornography. Once thought to be the domain of only men, women are finding themselves addicted as well. The prevalence of pornography is nearly ubiquitous, defying internet bandwidth limits. This can wreak havoc on marriages. But there is a way out, even for those in the grips of this addiction. There is confession, which puts us back in the state of grace, and the Eucharist strengthens us to remain there. But there is also the devotion to Mary, especially in the Rosary.

The Rosary and the scapular are your ways of mystically holding Mary's hand; she will lead you out of darkness and toward her son.

If your marriage is in trouble, turn to Mary.

If you have a storybook marriage, turn to Mary.

Always turn to Mary.

After all, if you are going to battle dragons, it is wise to enlist the help of the woman who was promised to crush the dragon's head.

Turn to Saint Joseph

It is a frequent slander against Catholics that we "worship" Mary, as though we think Mary is a deity. Of course, this is nonsense. We Catholics worship God alone, and this worship is titled *latria*. But we do greatly honor Mary. While each of the saints is owed *dulia* (honor), Mary is owed the highest honor: the Church calls this *hyperdulia*. Among the rest of the saints, Saint Joseph is owed *protodulia*, which is an honor owed to him alone. Pope Leo XIII explains, "In truth, the dignity of the Mother of God is so lofty that naught created can rank above it. But as Joseph has been united to the Blessed Virgin by the ties of marriage, it may not be doubted that he approached nearer than any to the eminent dignity by which the Mother of God surpasses so nobly all created natures."[480]

This classification is essential for Catholic families to remember. The Holy Family consisted of the Second Person of the Trinity and the Immaculate Mother of God, yet Saint Joseph was the head of the family. Pope Leo XIII continues, "Joseph became the guardian, the administrator, and the legal defender of the divine house whose chief he was."[481] Wives must honor their husbands and children are called to honor their father as the head of the family, even if he is the least among them.

But it is contingent upon husbands and fathers to earn that respect. That requires, in considerable measure, being holy ourselves. The fourth commandment demands that

---

[480] Leo XIII, *Quamquam Pluries*.
[481] Leo XIII, *Quamquam Pluries*.

children honor their fathers, but some fathers make this very difficult. Our job is to make it easier, which requires us to be holy. There was only one head of the Holy Family, yet we Catholic fathers are each called to be the heads of families who are collectively and individually called to holiness. Husbands must recognize that this headship has duties of piety. Our wives also deserve us to be holy. That means we lead the family in the Rosary, live sacramental lives, kneel before Our Lord and Our Lady, do spiritual reading, adorn our homes with sacramentals, and battle those dragons who tempt us.

Many studies have indicated that a mother's faith is essential to children but considerably less important than a father's. Fathers can profoundly form a child's impression of God.[482] What an extraordinary responsibility! Thus, we must pray for the grace to make a good and loving impression. We must remember, however, that we are imperfect; we will make mistakes. As I have told my children, "When you see me going to confession, the priest and I are not playing Scrabble there. I have sinned. I have to ask God for forgiveness too." In our finest moments, perhaps our children see Saint Joseph in us. We must pray that they do. And to help accomplish that, we should develop a devotion to Saint Joseph. That means asking for his intercession, reading books about him, and consecrating your life to him. Edward Healy Thompson's *The Life & Glories of Saint Joseph*, Father Donald Calloway's *Consecration to Saint Joseph*, and Devin Schadt's *Custos: Total Consecration Through Saint Joseph* would be excellent places to begin—or continue—your journey.

---

[482] Brown, "Father's faith."

One last point here. It has been said: if you wish to be a better father, love your wife. I believe that thirty years of marriage have illustrated that truth. And I have come to understand the inverse: if you want to be a better husband, love your children. And all of this is fostered through devotion to Saint Joseph.

Practice Patience and Kindness

Saint Paul begins his definitive litany of love in the thirteenth chapter of Corinthians by stating: "Love is patient and kind" (1 Cor 13:4). These are principal virtues necessary in marriage. Saint Augustine tells us, "The virtue of the soul that is called *patience*, is so great a gift of God, that we even preach the patience of Him who bestows it upon us."[483] Saint Augustine touches upon something that we husbands and wives must remember: God has been patient with each of us. Though I never deserved patience, God was patient with me through all my sins.[484] It is said that to forgive is divine, but patience is prior to forgiveness. If God is patient toward us, who are we to not pass that on to others? Who am I not to pass that on to my wife or my children?

Patience is also a transitive and beautiful virtue because it believes and hopes in its recipient. Early in our marriage, I had fallen out of the habit of praying the Rosary. I still prayed, of course, but the fifteen minutes of the Rosary just seemed too big a commitment. So Lisa prayed for me to start praying the Rosary again, although I didn't know it at

---

[483] Aquinas, *Summa Theologiae*, II-II, Q. 36, Art. 1.
[484] Lovasik, *The Hidden Power of Kindness*, 113.

the time. Very soon, I began praying it again, and we prayed it as a family. But that's not all: I started reading books about the history of the Rosary. I began writing columns and blogs about the Rosary. A few years later, I traveled the country giving speeches about the value and importance of the Rosary, offering free rosaries to everyone who attended. At one of those speeches, a woman told me her husband would not pray the Rosary with the family. My advice was to pray for him. Two years later, a woman came up to me and said, "You probably don't remember me, but two years ago, I listened to your speech about the Rosary." I assured her that I remembered. She told me, "I wanted to let you know that you changed my life. My husband has started praying the Rosary with the family." Lisa's patience changed lives. Her patience strengthened our marriage.

While envy has been defined as "sorrow for another's good," we might consider kindness to be joy for another's true good. While we must practice kindness toward everyone in our lives, it is vital in marriage. We must rejoice in their good: Saint Paul's letter tells us as much. Father Faber once commented, "Kindness has converted more sinners than either zeal, eloquence, or learning; and these three last have never converted anyone, unless they were kind also."[485] Kindness makes marriages thrive. A smile, a kiss, a kind word, an embrace, a bouquet, a note of encouragement, forgive quickly and permanently: these things are the lifeblood of a marriage.

---

[485] Lovasik, 9.

Find Good Role Models

One particularly troubling development in recent years is that Catholics have often chosen terrible role models. We admire celebrities whose movies clearly violate the sixth and ninth commandments (and we often view those movies). We buy sports jerseys with the names of men who have run away with younger women. At political rallies, we chant the names of politicians whose sexual deviance is well-documented. For good measure, we openly criticize those who disagree with our admiration of such characters. Leaving aside the strong likelihood of scandal for those around us, the role-modeling of such characters progressively shatters our perception of chastity and marital fidelity.

It is often lamented that there are no good role models today. That's nonsense. There are plenty of good role models available. But you must know where to look, and the beginning of that search sends us back in time. Years ago, Cardinal Eduard Gagnon, president of the Pontifical Council for the Family, gave a speech at a dinner I was blessed to attend. After he delivered a brief speech, he opened the floor to questions. Someone asked him how to nourish the Catholic faithful in America. The question was essentially, "In a world that is quickly losing sight of the divine, how can we help people focus on God?" I've never forgotten Cardinal Gagnon's answer: "Give them the lives of the saints." It was wise then but far more applicable today because we've largely forgotten what constitutes true heroism.

For many years, we Clark brothers began our homeschool day with breakfast, followed by morning prayers, which included a litany of the saints. No role models? Don't tell that to a Clark child. My mom read off a long list of heroes every morning, to which we all replied in unison, "Pray for us." My brother Daniel once joked that my mom would be in charge of reading heaven's roll call when she made it to heaven. We began our day by recognizing true heroism and real role models. My heroes growing up were Mary, Saint Joseph, Saint Paul, Saint Veronica, and Saint Tarcisius. Maybe they lived a hundred years ago; perhaps they lived two thousand years ago—that did not matter. What mattered was heroic virtue.

The German language has a word for the collective feeling and attitudes of an age: *zeitgeist*. Our American zeitgeist is antimarriage, affecting us in both discernable and hidden ways—even for those of us in storybook marriages. C. S. Lewis observes that everyone is influenced by his particular time, place, and societal moral codes. Lewis argues that we are all affected by this zeitgeist, even those "who seem most opposed to it."[486] But within the accidents of chronology and geography, we are prisoners only if we choose to be. Cardinal Gagnon and Lewis instructed that to escape from the damaging aspects of modern times—modernism—to look to the past. Lewis's answer was the "old books." Gagnon's recommendation was much more specific: biographies of the holy men and women. And for our purposes here, we can be even more precise. Our culture may surround us with divorce; thus, we must surround ourselves with the stories of married saints. We need to study the lives of canonized husbands and wives. Theirs are the real happily-ever-after stories. Their lives witness that the noble aspirations of Matrimony can be ultimately realized.

[486] Behr, *Saint Athanasius the Great of Alexandria*, loc. 6, Kindle.

Although the process for doing so is less clear, finding role models and marriage mentors in the present day is possible. That search should not begin with celebrities and politicians but with men and women in the pews. You might start that search with couples in your church who have been married for decades. In various parishes I have attended since we were first married, we had no trouble locating those heroic couples. Or rather, Providence carefully arranged that these faithful husbands and wives would bless our lives. They have provided Lisa and me with real-life lessons about being faithful in an unfaithful world and being happy in a sad world. Find out which couple in your parish has been married the longest, and congratulate them. Get to know them. Get to respect them. You might discover that their wisdom greatly benefits your marriage. If you want to learn carpentry, it makes sense to speak to someone who has been a carpenter for fifty years. The same is true for marriage. Look for mentors, and ask Saint Anthony to help you find them.

Saint Anthony, *pray for us*.

Conclusion

As any child can guarantee, there is a great prize for slaying a dragon. It is to win the hand and the heart of a princess and to live together happily ever after. Living happily ever after is not the mere fiction of storybooks. It is our calling. By virtue of our baptism and sanctifying grace, perfect happiness is our destiny because eternal life is eternal happiness.

Many years ago, Saint John Chrysostom wrote a letter to a young woman who had recently lost her husband of only five years. Chrysostom assured her that they would meet again in total and perpetual happiness. For their married love would know no end. He writes,

> For such is the power of love, it embraces, and unites, and fastens together not only those who are present, and near, and visible but also those who are far distant; and neither length of time, nor separation in space, nor anything else of that kind can break up and sunder in pieces the affection of the soul. But if you wish to behold him face to face . . . keep your bed in his honour sacred from the touch of any other man, and do your best to manifest a life like his, and then assuredly you shall depart one day to join the same company with him, not to dwell with him for five years as you did here, nor for 20, or 100, nor for a thousand or twice that number but for infinite and endless ages.[487]

There are no trials, tribulations, or death in heaven. There is only love—*perfect* love. And if those habits and things about your husband or wife drive you crazy, do not worry. We are made perfect in heaven and perfectly happy. As Saint Paul's Letter to the Corinthians assures us, "When the perfect comes, the imperfect will pass away" (1 Cor 13:10). No one does not "get along" in heaven. All of Chrysostom's words beautifully reflect Saint Paul's letter, "Love bears all things, believes all things, hopes all things, endures all things. Love never ends" (1 Cor 13:7–8).

Love never ends.

---

[487] *The Catholic Encyclopedia*, s.v. "Letter to a Young Widow."

Bibliography

"2015 Expenditures on Children by Families." US Department of Agriculture, updated January 6, 2017, https://www.fns.usda.gov/resource/2015-expenditures-children-families.

Ambrose. "St. Ambrose on Gen. 2-3." *Patristic Bible Commentary*, 327, https://sites.google.com/site/aquinasstudybible/home/genesis/st-ambrose-on-gen-2-3.

"Annulment Changes Backed by Vatican." *The New York Times*, June 23, 1970, 43, https://timesmachine.nytimes.com/timesmachine/1970/06/23/issue.html.

Anselm. *Cur Deus Homo.* Edinburgh: John Grant, 1909.

Aquinas, Thomas. "The Catechetical Instructions of St. Thomas." Accessed October 20, 2022, https://www.ewtn.com/catholicism/library/catechetical-instructions-of-st-thomas-12546.

———. *The Summa Theologiæ of St. Thomas Aquinas, Second and Revised Edition. Translated by the* Fathers of the English Dominican Province. London: Burns Oates & Washbourne, 1920. https://www.newadvent.org/summa/5042.htm#article2.

Aquila, Samuel. "Did Thomas More and John Fisher Die For Nothing?" *The National Catholic Register*, October 19, 2015, https://www.ncregister.com/blog/did-thomas-more-and-john-fisher-die-for-nothing.

Augustine. "The Enchiridion on Faith, Hope and Love." Translated by J. F. Shaw. Edited by Philip Schaff. In *Nicene and Post-Nicene Fathers, First Series.* Vol. 3. Buffalo, NY: Christian Literature Publishing Co., 1887.

Baker, Kenneth, trans. "J. Ratzinger 'On the Meaning of Sacrament.'" FCS Quarterly, *Spring 2011, 28–35;* https://static1.squarespace.com/static/569543b4bfe87360795306d6/t/57eec14637c58104eff2607b/1475264858984/MeaningofSacrament-Ratzinger.pdf.

Barringer, Felicity. "The Mainstreaming of Marxism in U.S. Colleges." *The New York Times*, October 25, 1989, https://www.nytimes.com/1989/10/25/us/education-the-mainstreaming-of-marxism-in-us-colleges.html.

Beal, John P., James A. Coriden, and Thomas J. Green, eds. *New Commentary on the Code of Canon Law*. New York: Paulist Press, 2000.

Beard, Charles. *Martin Luther and the Reformation in Germany Until the Close of the Diet of Worms*. London: Kegan Paul, Trench & Co., 1889.

Beauvoir, Simone de. *The Prime of Life: The Autobiography of Simone de Beauvoir*. Translated by Peter Green. New York: Paragon House, 1992

———. *The Second Sex*. Translated by H. M. Parshley. New York: Alfred A. Knopf, 1953.

Beauvoir, Simone de, and Betty Friedan. "Sex, Society, and the Female Dilemma: A Dialogue between Simone de Beauvoir and Betty Friedan." *The Saturday Review*, June 14, 1975, 18; https://www.unz.com/print/SaturdayRev-1975jun14-00012/.

Behr, John, trans. *Saint Athanasius the Great of Alexandria: On the Incarnation*. Yonkers: St. Vladimir's Seminary Press, 2011.

Bergsma, John, and Brant Pitre. *A Catholic Introduction to the Bible*. Vol. 1, The Old Testament. San Francisco: Ignatius Press, 2018.

Blackburn, Jim. "Why did Henry VIII need a dispensation to marry his brother's widow, Catherine of Aragon?" *Catholic Answers*, accessed October 17, 2022, https://www.catholic.com/qa/why-did-henry-viii-need-a-dispensation-to-marry-his-brothers-widow-catherine-of-aragon.

Blackman, Ann. "Books: The Friedan Mystique." *Time*, May 1, 2000, https://content.time.com/time/subscriber/article/0,33009,996777,00.html.

Bowle, John. *Henry VIII: A Biography*. New York: Dorset Press, 1990.

Brown, Matthew. "Father's faith: Perceptions of God may stem from dad-child relationships." *The Washington Times*, June 15, 2013, https://www.washingtontimes.com/news/2013/jun/15/fathers-faith-perceptions-god-may-stem-dad-child-r/#:~:text="Because%20regular%20church%20attendance%20is%20less%20common

%20for,Virginia%20and%20director%20of%20the%20National %20Marriage%20Project.

Bruce, Marie Louise. *Anne Boleyn. n.p.:* Sapere Books, 2020.

———. *The Making of Henry VIII.* Leeds, England: Sapere Books, 2021.

Burke, Cormac. *Covenanted Happiness: Love and Commitment in Marriage.* Dublin: Four Courts Press, 1990.

Burke, Tracey, and Mimi Gleason. *The Tet Offensive: January-April, 1968.* New York, Gallery Books, 1988.

Burleigh, Michael. *Earthly Powers: The Clash of Religion and Politics in Europe, from the French Revolution to the Great War.* HarperCollins e-books, 2009.

Butler, Alban. *Butler's Lives of the Saints: Complete Edition.* Vol. 3. Edited by Herbert J. Thurston and Donald Attwater. London: Burns & Oates, 1981.

Camm, Bede, ed. *The Lives of the English Martyrs: Declared Blessed by Pope Leo XIII in 1886 and 1895.* Vol. 1. London: Burns and Oates, 1904.

Carroll, Warren. *The Cleaving Of Christendom.* Front Royal, VA: Christendom Press, 2000.

"Catholic Marriage and Family in the United States." United Sates Conference of Catholic Bishops, accessed October 23, 2022, https://www.usccb.org/offices/public-affairs/catholic-marriage-and-family-united-states.

Cicognani, Amleto Giovanni. *Canon Law, Second, Revised Edition.* Translated by Joseph M. O'Hara and Francis Brennan. Philadelphia: The Dolphin Press, 1935.

Chesterton, G. K. "A Turning Point in History." In *The Fame of Blessed Thomas More: Being Addresses Delivered in His Honour in Chelsea, July 1929.* London: Sheed and Ward, 1929.

Chrysostom, John. *Homilies on Genesis.* "Homily 15." Accessed March 19, 2022. http://www2.iath.virginia.edu/anderson/commentaries/ChrGen.html#glossGen2:20.

———. "Homily 21 on the Gospel of John." Translated by Charles Marriott. Edited by Philip Schaff. *Nicene and Post-Nicene Fathers, First Series.* Vol. 14. Buffalo, NY: Christian Literature Publishing Co., 1889.

Churchill, Winston. "The Sinews of Peace ('Iron Curtain Speech')." International Churchill Society, March 5, 1946, https://winstonchurchill.org/resources/speeches/1946-1963-elder-statesman/the-sinews-of-peace/.

Clancy, Tom. *The Hunt for Red October.* New York: Penguin Publishing Group, 2018.

Clark, James G. *The Dissolution of the Monasteries: A New History.* New Haven: Yale University Press, 2021.

Coates, Tim. *The King's Great Matter: Letters of Henry VIII and His Court.* n.p.: Freckle, 2016.

Congregation for the Doctrine of the Faith. "Declaration of the Commission of Cardinals on the 'New Catechism.'" October 15, 1968, https://www.ewtn.com/catholicism/library/declaration-of-the-commission-of-cardinals-on-the-new-catechism-2060 In 1968.

Conrad, Robert J., Jr. *John Fisher and Thomas More: Keeping Their Souls While Losing Their Heads.* Gastonia, NC: TAN Books, 2021.

"Conservative Position: The Teaching of the Church and its Authority." *National Catholic Reporter*, April 19, 1967, 9. https://thecatholicnewsarchive.org/?a=d&d=ncr19670419-01.1.1&.

Curran, Charles E. *Loyal Dissent: Memoir of a Catholic Theologian.* Washington, D.C.: Georgetown University Press, 2006.

DeFerrari, Roy J., trans. *Denzinger: The Sources of Catholic Dogma.* Thirtieth Edition. London: B. Herder Book Co., 1957.

DeParmiter, Geoffrey C. *The King's Great Matter: A Study of Anglo-Papal Relations 1527-1534.* Oxford: Barnes & Noble, 1959.

DeSilver, Drew. "For most U.S. workers, real wages have barely budged in decades." Pew Research Center, August 7, 2018, https://www.pewresearch.org/fact-tank/2018/08/07/for-most-us-workers-real-wages-have-barely-budged-for-decades/.

Diethelm, Walter. *Saint Pius X: The Farm Boy Who Became Pope.* San Francisco: Ignatius Press, 1994 .

"Dio ci guardi dall'aver paura . . ." *Liberta e Persona.* December 29, 2013. http://www.libertaepersona.org/wordpress/2013/12/dio-ci-guardi-dallaver-paura/.

Dods, Marcus, ed. & trans. *The Works of Aurelius Augustine, Bishop of Hippo.* Vol. 2, *The City of God.* Edinburgh: T & T Clark, 1871.

Doidge, Norman. *The Brain That Changes Itself: Stories of Personal Triumph from the Frontiers of Brain Science.* New York: Viking, 2007.

Elliott, Peter J. *What God Has Joined: The Sacramentality of Marriage.* New York: Alba House, 1990.

Estevez, Jorge Arturo Medina. "Holy Communion for Divorced and Re-married?" Catholic Culture, May 3, 2006, https://www.catholicculture.org/culture/library/view.cfm?recnum=7010.

"Family Engagement." Early Childhood Learning and Knowledge Center. July 2, 2020, https://eclkc.ohs.acf.hhs.gov/family-engagement/article/appreciating-how-fathers-give-children-head-start#father.

Finnegan, John T. "The Capacity to Marry." *The Catholic Lawyer*, Summer, 1969.

Flynn, John. "Data Show Benefits of Fathers." Fathers for Good (website), accessed October 21, 2022, http://www.fathersforgood.org/ffg/en/fathers_essential/benefit.html.

Ford, John C. "Marriage: Its Meaning and Purposes." *Theological Studies* (September 1, 1942): http://cdn.theologicalstudies.net/3/3.3/3.3.2.pdf.

Foussianes, Chloe. "The True Story of *Ms.* Magazine, and What It Meant for Feminist Publishing." *Town & Country*, April 25, 2020, https://www.townandcountrymag.com/leisure/arts-and-culture/a32131889/gloria-steinem-ms-magazine-true-story/#:~:text=For%20many%2C%20Ms.%20appeared%20to%20be%20the%20mouthpiece,bring%20awareness%20to%20those%20crucial%2C%20previously%20little-covered%20issues.

Francis (pope). *Amoris Laetitia*, https://www.vatican.va/content/dam/francesco/pdf/apost_exhortations/documents/papa-francesco_esortazione-ap_20160319_amoris-laetitia_en.pdf.

———. "General Audience." May 20, 2015, https://www.vatican.va/content/francesco/en/audiences/2015/documents/papa-francesco_20150520_udienza-generale.html.

Fraser, Antonia. *The Wives of Henry VIII.* New York: Vintage Books, 1994 .

"Frequently Requested Church Statistics." Center for Applied Research in the Apostolate. Accessed October 29, 2022, http://cara.georgetown.edu/frequently-requested-church-statistics/.

Friedan, Betty. *Life So Far.* New York: Simon and Schuster Paperbacks, 2006.

———. *The Feminine Mystique.* New York: Dell Publishing, 1963

Friedmann, Paul. *Anne Boleyn: A Chapter of English History, 1527-1536.* Vol. 1. n.p.: Lume Books, 2015.

"Full text of Benedict XVI essay: 'The Church and the scandal of sexual abuse.'" *Catholic News Agency*, April 10, 2019, https://www.catholicnewsagency.com/news/41013/full-text-of-benedict-xvi-essay-the-church-and-the-scandal-of-sexual-abuse.

Garner, Bryan A., ed. *Black's Law Dictionary.* Abridged Eighth Edition. St. Paul: Thomson West, 2005.

Gaudium et Spes. The Vatican Website. December 7, 1965, https://www.vatican.va/archive/hist_councils/ii_vatican_council/documents/vat-ii_const_19651207_gaudium-et-spes_en.html.

Gee, Henry, and William John Hardy, eds. *Documents Illustrative of English Church History.* London: MacMillan and Co., 1910.

Godfrey-Howell, Catherine. *Consensual Incapacity to Marry.* South Bend: St. Augustine's Press, 2020.

Grall, Timothy. "Custodial Mothers and Fathers and Their Child Support: 2017." U.S. Census Bureau, May 2020, https://www.census.gov/content/dam/Census/library/publications/2020/demo/p60-269.pdf.

Grappone, Antonio. "Divorce and Remarriage in the Early Church." Zenit, February 12, 2014, https://www.ewtn.com/catholicism/library/divorce-and-remarriage-in-the-early-church-1819.

Gregorovius, Ferdinand. *Lucrezia Borgia.* Las Vegas: Histria Books, 2020.

Hall, Basil. "Martin Bucer in England." In D. F. Wright, ed. *Martin Bucer: Reforming Church and Community.* Cambridge: Cambridge University Press, 1994.

"Happy 80th Birthday Gloria Steinem: 8 of Her Funniest Quips." *Time* Magazine, March 25, 2014, https://time.com/36046/gloria-steinem-8-funny-quotes-80-birthday/.

Hefner, Hugh M. *The Playboy Philosophy.* n.p., no publisher, 1962.

Hendricks, Lawrence. *The London Charterhouse: Its Monks and Its Martyrs.* London: Kegan Paul, Trench & Co., 1889.

Hook, Judith. *The Sack of Rome: 1527*. New York: Palgrave Macmillan, 2004.

Horowitz, Daniel. *Betty Friedan and the Making of the Feminine Mystique*. Amherst: University of Massachusetts Press, 2000.

Houghton, William D. *Houghton Ancestors: A 1,000 Year Historical Adventure*. n.p., William D. Houghton, 2010.

"How Many People are on Porn Sites Right Now? (Hint: It's a Lot.)" Fight the New Drug, April 5, 2022, https://fightthenewdrug.org/by-the-numbers-see-how-many-people-are-watching-porn-today/.

Hunter-Kilmer, Meg. "Saints Timothy and Maura, newlyweds martyred together." *Aleteia*, April 27, 2017, https://aleteia.org/2017/04/27/saints-timothy-and-maura-newlyweds-martyred-together/.

Ives, E. W. *Anne Boleyn*. Oxford: Basil Blackwell, 1986.

Janaro, John. *Never Give Up: My Life and God's Mercy*. Cincinnati: Servant Books, 2010.

Jedin, Hubert. *A History of the Council of Trent*. Vol. I. Translated by Dom Ernest Graf. St. Louis: B. Herder Book Co., 1957.

———. *A History of the Council of Trent*. Vol. 2, *The First Sessions at Trent: 1545-47*. Translated by Ernest Graf. Edinburg: Thomas Nelson & Sons, Ltd., 1961.

Joannes, F. V. *The Bitter Pill: Worldwide Reaction to the Encyclical* Humanae Vitae. Philadelphia: Pilgrim Press, 1970.

John XXIII (pope). *Pacem in Terris*. https://www.vatican.va/content/john-xxiii/en/encyclicals/documents/hf_j-xxiii_enc_11041963_pacem.html.

John Paul I (pope). "Address of John Paul I to a group of American Bishops on their Ad Limina Visit." September 21, 1978, https://www.vatican.va/content/john-paul-i/en/speeches/documents/hf_jp-i_spe_21091978_us-bishops.html.

John Paul II (pope). "Address of His Holiness John Paul II to the Tribunal of the Roman Rota." February 10, 1995, https://www.vatican.va/content/john-paul-ii/en/speeches/1995/february/documents/hf_jp-ii_spe_19950210_roman-rota.html#:~:text=ADDRESS%20OF%20HIS%20HOLINESS%20JOHN%20PAUL%20II%20TO,of%20the%20Studio%20Rotale%20and%20the%20rotal%20advocates.

———. "Address of John Paul II to the Members of the Tribunal of the Roman Rota for the Inauguration of the Judicial Year." January 29, 2004, https://www.vatican.va/content/john-paul-ii/en/speeches/2004/january/documents/hf_jp-ii_spe_20040129_roman-rota.html.

———. "Address of John Paul II to the Tribunal of the Roman Rota." January 24, 1981, https://www.vatican.va/content/john-paul-ii/en/speeches/1981/january/documents/hf_jp-ii_spe_19810124_roman-rota.html.

———. "Address of John Paul II to the Tribunal of the Roman Rota." January 25 1988, https://www.vatican.va/content/john-paul-ii/en/speeches/1988/january/documents/hf_jp-ii_spe_19880125_roman-rota.html.

———. "Apostolic Letter issued Motu Proprio Proclaiming Saint Thomas More Patron of Statesmen and Politicians." Vatican City: Libreria Editrice Vaticana, 2000.

———. *Centesimus Annus.* https://www.vatican.va/content/john-paul-ii/en/encyclicals/documents/hf_jp-ii_enc_01051991_centesimus-annus.html.

———. *Familiaris Consortio.* Vatican City: Libreria Editrice Vaticana, 1981.

———. *Gratissimam Sane.* Letter, 1994, https://www.vatican.va/content/john-paul-ii/en/letters/1994/documents/hf_jp-ii_let_02021994_families.html.

Johnson, Paul. *Heroes.* n.p., HarperCollins e-books.

———. *Intellectuals.* New York: Harper & Row, 1988.

Kendra, Robert J. "American Annulment Mills." *Homiletic and Pastoral Review*, December, 2005, 14, https://marysadvocates.org/wp-content/uploads/2018/05/kendra-HPR.pdf.

Knap, Patty. "Homeschooling is Bringing Us More Priests." *National Catholic Register*, April 20, 2018, https://www.ncregister.com/blog/homeschooling-is-bringing-us-more-priests.

Koedt, Anne, Ellen Levine, and Anita Rapone, eds. *Radical Feminism.* New York: Quadrangle, 1973.

Landry, Roger. "Without Vocations, There Will Be No Eucharistic Revival." *The National Catholic Register*, August 10, 2022, https://www.ncregister.com/blog/vocational-key-to-ongoing-eucharistic-revival.

Layden, Mary Anne, and Mary Eberstadt. *The Social Costs of Pornography: A Statement of Findings and Recommendations.* Princeton: The Witherspoon Institute, 2010.

Leo XIII (pope). *Rerum Novarum.* 1891, https://www.vatican.va/content/leo-xiii/en/encyclicals/documents/hf_l-xiii_enc_15051891_rerum-novarum.html.

———. *Quamquam Pluries.* 1889, https://www.vatican.va/content/leo-xiii/en/encyclicals/documents/hf_l-xiii_enc_15081889_quamquam-pluries.html.

Levering, Matthew. *Engaging the Doctrine of Marriage: Human Marriage as the Image and Sacrament of the Marriage of God and Creation.* Eugene, OR: Cascade Books, 2020.

———. *The Indissolubility of Marriage.* San Francisco: Ignatius, 2019.

Lovasik, Lawrence G. *The Hidden Power of Kindness: A Practical Handbook for Souls Who Dare to Transform the World, One Deed at a Time.* Manchester, NH: Sophia Institute Press, 1999.

Lull, Timothy F., ed. *Martin Luther's Basic Theological Writings.* Minneapolis: Fortress Press, 2005.

Luther, Martin. *Works of Martin Luther.* Vol. 5. Grand Rapids, MI: Baker Book House, 1982.

Mann, Stephanie. "The Man Who Was Almost Pope: Reginald Cardinal Pole." *The National Catholic Register*, November 30, 2016, https://www.ncregister.com/blog/the-man-who-was-almost-pope-reginald-cardinal-pole.

Mattingly, Garrett. *Catherine of Aragon.* New York: Vintage Books, 1941.

Marshner, William H. *Annulment or Divorce?: A Critique of Current Tribunal Practice and the Proposed Revision of Canon Law.* Front Royal, VA: Crossroads Books, 1978.

Martin, Michelle. "Tribunal Field delegates help people with annulment process." *Chicago Catholic*, August 5, 2020, https://www.chicagocatholic.com/chicagoland/-/article/2020/08/05/tribunal-field-delegates-help-people-with-annulment-process.

Mayor, John E. B., ed. *The English Works of John Fisher, Bishop of Rochester, Part 1.* London: The Early English Text Society, 1876.

McIntyre, Douglas A. "Skyrocketing Costs of Child Care: 1960 to Today." 24/7 Wall St, June 24, 2011, https://247wallst.com/invest

ing/2011/06/24/the-fifty-year-soaring-cost-to-raise-a-child/3/#:~:text=2000%20%3E%20Total%20Cost%20to%20Raise%20Child%20%28Not,Raise%20Child%20%28Inflation%20Adjusted%20for%202011%20dollars%29%3A%20%24216%2C975.

McKeon, Richard, ed. *The Basic Works of Aristotle.* New York: The Modern Library, 1941.

McLaughlin, Dillon. "A Comprehensive History of the Rise and Fall of *Playboy* Magazine." Cool Material, accessed October 20, 2022, https://coolmaterial.com/media/history-of-playboy-magazine/.

Medved, Michael. *Hollywood vs. America: Popular Culture and the War on Tradition.* n.p., HarperCollins e-books, 2011.

Meeker, Meg. *Strong Fathers, Strong Daughters: 10 Secrets Every Father Should Know.* Washington, D.C.: Regnery Publishing.

Meier, John P. *The Vision of Matthew: Christ, Church, and Morality in the First Gospel.* New York: Paulist Press, 1979.

Messenger, E. C. *Two In One Flesh, Part 2: The Mystery of Sex and Marriage In Catholic Theology.* Westminster, MD: The Newman Press, 1948.

Miller, Leila, "When Does the Church Tolerate Divorce." Catholic Answers, June 29, 2018, https://www.catholic.com/magazine/online-edition/when-does-the-church-tolerate-divorce.

Mitchell, Peter M. *The Coup at Catholic University: The 1968 Revolution in American Catholic Education.* San Francisco: Ignatius Press, 2015.

Montagna, Diane. "(FULL TEXT) Seeking Clarity: A Plea to Untie the Knots in 'Amoris Laetitia.'" *Aleitia*, November 14, 2016, https://aleteia.org/2016/11/14/full-text-seeking-clarity-a-plea-to-untie-the-knots-in-amoris-laetitia/.

Morrissey, Una, trans. *The Sermons of the Cure of Ars.* Fort Collins, CO: Roman Catholic Books, 1959.

Murray, Gerald. "World Over - 2018-01-11 – Controversy on Amoris Laetitia, Fr. Gerald Murray with Raymond Arroyo." YouTube, 6:00–8:10, https://www.youtube.com/watch?v=2qpArUYqXno.

Murray, Gerald E., and Diane Montagna. *Calming the Storm: Navigating the Crises Facing the Catholic Church and Society.* Steubenville, OH: Emmaus Road Publishing, 2022 .

"Musonius Rufus | Lectures | 14." Red Zambala (website), accessed January 12, 2023, https://philosophy.redzambala.com/musonius-rufus/musonius-rufus-lectures-14.html.

"Nature of Marriage (Sig. Apost., 30 Dec., 1971) Private." https://web.archive.org/web/20190719065842/http://www.clsadb.com/document/ff003213-73d8-4ce2-bd6b-b0b041caa78e.

Newman, John Henry. *An Essay on the Development of Christian Doctrine*. Notre Dame: University of Notre Dame Press, undated.

Nicholas, Mary A., and Paul Kengor. *The Devil and Bella Dodd: One Woman's Struggle against Communism and Her Redemption.* Gastonia, NC: TAN Books, 2022.

Noonan, John T., Jr. *Contraception: A History of Its Treatment by the Catholic Theologians and Canonists.* New York: The New American Library, 1967.

O'Connell, Gerald. "Pope Francis meets with Father James Martin in private audience." *America*, September 30, 2019, https://www.americamagazine.org/faith/2019/09/30/pope-francis-meets-father-james-martin-private-audience.

"Origins of the Defender of the Bond: From Roman Law to the Defender in the *Ius Vigens.*" Northwest Region Canon Law Conference, May 3, 2017, accessed October 22, 2022, https://www.jgray.org/scripture/defender.pdf.

Paglia, Camille. *Sexual Personae: Art And Decadence From Nefertiti To Emily Dickinson.* New York: Vintage Books, 1991.

Pakaluk, Michael. "Lambeth, 90 Years Later." *The Catholic Thing*, September 1, 2020, https://www.thecatholicthing.org/2020/09/01/lambeth-90-years-later/.

"Patristic Bible Commentary." 1 Corinthians, Chapter 11, accessed October 23, 2022, https://sites.google.com/site/aquinasstudybible/home/1-corinthians/st-thomas-aquinas-on-1-corinthians/chapter-1/chapter-2/chapter-3/chapter-4/chapter-5/chapter-6/chapter-7/-7-15-10-33/chapter-11.

Parker, Kathleen. *Save the Males.* New York: Random House, 2010.

Paul VI (pope). *Humanae Vitae.* Vatican City: Libreria Editrice Vaticana, 1968.

Paul, Pamela. "Are Fathers Necessary?" *The Atlantic*, July/August 2010, https://www.theatlantic.com/magazine/archive/2010/07/are-fathers-necessary/308136/.

———. *Pornified: How Pornography is Damaging Our Lives, Our Relationships, and Our Families.* New York: Times Books, 2005.

Pedersen, F. A., et al. "Parent-Infant and Husband-Wife Interactions Observed at Five Months." In *The Father-Infant Relationship.* New York: ed. F. Pedersen, 1980.

Perry, Samuel L., and Cyrus Schleifer. "Till Porn Do Us Part? A Longitudinal Examination of Pornography Use and Divorce." The Journal of Sex Research 55, no. 3, 284–296, https://www.tandfonline.com/doi/full/10.1080/00224499.2017.1317709.

Peters, Edward N. *Annulments and the Catholic Church: Straight Answers to Tough Questions.* West Chester, PA: Ascension Press, 2004.

———. "Fr. James Martin, S.J., and accusations of heresy." *The Catholic World Report*, October 2, 2017, "https://www.catholicworldreport.com/2017/10/02/fr-james-martin-and-accusations-of-heresy/.

———. *The 1917 or Pio-Benedictine Code of Canon Law.* San Francisco: Ignatius Press, 2001.

Pilon, Mark A. "Streamlining Annulments." *Homiletic and Pastoral Review*, November 14, 2014, https://www.hprweb.com/2014/11/streamlining-annulments/#fn-12478-6.

Pius IX (pope). *The Syllabus of Errors.* https://www.ewtn.com/catholicism/library/syllabus-of-errors-9048.

Pius X (pope). *Iamdudum.* Vatican City: Libreria Editrice Vaticana, 1911.

Pius XI (pope). *Casti Connubii.* Vatican City: Libreria Editrice Vaticana, 1930.

———. *On Christian Education*, 1929, https://www.vatican.va/content/pius-xi/en/encyclicals/documents/hf_p-xi_enc_31121929_divini-illius-magistri.html.

"Pontifical Commission on Birth Control – Final Report (1966)." Wijngaards Institute for Catholic Research, accessed October 21, 2022, https://www.wijngaardsinstitute.com/papal-report-contraception-1966/.

PopulationPyramid.net. "United States of America, 1972." Accessed October 20, 2022, https://www.populationpyramid.net/united-states-of-america/1972/.

"Pre-Cana: Living Our Faith in Love." The Marriage Group, accessed October 23, 2022, https://themarriagegroup.com/courses/pre-cana/?gf_protect_submission=1#gf_4.

Probst, Ferdinand. *Katholische Moraltheologie.* Tubingen, 1848-1850.

Raeburn, Paul. *Do Fathers Matter? What Science Is Telling Us About the Parent We've Overlooked.* New York: Scientific American/Farrar, Straus and Giroux, 2014.

Ratzinger, Joseph. "Letter to Father Charles Curran." Congregation for the Doctrine of the Faith. July 25, 1986, https://www.vatican.va/roman_curia/congregations/cfaith/documents/rc_con_cfaith_doc_19860725_carlo-curran_en.html.

Ratzinger, Joseph. "The Dutch Catechism: A Theological Appreciation." *The Furrow*, December 1971, 741.

"Religion: Catholic Freedom v. Authority." *Time* Magazine, Nov. 22, 1968, https://content.time.com/time/subscriber/article/0,33009,841458-2,00.html.

Reynolds, E. E. *The Field is Won: The Life and Death of Saint Thomas More.* Milwaukee, The Bruce Publishing Company, 1969.

Ridgway, Robert G. "*The Record: The Following Is A List Of Countries That Have Gone Communist In The Past 24 Years.*" Minneapolis: Citizens for Goldwater-Miller, [Summer-Fall] 1964, accessed October 22, 2022. https://bostonraremaps.com/inventory/barry-goldwater-anti-communism-1964/.

Roberts, Paul Craig. "My Time With Soviet Economics." Institute for Political Economy, accessed October 21, 2022, https://www.paulcraigroberts.org/2002/10/07/my-time-with-soviet-economics-2/.

"Roman Catholics: Catechism in Dutch." *Time* Magazine, Dec. 1, 1967, http://content.time.com/time/subscriber/article/0,33009,712033,00.html.

Romano, Lois. "The Convictions of Father Curran." *Washington Post*, September 4, 1986, https://www.washingtonpost.com/archive/lifestyle/1986/09/04/the-convictions-of-father-curran/9926606a-67b0-4569-8f3d-b1b31536096b/.

Rosen, R. D. *Psychobabble: Fast Talk and Quick Cure in the Era of Feeling.* New York: Avon Books, 1979.

Rutler, George. *The Cure d'Ars Today: St. John Vianney.* San Francisco: Ignatius Press, 1988.

Sack, Brian. "Those Who Pre-Cana Don't Really Wanna." January 15, 2004, https://www.banterist.com/those_who_preca/.

Sary, Pal. "The Changes of the Rules of Divorce in the Christian Roman Empire." *Days of Law.* n.p., Masaryk University, 2010.

Savage, John J., trans. *The Fathers of the Church.* Vol. 42, *Saint Ambrose: Hexameron, Paradise and Cain and Abel.* Washington, DC, The Catholic University of America Press, 1961.

Scarisbrick, J. J. *Henry VIII.* New Haven: Yale University Press, 1997.

Schoof, Ted, ed. *The Schillebeeckx Case, official exchange of letters and documents in the investigation of Fr. Edward Schillebeeckx, O.P. by the Sacred Congregation for the Doctrine of the Faith, 1976-1980.* Translated by Matthew J. O'Connell. New York: Paulist Press.

Schroeder, H. J., trans. *Canons and Decrees of the Council of Trent.* Charlotte, NC: TAN Books, 2011.

Schwarzer, Alice. *Simone de Beauvoir Today: Conversations 1972-1982.* London: The Hogarth Press, 1984.

"Selecting the Ground." The Archdiocese of Newark, accessed October 22, 2022, https://www.rcan.org/www.rcan.org/offices-and-ministries/metropolitan-tribunal-whatisannulment.

Smith, S. B. *Elements of Ecclesiastical Law.* Vol. 2, *Ecclesiastical Trials.* New York: Benziger Brothers, 1887.

Smyth, Kevin, trans. *A New Catechism: Catholic Faith for Adults.* New York: Herder and Herder, 1970.

Stark, Rodney. *Bearing False Witness: Debunking Centuries of Anti-Catholic History.* West Conshohocken: Templeton Press, 2016.

Stephenson, Alan M. G. *The First Lambeth Conference: 1867.* London: S.P.C.K., 1967.

Stern, Sydney Ladensohn. *Gloria Steinem: Her Passions, Politics, and Mystique.* Secaucus, NJ: Carol Publishing Group, 1997.

Stoelker, Tom. "Building a Bridge Between the Catholic Church and the LGBT Community." *Fordham News*, September 6, 2017, video beginning at 59:38, https://news.fordham.edu/inside-fordh

am/lectures-and-events/building-bridge-catholic-church-lgbt-community/.

Symonds, Kevin. "Rethinking Bella Dodd and Infiltration of the Catholic Priesthood." *Homiletic and Pastoral Review*, December 24, 2021, https://www.hprweb.com/2021/12/rethinking-bella-dodd-and-infiltration-of-the-catholic-priesthood/.

Taborda, Joana. "Getting a Divorce in Portugal." Expatica, accessed October 19, 2022, https://www.expatica.com/pt/living/love/getting-a-divorce-in-portugal-1174558/#:~:text=Portugal%20has%20a%20complicated%20history%20with%20divorce.%20The,Vatican%20Church%20prohibited%20divorce%20for%20all%20Catholic%20weddings.

Tertullian. "On Exhortation to Chastity." Translated by S. Thelwall. Edited by Alexander Roberts, James Donaldson, and A. Cleveland Coxe. *Ante-Nicene Fathers.* Vol. 4. Buffalo, NY: Christian Literature Publishing Co., 1885.

The Catholic Encyclopedia. Vol. 4. New York: Robert Appleton Company, 1908.

"The Process." Archdiocese of Newark, accessed January 18, 2023, https://www.rcan.org/offices-and-ministries/metropolitan-tribunal/guide-petitioners-statement#:~:text=Determining%20Jurisdiction%20A%20Tribunal%20must%20have%20jurisdiction%20in,wish%20to%2C%20and%20prevents%20"shopping%20around"%20among%20Tribunals.

The Roman Martyrology. Translated by the Most Rev. Archbishop of Baltimore. Baltimore: John Murphy Company, 1916.

Thevathasan, Pravin. "Bernard Häring and his Medical Ethics." 2017, accessed October 22, 2022, http://www.christendom-awake.org/pages/pravin/haring-ethics.htm.

Thomson, Ian. "Martin Luther: Renegade and Prophet by Lyndal Roper – review." *The Guardian*, June 26, 2016, https://www.theguardian.com/books/2016/jun/26/martin-luther-renegade-prophet-lyndal-roper-review.

Treggiari, Susan. "Divorce Roman Style: How Easy and how Frequent was it?" In *Marriage, Divorce, and Children in Ancient Rome.* Edited by Beryl Rawson. Oxford: Clarendon Press, 1996.

Van de Wiel, Constant. *History of Canon Law*. Louvain: Peeters Press, 1991.

Vasoli, Robert H. *What God Has Joined Together: The Annulment Crisis in American Catholicism*. New York: Oxford University Press, 1998.

Venker, Suzanne, and Phyllis Schlafly. *The Flipside of Feminism: What Conservative Women Know -- and Men Can't Say*. Washington, D.C.: WND Books, 2010.

Verny, Thomas, with John Kelly. *The Secret Life of the Unborn Child*. New York: Dell Publishing, 1982.

Walton, Clifford Stevens. *The Civil Law in Spain and Spanish America*. Washington, D.C.: The W. H. Lowdermilk & Co., 1900.

Website of Anglican Communion. Resolution 15, accessed October 20, 2022. https://www.anglicancommunion.org/resources/document-library/lambeth-conference/1930/resolution-15-the-life-and-witness-of-the-christian-community-marriage?author=Lambeth+Conference&year=1930.

Website of Anglican Communion. Resolution 41, accessed October 20, 2022. https://www.anglicancommunion.org/resources/document-library/lambeth-conference/1908/resolution-41.aspx.

Website of Anglican Communion. Resolution 68, accessed October 20, 2022. https://www.anglicancommunion.org/resources/document-library/lambeth-conference/1920/resolution-68-problems-of-marriage-and-sexual-morality.aspx.

Website of Anglican Communion. Resolution 70, accessed October 20, 2022. https://www.anglicancommunion.org/resources/document-library/lambeth-conference/1920/resolution-70-problems-of-marriage-and-sexual-morality.aspx.

Weidenkopf, Steve. "Father Ignatius Maternowski: D-Day Chaplain." *Catholic Answers*, June 4, 2019, https://www.catholic.com/magazine/online-edition/father-ignatius-maternowski-d-day-chaplain.

Westermarck, Edward. *A Short History of Marriage*. London: Macmillan and Co, 1926.

"What the Early Church Believed: Marriage." Catholic Answers, accessed October 29, 2022, https://www.catholic.com/tract/the-permanence-of-matrimony#:~:text=In%20the%20midst%20of%20the%20Greco-Roman%20culture%2C%20which,easy-divorce%20culture

%20%28Catechism%20of%20the%20Catholic%20Church%201614–1615%29.

Wiltgen, Ralph M. *The Rhine Flows into the Tiber.* Devon, England: Augustine Publishing Company, 1979.

Witte, John, Jr. *From Sacrament to Contract: Marriage, Religion, and Law in the Western Tradition.* Second Edition. Louisville, KY: Westminster John Knox Press, 2012.

Wooden, Cindy. "Vatican releases suggestions for lengthier, revamped marriage preparation." *Northwest Catholic*, June 15, 2022, https://nwcatholic.org/news/cindy-wooden-catholic-news-service/vatican-releases-suggestions-for-lengthier-revamped-marriage-preparation.

World Atlas. "Countries with the Largest Anglican Populations." Accessed October 20, 2022. https://www.worldatlas.com/articles/countries-with-the-largest-anglican-populations.html.

Wrenn, Michael J. *Catechisms and Controversies: Religious Education in the Postconciliar Years.* San Francisco: Ignatius Press, 1991